The
11 Contracts
That Every Artist, Songwriter, and Producer Should Know

To access online media visit:
www.halleonard.com/mylibrary
Enter code

5959-7087-1612-3037

The
11 Contracts

That Every Artist, Songwriter, and Producer Should Know

STEVE GORDON, ESQ.

RYANNE PERIO, ESQ.
Executive Editor

BLAIR MACLIN
Associate Editor

ERIC DICKSTEIN
Associate Editor

HAL LEONARD BOOKS
AN IMPRINT OF HAL LEONARD LLC

Published in 2017 by Hal Leonard Books
An Imprint of Hal Leonard LLC
7777 West Bluemound Road
Milwaukee, WI 53213

Trade Book Division Editorial Offices
33 Plymouth St., Montclair, NJ 07042

The SmallsLIVE Artists' Internet Revenue Share Agreement is used by permission of Spike Wilner.

The model band agreement, "Band Agreement: Equal Partners," is used by permission of Wallace Collins, Esq.

Printed in the United States of America

Book design by Lynn Bergesen, UB Communications

Library of Congress Cataloging-in-Publication Data

Names: Gordon, Steve (Steve R.), author.
Title: The 11 contracts that every artist, songwriter, and producer should
    know / Steve Gordon, Esq.
Other titles: Eleven contracts that every artist, songwriter, and producer
    should know
Description: Montclair : Hal Leonard Books, 2017.
Identifiers: LCCN 2016053042 | ISBN 9781495076701 (hardcover)
Subjects: LCSH: Music trade—Vocational guidance—United States. | Musicians'
    contracts—United States. | Music trade—Law and legislation—United
    States. | Sound recording industry—Law and legislation—United States.
Classification: LCC ML3795 .G753 2017 | DDC 780.23—dc23
LC record available at https://lccn.loc.gov/2016053042

ISBN: 978-1-4950-7670-1

www.halleonardbooks.com

For Sonia,
I do it all for you

CONTENTS

INTRODUCTION

There are usually two basic versions of even a simple agreement in the music business: one that represents the best interests of creators, including artists, songwriters, and producers, and another that represents the interests of the companies that do business with them, such as record labels, publishers, and managers. These parties frequently have different or even opposite objectives. For instance, record labels often will try to tap into artists' income beyond record sales, such as monies from live performances, merchandise, and music publishing. However, it is in the artist's best interest to retain as much income from these other sources as possible.

Other agreements, however, such as contracts between co-songwriters or band members, are meant to delineate the rights and duties of similarly situated individuals in order to avoid disputes that might otherwise arise. But, even with regard to these agreements, the parties may wish for different things.

In this book, I present the contracts you are most likely to encounter in your music career. This book also provides introductions on each kind of agreement and commentary inserted into the contracts themselves so that you can understand exactly what you are agreeing to.

I focus on the types of agreements typically offered to *indie* artists, songwriters, and producers taking the step to the next level of their careers. By the time you are offered a deal with a major record label or publisher, *if* that ever happens, you will be able to pay for the services of an experienced music attorney, or the company may even advance you additional funds to pay for a lawyer. This book is intended to help you on your journey, wherever it may lead.

Here are abbreviated introductions to each chapter, designed to help you get the most out of this book:

Chapter 1. Management Agreements

I will guide you through a standard agreement between an artist and a manager, first from the point of view of the manager, then from the point of view of the artist.

Chapter 2. Production Company Deals (. . . and the Contract from Hell Which No Artist Should Sign)

Production companies are not labels. Their function is to produce masters and shop for deals with record labels. Production companies don't deserve (although they often try) to get the artist to sign a "360" deal under which the company would receive a slice of every dollar the artist earns in the entertainment business including touring, merch, and publishing, as well as record sales. This chapter shows you what a *fair* deal with a production company looks like, as well as the "contract from hell" that you should never sign.

Chapter 3. Artist Recording Contracts with Record Companies

Once you have a major record deal, you won't need this book, as you'll be able to afford a music lawyer who can provide you with individualized advice and answer all your questions. But, if you get a deal with an indie record label that can only pay a modest advance, this chapter will show you what a fair deal looks like.

Chapter 4. A Simple Guide to Sync Deals

You work at a bar, but your girlfriend knows someone at an ad agency who is working on a commercial for Budweiser. They send you a "submission form" for a demo that states you will submit music on a spec on a "work for hire" basis. What do you do next? Don't sign it! Read this chapter first.

Chapter 5. Producer Agreements

You are an artist and want to hire a producer. Or, you are a producer. This chapter offers three different contracts that range from pro-artist to pro-producer and explains the issues from both the producer's as well as the artist's point of view.

Chapter 6. Music Publishing and Songwriter Contracts

One "hit" song can subsidize, or even pay for, the rest of your life and even the lives of your children. Learn how to make and keep the money.

Chapter 7. Music and the Movies: Composer Agreements (Written with Robert Seigal, Esq.)

So you want to write music for movies? This is a guide on how not to get screwed.

Chapter 8. Live Performance and Booking Agreements (A Lawyer's Guide to Structuring Paid Music Gigs)

Tips for making money and how not to let booking agents and clubs cheat you. Learn what's fair!

Chapter 9. Music Video Production Contracts

Making a music video? Use this form to hire a producer/director that's fair for both you and them. Also, learn what you can legally include in your music video and what you need a release to include.

Chapter 10. Band Agreements and Essential Business Actions a Band (or Solo Artist) Can Take at Little to No Cost Without the Services of an Attorney

The first part of this chapter provides a roadmap for putting your legal house in order, even if you can't afford an attorney. The second part tells you when you need a band agreement and what it should contain.

Chapter 11. Investment Agreements

Your rich aunt wants to give you money so you can quit your day gig and do music full time. This section will help you structure an agreement that is fair to both you and your investor.

DISCLAIMER

This book, including the form agreements contained in it, has been created for informational purposes only and does not constitute legal advice. This book should be used as a guide to understanding the music business and law, not as a substitute for the advice of qualified counsel.

CHAPTER 1

MANAGEMENT AGREEMENTS

INTRODUCTION: THE ROLE OF THE MANAGER

Managers have never played a more important role in the music business than they do today. If you have taken or are ready to take the next step in your music career, you probably need one.

A good manager advances the career of his or her client in a variety of ways. Traditionally, a manager would provide advice on all aspects of the artist's professional life, use his or her relationships to generate opportunities, negotiate deals, and help the artist select other members of the "team," such as accountants, lawyers, booking agents, and publicists. However, a manager's principal job was searching for the "holy grail"—shopping the artist to record labels, particularly the majors, with the hope of signing a lucrative recording agreement. Signing a record deal would mean a payday for both the artist and the manager. Managers work on commission, so the goal was to sign the artist with a major label and negotiate the largest advance possible. In the '90s, when I was a lawyer for Sony Music, we paid advances to new artists ranging from $250,000 to upwards of $500,000. If the artist caught fire, both the artist and the manager could become very wealthy from record sales alone. Those days are largely gone.

Starting in 1999, income from recorded music has declined more than 75%, accounting for inflation. As a result, the major labels (Sony, Universal, and Warner, along with their affiliates) sign fewer artists and pay those new artists far more modest advances. An artist may never get a deal or may be dropped from the label's roster much faster than in the past, when labels had spare cash to support a developing artist. For instance, Bruce Springsteen did not catch fire until after Columbia (now a Sony affiliate) released two of his albums. But, Columbia had faith and supported him through the early disappointments. Today, with the major labels fighting to survive, a story like that is far less likely to occur. Labels would rather put their resources behind already established acts, where a return on investment is more certain.

In the past, once the artist was signed to the major label, the manager's primary function became to serve as liaison between the record company and the artist. The manager lobbied the label to do more, spend more, and focus more on his or her artist. However, due to budget cuts and massive layoffs at the labels, today's manager does a lot of the work that the label used to do. In these days of financial insecurity in the record business, the manager's role is more important than ever. For example, the manager may take over social networking, search for opportunities to get the artist's music in movies or commercials, or find branding opportunities with sponsors. And, if the artist can't find an acceptable record deal, the manager may become the artist's de facto label and take on the responsibility of crowd funding or securing funding from investors in order to produce records, arrange physical and digital distribution, and do everything else record companies traditionally did.

Pro-Manager Agreement with Pro-Artist Commentary

In the first contract below, I critique a standard pro-management agreement and explain in the comments the changes an artist should negotiate. There are a number of important terms where the interests of the manager are directly adverse to the interests of the artist. For example, it is generally in the manager's interest to have a long initial term and several options to extend the duration of the agreement. The artist, conversely, will want to be able to get out of an agreement quickly if the manager is not meeting the artist's goals. This issue is addressed in the comments for the first paragraph of the pro-management agreement.

Most management agreements base the manager's commission, which is normally 15% to 20%, on gross income that an artist earns from any activities in the entertainment business. It is crucial for the artist to insist that monies paid to the artist, or on the artist's behalf, for recording costs, touring expenses and other business expenses are not included in gross income. For instance, if a record company gives an artist an advance of $100,000 and the artist spends $80,000 on recording costs, the manager should not calculate her commission on the $100,000. If the contract allows him or her to do so, he or she would be entitled to $20,000 and the artist would be left with nothing. This issue is addressed in the comments for subparagraphs 11(b) and (d).

Another very important provision is whether the manager has the right to receive a commission from any contract negotiated during the term—even after the management contract terminates. Pro-manager agreements will usually include such a provision, while the artist will want to terminate the manager's right to commission his income when the contract ends. The manager's position is that if the manager lands a multi-album deal or long-term publishing agreement, the manager should continue to receive money because she helped create that source of income. The compromise is called a "sunset clause." Under this clause the manager still receives income from contracts negotiated during the term of the agreement, but that amount of income declines over time and eventually ends within a reasonable time. An example of a sunset provision is included in the comments for paragraph 13 in the pro-management agreement, and is also contained in the pro-artist agreement provided in this installment.

Other terms are "boilerplate"—standard legal phrases that are important to the agreement but equally protect the interests of both parties. I will point out these terms and explain their significance as well. One example is paragraph 29, which states that any amendment to the contract must be made in writing and signed by both parties.

Pro-Artist Management Agreement

The second contract provides an example of a pro-artist management agreement. The contract your new manager presents you with will often start out resembling the pro-manager agreement, and the closer you can negotiate it to the pro-artist agreement, the better.

PRO-MANAGER AGREEMENT

EXCLUSIVE MANAGEMENT AGREEMENT

THIS AGREEMENT ("Agreement") is entered into on _____, 2017 by and between _____ Management Inc. ("Manager") with an address at _____, and _____ (the "Artist") residing at _____.

1. ENGAGEMENT & TERM: (a) Artist hereby engages Manager as Artist's sole and exclusive personal representative and manager for a period of two (2) years, commencing from the date hereof (hereinafter referred to as the "Initial Term"). Artist hereby grants Manager three (3) consecutive options to extend the term of this Agreement for an additional period of one (1) year each upon all of the terms and conditions herein, and each option shall commence automatically unless Manager submits notice to Artist to the contrary not later than thirty (30) days prior to the expiration of the Initial Term. The Initial Term and any and all option periods of this Agreement shall hereinafter be referred to as the "Term."

Perhaps the most important provision in a management agreement is the "Term," i.e., the duration of the agreement. In this pro-manager agreement, the Manager has the right to represent the Artist for an initial period of two years followed by three options, to be exercised in the Manager's sole discretion, to extend the term for one year each. Essentially, the Manager has up to five years to collect a commission (see Para. 11 below) from the Artist's income, whether the Manager actually helps the Artist become more successful or not.

In a pro-artist agreement, the initial term could be one year, 18 months or even two years. But at the end of the term, the Manager would only have the right to extend the term if certain performance goals are reached. For instance, the Manager may only have the right to extend the Term for another year if the Artist has earned a minimum amount of money ($100,000, for example), or has entered into a record deal with a major label. The rationale is, if these events don't occur, the Manager hasn't been doing a good job of getting the Artist to the next level. Each subsequent right to extend the duration of the agreement should be tied to an even higher performance goal.

---

2. MANAGEMENT SERVICES: Manager agrees to use best efforts to devote itself to Artist's career and to do all the things necessary and desirable to promote Artist's career and earnings therefrom.

The "Manager's Services" provision in most management agreements, whether pro-management or pro-artist, is generally a boilerplate list of a Manager's duties. As discussed in the Intro, boilerplate are standard legal provisions that generally do not favor one party or the other, and therefore are not usually negotiated. Nonetheless, the Artist should carefully read through this section of the contract to see if there is anything potentially harmful, such as a power of attorney in favor of the Manager, which would allow the Manager to execute contracts and other legal documents on the Artist's behalf without her knowledge or approval.

These duties shall consist of such activities as working to secure deals with record companies, booking agents, song publishers and music instrument manufacturers, and advising Artist on the recording process, song selection, producers, packaging design for records, etc. Artist hereby authorizes and empowers Manager, and Manager agrees subject to the limitations set forth in Paragraphs 4 through 6 of this Agreement:

(a) to represent, advise and assist Artist in fixing the terms governing all manner of disposition, use, employment or exploitation of Artist's talent and the products thereof;

(b) to supervise Artist's professional employment and on Artist's behalf, to consult with employers and prospective employers so as to assure the proper use and continued demand for Artist's services;

(c) to be available at reasonable times and places, subject to Paragraph 5 below, in order to confer with Artist, in connection with all matters concerning Artist's professional career, business interests, employment and publicity;

(d) to advise Artist with respect to the exploitation of Artist's personality in all media and in connection therewith to approve and permit for the purpose of trade, advertising, publicity and otherwise, the use, dissemination, reproduction or publication of Artist's name, photographic likeness, voice and artistic and musical materials;

(e) to engage, discharge and direct such theatrical agents, booking agencies, and employment agencies as well as other firms, persons or corporations who may be retained for the purpose of securing contracts, engagements or employment for Artist;

Subsection 2(e) should be modified to make the engagement or discharge of theatrical agents, booking agents and others subject to the approval of both the Manager and the Artist.

(f) to advise Artist in all dealings with unions and guilds; and

(g) to generally promote the best interest, professional and artistic value, profit, benefit and advantage of the Artist.

3. ARTIST'S OBLIGATIONS: Artist understands and agrees that:

(a) Artist shall be solely responsible for payment of all fees and expenses incurred by Artist, including but not limited to booking agency fees, union dues, publicity auditing fees, travel expenses for the Artist or for any employee of or assistant to the Artist, wardrobe expenses, and all other costs and expenses incurred by Artist, but in no event shall Artist be responsible for any expenses related directly to Manager's general overhead expense. Artist shall be responsible for reimbursing Manager for any and all direct expenses incurred by Manager, for which Manager provides receipts, vouchers and/or other documentation.

In regard to the last sentence in 3(a), a few words planted in an innocuous looking paragraph like this can be a land mine for the Artist. The problem is that "direct expenses" are not defined. The Manager could arguably deduct from the Artist's income any expense so long as the Manager kept receipts. This provision should be modified to clarify that the expense must be directly in further-ance of the Artist's career, plus any expense over some minimum amount such as $100 must be pre-approved by the Artist, and that any amount over $250 per month must be pre-approved.

(b) Nothing herein shall be construed to create an obligation on the part of Manager to advance any monies to Artist.

(c) In the event Manager does advance monies to Artist or, solely at Artist's request, to any employee of Artist or anyone else on Artist's behalf, Manager shall be entitled to recover the sum or sums advanced from Artist's Gross Earnings as defined in Paragraph 12.

(d) No advance made by Manager to Artist or to any employee of Artist shall be construed to create an obligation for Manager to make any further advances to Artist or to any employee of Artist.

(e) In the event that Manager incurs costs or expenses in connection with its duties here-under, including, but not limited to travel expenses and entertainment expenses related to the promotion of Artist's career or for any of the categories described in sub-paragraph 3(a) herein ("Manager Expenses"), Artist agrees that Manager shall have the right to reimburse itself for such Manager Expenses, after deduction of its Commission, from Artist's Gross Earnings as defined in Paragraph 12.

Subsection (e) is not as prejudicial to the Artist as the last sentence of subsection (a) because it ties the Manager's expenses to the promotion of the Artist's career, but it still gives the Manager too much discretion. For instance, this language would arguably give the Manager the right to deduct the cost of a vacation if the Manager had a single meeting regarding the Artist's career. Again the contract should include a clause providing that any expense over some minimum amount such as $100 must be pre-approved by the Artist and that any amount over $250 per month must be pre-approved.

(f) Artist shall not form or enter into any group, association or other entity for purposes of recording records, tapes or audio/visual devices, or for the purpose of performing live en-gagements, or for the purpose of performing in television, theater or motion pictures, without first obtaining Manager's approval.

(g) Artist warrants that Artist will actively pursue Artist's career in the entertainment indus-try and will follow all advice and counsel proffered by Manager hereunder.

Subsection (g) should be modified by inserting the word "reasonable" immediately before the words "advice and counsel." Otherwise, the Artist would be in breach if she didn't follow every piece of advice the Manager handed down, no matter whether that advice is brilliant or utterly terrible. Every human is fallible, even the most successful manager.

(h) Artist and Manager hereby agree that the selection of Artist's road manager shall be decided by Manager.

> Subsection (h) should give the Artist approval rights over selection of the road manager because the Artist must practically live with the road manager when on tour.

4.   OTHER ARTIST: Artist understands that Manager may represent and continue to represent other persons, artists and performers, and Artist agrees that Manager shall not be required to devote Manager's entire time and attention to fulfilling Manager's obligations under this Agreement.

> Paragraph 4 is reasonable but if the individual who the Artist wants to manage her is part of a firm including other managers, a pro-artist agreement would supplement this paragraph with a "key man" clause. The following is an example of such a provision:
> "During the Term, _____ shall be primarily responsible for Manager's activities under this Agreement. Notwithstanding the foregoing, it is understood and agreed that _____ may delegate day-to-day responsibilities to other employees of Manager provided _____ remains primarily responsible for the activities and services provided by Manager. Notwithstanding anything to the contrary contained herein, in the event that _____ shall cease to be employed by Manager or shall cease to be primarily responsible for Manager's activities hereunder ('Key-Man Event'), Artist shall have the right to terminate the Term of this agreement effective upon the date of Artist's notice to Manager of such Key-Man Event."

5.   MEETINGS: Manager shall not be required to travel or to meet with Artist at any particular times or places except in Manager's discretion and provided that arrangements have been made for costs and expenses of such travel to be paid for by Artist, but if said costs and expenses are paid by Manager, the full amount of such costs and expenses shall be recoupable from the Artist as provided in paragraph 3 above.

> While it is reasonable not to require the Manager to travel long distances to meet with the Artist if, for example, the Artist is on the road, the Manager should make himself reasonably available to meet with the Artist at other times. Moreover, the Artist should have the right to approve any travel expenses if the Manager and Artist decide that the Manager should travel to meet with the Artist.

6.   BOOKING AGENT: It is further understood and agreed by and between the Parties hereto that the obtaining of employment for Artist by Manager is not an obligation of Manager under this Agreement, that Manager is not an employment agent or theatrical agent, that Manager has not offered or attempted or promised to obtain, seek or procure employment or engagements for Artist and that Manager is not obligated, authorized, licensed or expected to do so. Manager may provide assistance in negotiating with theatrical booking agents or other persons, firms or corporations for the purpose of obtaining engagements for Artist, in which event the compensation to be paid to said theatrical booking agents, or other

third parties for obtaining such bookings or engagements shall be paid by Artist in addition to the compensation payable to Manager hereunder. Artist and Manager hereby agree that the selection of booking agent(s) must be approved by Manager.

> The Manager needs this provision because an employment agency license is legally required in most states, including California and New York, in order to solicit employment. Most managers don't have these licenses because securing an employment agency license usually requires posting a bond and other formalities. But, to solicit employment without a license would, in most states, subject the Manager to civil and even criminal penalties. The boilerplate language included in this paragraph is designed to avoid placing the Manager in jeopardy of these penalties.

7. EXCLUSIVITY:

(a) Artist shall not, during the Term of this Agreement, engage any other person, firm or corporation or otherwise, to act on her behalf in the capacity of a personal manager or to perform any of the services or undertakings of Manager as provided for herein.

> The Manager does not want to compete with third parties for the Artist's attention, nor does he want to share his commission. However, there are some occasions where it is reasonable for an Artist to have more than one Manager. For instance, suppose that the Artist has a separate career as a novelist in addition to his music career. The Artist may wish to have separate representation for his career as a writer. This issue also arises in the definition of "Entertainment Business." See Paragraph 11(c) below.

(b) Notwithstanding the foregoing, nothing contained in this Agreement shall be construed as limiting Artist's ability to retain legal advice and counsel or financial investment advice.

8. USE OF NAME & LIKENESS: Artist agrees that Manager may publicly represent itself as Artist's exclusive manager, and for the purposes of this Agreement, Artist grants Manager the right to use Artist's likeness, photograph, and approved biographical material and the like as in Manager's reasonable discretion shall be advisable.

> A pro-artist contract would limit the Manager's right to use the Artist's "likeness" and "photo-graph" to those images that the Artist has approved.

9. PERFORMANCE OBLIGATIONS:

(a) Artist will use best efforts to perform such services at such times and at such places as Manager directs.

> This provision should be modified because it gives too much power to the Manager. The Manager will be protected if the Artist fails to pursue her career (see Paragraph 17), but the Artist should not have to do everything the Manager "directs."

(b) For the purposes of this Agreement, Artist grants Manager the right to use Artist's likeness, photograph, and approved biographical material and the like as in Manager's reasonable discretion shall be advisable. Artist will comply with the rules and obligations covering such services in all respects.

See comment for Paragraph 8.

10. ARTIST NOT A MINOR: Artist warrants and represents that she is an adult and not a minor under the laws governing this Agreement and the performance hereunder.

In most states if the Artist is a minor she can rescind or nullify the entire agreement. For instance, in New York, any person under the age of 18 can rescind an agreement that requires a period of years to take place. A manager entering into a deal with a child should consider a legal process having a judge "affirm" that the contract is fair. This judicial process generally costs between $5,000 to $10,000 in legal fees, and that cost should not be chargeable to the Artist.

11. COMPENSATION:

(a) As compensation for services to be rendered hereunder, Artist hereby agrees to pay Manager a sum equal to Twenty Percent (20%) of one hundred percent (100%) of Artist's "Gross Earnings" as defined in paragraph 11(b) (hereinafter the "Commission").

15% to 20% of gross earning is standard. Since this is a pro-management agreement, the commission is 20%.

(b) The term "Gross Earnings", as used herein, refers to the total of all earnings, whether in the form of salaries, earnings, fees, bonuses, royalties, advances against royalties, sponsorship fees, endorsement fees, residuals, deferred compensation, union payments in connection with Artist services, interest, shares of profits, or any other kind or type of income which is reasonably related to Artist's career in the "Entertainment Business" as defined below.

This clause is the standard "pro-management" definition of gross earnings. It would be better for the Artist to have a "net" deal, but this is hard to get. A net deal would exclude income that the Artist needs to spend to make money. In other words, the Artist's expenses in connection with her career are taken off the top, and the Manager's cut is taken as a percentage of the remainder. As we discussed in the introduction, it is essential that agreement spells out specific exclusions to "Gross Earnings." See comments in connection with Paragraph 11(d) below.

(c) The "Entertainment Business" shall include live performance, personal engagements, amusement, music recording, music publishing (and all income derived from music publishing), music production (including but not limited to income earned in connection with Artist's rendering producer or re-mixer services), Artist production company, Artist record label, motion picture, endorsements and branding, theatrical and advertising fields and all similar areas whether now known or hereafter devised in fields and all similar areas whether now known or hereafter devised in any media and throughout the world, in which Artist's artistic talents are developed and exploited, received by Artist or by any person, firm or corporation (including Manager) on Artist's behalf, including but not limited to Artist's heirs, executors, administrators or assigns.

This definition of the "Entertainment Business" is defined in the broadest possible terms because it is in the Manager's interest to apply his commission to ANY and ALL income that the Artist makes in the entertainment industry, from selling records to writing a cook book. The Manager will argue that creating success in any area of the entertainment business such as music will create opportunities in other areas. The Artist should try to at least "carve-out" forms of income that the Artist does not need the Manager's help to make or sustain. See comments to Paragraph 12 below.

(d) Notwithstanding anything to the contrary above, Gross Earnings, as used herein shall specifically exclude (i) any actual recording or video production costs paid to unaffiliated and unrelated third parties in connection with Artist's recording or video performance, (ii) income derived by Artist from any business investments and non-entertainment industry related activities, or (iii) money used for sound and lights and/or actual tour support expenses.

A totally pro-management agreement would not even have these deductions, but they are essential to protect the Artist. For instance, subsection (i) excludes recording costs. Suppose the Artist's record deal provides that a label will pay an advance of $50,000 inclusive of recording costs, and the Artist spends $35,000 to make an album including studio time, producers, side musicians, and mixing. Without (i) the Manager's Commission would be $10,000 (20% of $50,000), and the Artist would end up with $5,000. Plus the Artist would still be responsible for paying all her other expenses such as food, rent, and taxes.

Subsection (iii) is also an essential exclusion. Here's why: If the Artist is unsigned and paying for the costs of touring, unless the management agreement is carefully negotiated, the Artist could easily end up being left with little or nothing, or even owing the Manager money. For instance, if the Artist makes a total of $15,000 playing live gigs on a tour, the expenses—such as a tour bus, gas, hotel, etc.,—could end up costing $12,000. The Manager's commission would be 20% of $15,000 or $3,000, leaving the Artist with exactly nothing.

The bottom line is that all reasonable expenses such as production costs including videos and records, touring costs including light and sound expenses as well as travel and accommodations, have to be spelled out in the Agreement and deducted from "Gross Earnings." The quibbling starts when the attorneys try to define reasonable expenses. For instance, if the Artist has to fly to a gig, the Manager's attorney may insist that she flies coach, spends less than $50 a day on food, rent an economy car, and stay at no better than a 3 star hotel. The Artist's attorney will want to deduct car rental and any other costs that the venue does not cover.

---

12. <u>CARVE-OUTS</u>: Notwithstanding anything to the contrary in the foregoing, Manager shall not be entitled to its Commission in regard to any income paid to Artist as a free-lance make-up artist.

Carve out clauses are designed to exclude income that it may be unfair for a Manager to commission. For instance, in this case, the Artist may be an aspiring singer/songwriter who has been making a living as a freelance make-up artist. She is not hiring the Manager to make her more money from being a make-up artist. So it is reasonable to "carve out" that income from "Gross Earnings."

13. POST-TERM COMPENSATION: The compensation agreed to be paid to Manager pursuant to paragraph 11 hereof, or any other provision of this Agreement, shall be based upon Artist's Gross Earnings (as herein defined) earned by Artist or received by Artist, Manager or Business Manager during the Term of this Agreement. Notwithstanding the foregoing, Artist likewise agrees to pay Manager in perpetuity, compensation following the expiration or termination of this Agreement with respect to any and all engagements, contracts and agreements, or extensions or amendments thereto, entered into during the Term or offers initiated or negotiated during the Term and consummated or executed within three (3) months following the expiration of the Term hereof.

An off-the-shelf pro-management agreement will have absolutely no time limits on the Manager's right to receive a commission from agreements entered into during the term. It will state, as this agreement does, that any contract entered into during the term, or any "extensions or amendments" of that contract will be subject to the Manager's commission. This means that as long as the Artist is with the same label or music publisher that the Manager originally helped the Artist sign with, the Artist would be obligated to continue paying the Manager for any income derived from that contract FOREVER. Many successful artists such as Bruce Springsteen, Billy Joel, and Bob Dylan have been with the same the record company for decades. For example, Bob Dylan signed with Columbia Records in 1961 and is still with that label. If he signed this agreement, he would still be paying the Manager for any monies Columbia is paying him.

To prevent the Artist from owing the Manager long after the term has expired, the Artist should negotiate a "sunset clause." Sunset clauses specify that even if the Artist is making money from a contract originally entered into during the term of the agreement, the Manager will not receive a commission after the termination of the agreement. Or, at least, the Manager should not receive his full commission. Here is a typical sunset clause:

"Following the Term, artist shall pay manager's commission ("post term commission") with respect to artist's gross earnings, as and when collected, derived from agreements entered into during the Term as follows:

Post-Term Years/ Commission

1	/	12.5%
2	/	7.5%
3–4	/	2.5%
5+	/	0%"

Sunset clauses reward managers for their work during the term of the agreement and at the same time afford the Artist the ability to sign with another manager and avoid paying two full commissions.

14. ARTIST'S INCORPORATION: In the event that Artist forms a corporation during the Term hereof for the purpose of furnishing and exploiting Artist's artistic talents, Artist agrees

that the Gross Earnings of such corporation prior to the deduction of any taxes, expenses or other deductions shall be included as part of Artist's Gross Earnings as herein defined.

A totally pro-manager agreement would also include a clause allowing the Manager to commission in perpetuity "any product of Artist's talents including musical compositions." This is sometimes referred to as a manager's "pension" clause because one great song can generate income for a lifetime or longer.

---

15. PAYMENT OF GROSS EARNING; REIMBURSEMENT OF MANAGER EXPENSES:

(a) Artist shall be entitled to retain an accountant or other music business professional to act as a business manager ("Business Manager"), provided that Manager shall have the absolute right to approve the Business Manager. The Business Manager shall have the obligation to collect and receive all Gross Earnings with respect to which Manager's Commission is payable. The Business Manager shall also handle Artist's accounting activities including, without limitation, payment to Manager of Manager's Commission due hereunder and reimbursement to Manager of Manager's Expenses. Artist shall direct said Business Manager to pay Manager its Commission from one hundred percent (100%) of Gross Earnings and Manager's Expenses within five (5) days of receipt of any Gross Earnings during the Term and thereafter so long as Manager is entitled to receive its Commissions hereunder. Manager shall receive a written accounting statement each month during the Term in which Artist receives Gross Earnings. Said accounting statement shall set forth all Gross Earnings received by the Business Manager hereunder during the prior month, specifying the source, and the amount received or earned from each source. It is understood that the Business Manager is generally paid a commission of five percent (5%), but the Business Manager's compensation shall be mutually approved by Manager and Artist.

Who collects the money? Many good managers do not want to collect the money and prepare accounting statements to an artist because that can be a time consuming job in itself. These managers would prefer to use their time to generate opportunities. The Artist, in turn, may not feel completely comfortable relying on the Manager to pay him. A good alternative, at least when the Artist is making significant income, is for the parties to mutually approve a third party "business manager" (usually a certified accountant) who can collect and accurately account to both the Artist and the Manager.

The business manager can also be responsible for paying the Artist's taxes, managing the Artist's money (so she doesn't spend it too quickly), and advising the Artist on investment opportunities. Business managers usually receive a 5% fee for these services. Again, just as in the deal between the Artist and the Manager, that fee should be a percentage of the Artist's income excluding income that the Artist must spend for production costs, touring, and other reasonable expenses.

(b) Until such time as Artist has retained a Business Manager (who, as set forth above, shall be subject to Manager's approval), Manager shall have the exclusive right to collect any and all Gross Earnings as defined in Paragraph 11 of this Agreement. Manager shall deduct Manager's Commission of twenty percent (20%) of one hundred percent (100%) Gross Earnings, and thereafter deduct Manager's Expenses, and then pay Artist the balance of Gross Earnings. Manager agrees to disburse to Artist any and all sums collected by Manager and due to Artist promptly after receipt of said sums by Manager after deducting its Commission and Expenses. In the event that any party actually pays any Gross Earnings to Artist instead of Manager, Artist agrees to immediately pay Manager that portion of those Gross Earnings that equals Manager's Commission. Artist shall execute any document that may be legally required for Manager to collect or receive any Gross Earnings.

16. <u>POWER OF ATTORNEY</u>: Artist hereby grants, assigns and conveys to the Manager the right to sign the following types of contracts, instruments or legal documents on his behalf: (a) a personal appearance engagement for up to three days and/or nights; and (b) any other contract, instrument or legal document if the Artist is unavailable and the Manager has the Artist's verbal, email or fax approval.

Some managers will ask for the right to enter into agreements on behalf of an artist. The Artist may wish to give the Manager the right to sign agreements on his behalf, but only after the Manager consults with him, apprises him of the terms of any agreement, and the Artist accepts the contract. If I represented the Artist, I would subject (a) to the Artist's approval as well as (b) "any other contract."

---

17. <u>SUSPENSIONS & EXTENSIONS</u>: Manager shall have the right to suspend the running of the Term of this Agreement and its obligations hereunder upon written notice to Artist, if for any reason Artists fails cooperate with Manager or fails to actively pursue her entertainment business career or if the ability of Artist to perform shall become physically or mentally impaired, as a result of such impairment Artist becomes unable to comply with any of his material obligations hereunder. Such suspension shall be for the duration of Artist's failure to perform and the Term of this Agreement (including any options or renewal terms) shall be automatically extended by such number of days equal to the total number of days of any such suspension pursuant to this paragraph.

The term of a management contract should arguably be suspended if the Artist "fails to actively pursue her entertainment business career or if the ability of Artist to perform shall become physically or mentally impaired," but "failure to cooperate" is too broad. A pro-artist contract would delete this language.

---

18. <u>REPRESENTATIONS & WARRANTIES</u>: The Artist hereby represents and warrants that she has not entered into any agreement or contract which shall in any way interfere or conflict, or which does in any way interfere or conflict, with Artist's obligations hereunder. Artist further

agrees that she shall hold Manager harmless and indemnify Manager from any and all claims arising out of such lack of disclosure and from any and all loss, damage, liability or expense, including cost of suit and reasonable attorneys fees, resulting from or arising out of such lack of disclosure. The parties further agree to indemnify and hold each other harmless from any and all claims and from any and all loss, damage, liability or expense, including cost of suit and reasonable attorneys fees, resulting from or arising out of the breach of any agreement, representation or warranty made by either party herein.

19. AUDIT: The Parties hereby agree that a certified public accountant or attorney may inspect and audit the books and the records of either Party or Business Manager to ascertain the accuracy of any statement rendered pursuant to this Agreement. The aforementioned audit and/or inspections, if any, shall only be upon receipt of written notice within thirty (30) days and at the principal place of business where such books and records are maintained with respect to the Artist may not assign this Agreement or any of the rights granted herein.

Whether the Artist or the Manager collects the money, there should be an accounting and audit provision applying to that party.

---

20. DEFAULT: It is agreed that no Party herein shall be deemed to be in breach or default hereunder, which breach or default would otherwise be deemed a material breach or default, unless and until the aggrieved Party shall first give to the Party allegedly in breach of default written notice by certified or registered mail, return receipt requested, describing the exact service which the aggrieved Party requires of the Party allegedly in breach or default. The Party allegedly in breach or default shall thereafter have a period of thirty (30) consecutive days to remedy such breach or default.

21. ASSIGNMENT: Manager may assign this Agreement or any of the rights hereunder to any person, firm, or corporation which has regular business in the entertainment industry including a corporation in which the Manager is a principal. Notwithstanding the foregoing, Artist may not assign this Agreement or any of the rights granted herein.

The Artist will want to modify this clause to allow the Manager to assign the agreement ONLY to a corporation in which the Manager is a principal, and not "to any person, form or corporation." Otherwise the Artist may wind up with a person as a manager that she doesn't even know.

---

22. INJUNCTIVE RELIEF: The services to be rendered by the Artist hereunder are personal, unique and irreplaceable, and any breach or threatened breach of this Agreement by the Artist shall cause irreparable harm and shall entitle Manager to injunctive relief in addition

to and without limiting any other remedy that may be available to the Manager or other parties.

> The Manager can use this clause to enforce the provisions of the Agreement including payment of the Manager's Commission, and to annul any other management deal the Artist may wish to enter into.

23. GOVERNING LAW: This Agreement shall be construed and interpreted according to the laws of New York. The parties hereto agree that any controversy arising under this Agreement shall be adjudicated under the jurisdiction of a competent court within the State of New York.

> It would be advantageous to the Artist if the jurisdiction of any court adjudicating a dispute under this Agreement is the state in which the Artist resides.

24. NOTICES & APPROVALS: All notices and approvals required by this Agreement (including approvals required under Paragraph 16 above) must be in writing and delivered to the other Party by certified mail or by electronic mail (i.e., e-mail) to the following email addresses:

TO MANAGER: _____@_____.com (or other email address as specified by manager from time to time)

TO ARTIST: _____@_____.com (or other email address as specified by Artist from time to time)

> Older forms would not include notice by e-mail.

25. WAIVER: A waiver of any provision or breach of this Agreement at any time shall not constitute a waiver of any other provision nor shall it constitute a waiver of the same provision or any other breach at any subsequent time. Any provision or clause of this Agreement which is deemed invalid or unenforceable, at law or otherwise, shall not affect the validity and binding nature of the rest of this Agreement.

26. MEANING OF TERMS: Every word or phrase defined herein shall, unless herein specified to the contrary, have the same meaning throughout. As used herein, wherever applicable, and as the context shall so require, the singular shall include the plural and the plural shall include the singular. Termination or discharge of this Agreement, or any provisions thereof, shall be binding unless confirmed by a written instrument signed by the Party sought to be changed. The headings of the paragraphs herein are intended for convenience only, and shall not be of any effect in construing the contents of this Agreement.

27. <u>ENTIRE AGREEMENT</u>: This Agreement sets forth the entire agreement between the Parties hereto, and no modification, amendment, waiver or change shall be valid except in a writing signed by both parties.

IN WITNESS WHEREOF, the parties hereto have executed this Agreement the day and year herein above the first written:

ARTIST:

_____

MANAGER:

_____

Authorized Signatory

PRO-ARTIST AGREEMENT

EXCLUSIVE MANAGEMENT AGREEMENT

THIS AGREEMENT ("Agreement") is entered into as of _____, 2017 (the "Effective Date") by and between _____ Management Inc. ("Manager") with an address at _____, and _____ ("Artist") having an address at _____.

1. TERM.

(a) The term of this Agreement shall commence on the date hereof and shall continue for a period of eighteen (18) months from the Effective Date (the "Initial Term").

(b) Solely in the event the Initial Term Threshold Amount (as defined herein) has been attained during the Initial Term, Artist hereby grants to Manager the option, to extend the Initial Term for an additional eighteen (18) month period (the "First Extended Term"). "Initial Term Threshold Amount" shall mean Two Hundred Thousand Dollars ($200,000) or more in Gross Earnings (as defined herein) earned in the aggregate during the Initial Term with respect to Entertainment Activities (as defined herein). For purposes of calculating the Initial Term Threshold Amount: monies earned from Wedding Singing shall not be included.

(c) Solely in the event the First Extended Threshold Amount (as defined herein) has been attained during the First Extended Term, Artist hereby grants to Manager the option, to extend the First Extended Term for an additional eighteen (18) month period (the "Second Extended Term"). "First Extended Term Threshold Amount" shall mean Three Hundred Thousand Dollars ($300,000) or more in Gross Earnings (as defined herein) earned in the aggregate during the First Extended Term with respect to Entertainment Activities (as defined herein). For purposes of calculating the First Extended Term Threshold Amount monies earned from Wedding Singing shall not be included.

(d) Solely in the event the Second Extended Threshold Amount (as defined herein) has been attained during the Second Extended Term, Artist hereby grants to Manager the option, to extend the Second Extended Term for an additional twelve (12) month period (the "Third Extended Term"). "Second Extended Term Threshold Amount" shall mean Three Hundred Fifty Thousand Dollars ($350,000) or more in Gross Earnings (as defined herein) earned in the aggregate during the Second Extended Term with respect to Entertainment Activities (as defined herein). For purposes of calculating the Second Extended Term Threshold Amount monies earned from Wedding Singing, as defined in subparagraph 2(e) below, shall not be included.

(e) The Initial Term, the First Extended Term (if applicable), the Second Extended Term (if applicable) and the Third Extended Term (if applicable) shall be individually and collectively referred to herein as the "Term."

2. <u>SERVICES.</u>

(a) Artist hereby engages Manager as Artist's sole and exclusive personal manager in all respects of the entertainment industry including, without limitation, live performance, music, music recording, music publishing, motion pictures, film, television, literary, dramatic and theatrical, merchandising or sponsorships ("Entertainment Activities") throughout the world for the Term, and Manager accepts such engagement subject to the terms and conditions of this Agreement (the "Management Services").

(b) Without limiting any of the terms hereunder, during the Term, Manager agrees to use all reasonable efforts to promote, develop, and advance Artist's professional career, and to advise and counsel Artist with respect to all Entertainment Activities, including, but not limited to:

(i) advising and counseling in any and all matters pertaining to publicity, public relations, and advertising;

(ii) advising and counseling with relation to the adoption of a proper format for presentation of Artist's talents, and in the determination of proper style, mood, setting, and characterizations in keeping with Artist's talents;

(iii) advising and counseling regarding the selection of artistic talent to assist, accompany, or embellish Artist's artistic presentation and advising and counseling in connection therewith;

(iv) advising and counseling with regard to general practices in the entertainment and amusement industries, and with respect to such matters of which Manager may have knowledge concerning compensation and privileges for similar artistic values;

(v) advising and counseling concerning the selection of theatrical agencies, business managers, and persons, firms, and corporations who will advise and counsel Artist, and will seek and procure employment and engagements for Artist;

(vi) to the extent permitted by law, advising and counseling in connection with the negotiations of all agreements affecting Artist's career;

(vii) subject to approval by Artist, coordinating the professional schedules of Artist;

(viii) with Artist's prior written consent, causing the audit and examination of books and records of parties which Artist has contractual or other rights to audit and to examine; and

(ix) performing any other services customarily performed by a personal manager in the entertainment industry, provided, however, that Manager shall not be obligated to seek, solicit, obtain, or procure any other employment or engagements for Artist, but shall consult with and assist licensed booking agents in doing so.

(c) Manager shall be required to render all customary and reasonable services called for by this Agreement as and when reasonably required. Manager shall not, however, be required to travel to meet with Artist at any particular place, except in Manager's reasonable discretion or as may be reasonably necessary to perform Manager's function hereunder, and subject to satisfactory arrangements for payment or reimbursement of the reasonable costs and expenses of such travel.

(d) Artist acknowledges that nothing contained herein shall prohibit Manager from providing similar services for others or from engaging in other business activities during the Term.

(e) Notwithstanding the foregoing terms and conditions, Artist hereby acknowledges that Manager shall not be required to render the Management Services with respect to Artist's services as a wedding singer ("Wedding Singing"). Monies earned by Artist in connection with Wedding Singing shall not be commissionable by Manager hereunder.

3. MANAGER'S AUTHORITY.

(a) During the Term hereof, Manager is authorized and empowered for Artist and on Artist's behalf, after written approval from Artist (email approval shall suffice) provided that Manager shall not be required to obtain Artist's written approval and oral approval shall suffice in any instance where the exigencies of the event require immediate action, to do the following: (i) to approve and permit any and all publicity and advertising relating to Artist's career in the entertainment industry; (ii) to approve and permit the use of Artist's name, approved photographs, approved likenesses, voice, sound effects, approved caricatures, literary, artistic and musical materials for purposes of advertising and publicity, and in the promotion and advertising of any and all products and services relating to Artist's career in the entertainment industry. Artist will provide to Manager, upon Manager's request, an appropriate number of photographs and images approved by Artist ("Subject Materials") for the aforementioned purposes; provided, if Artist provides Manager with new Subject Materials and requests Manager to cease with using the existing Subject Materials, Manager shall cease with using such existing Subject Materials; and (iii) with Artist's prior written consent in each instance, to engage, as well as discharge and/or direct for Artist and in Artist's name, theatrical agents, business managers, and employment agencies, as well as other persons.

(b) Notwithstanding any other provision contained in this Agreement, Manager shall not execute, pursuant to the authority granted to Manager in paragraph 3(a) above, on behalf of Artist, any book publishing, booking agency, motion picture, television, theatrical, sponsorship, endorsement or any merchandising contract, or any other agreement. As a general practice, Manager will make good faith efforts to not utilize its authority as set forth above except for short engagements and minor publicity matters. Manager will communicate regularly with Artist regarding all of the above and shall act under Artist's general direction.

4. <u>COMMISSION.</u>

(a) With respect to Term Products (as defined herein), Term Services (as defined herein) and Pre-Term Products (as defined herein), Artist shall pay Manager fifteen percent (15%) of Artist's Gross Earnings earned, received and/or credited to Artist ("Manager's Commission"), as and when collected, on the terms and conditions more particularly set forth below.

(b) For the purposes of this Agreement, subject to the terms and provisions of this Agreement, the term "Gross Earnings" shall mean the total of all earnings and other consideration, whether in the form of salary, bonuses, royalties (or advances against royalties), settlements, payments, fees, interests, property, percentages, shares of profits, stock, merchandise or any other kind or type of income or remuneration, related to Artist's career in the entertainment industry in which Artist's artistic talents or services are exploited that is received at any time by Artist, or by any person or entity (including Manager) on Artist's behalf. If Artist receives, as all or part of Artist's compensation for activities in the entertainment and literary fields, stock or the right to buy stock in any corporation or if Artist becomes the packager or owner of all or part of an entertainment property, whether as an individual proprietor, stockholder, partner, joint venturer or otherwise, Manager's percentage shall apply to said stock, right to buy stock, individual proprietorship, partnership, joint venture or other form of interest (only to the extent such interests are in lieu of compensation for Artist's services); and Manager shall be entitled to Manager's percentage share thereof. If any corporation, partnership, trust, joint venture, association, proprietorship or other business entity in which Artist has a direct or indirect interest shall receive any compensation for permitting or contracting for the use of the Artist's services, name, image, voice, likeness or endorsement, then such compensation shall be deemed to be "Gross Earnings" received by Artist for the purpose of this Agreement.

(c) Notwithstanding the foregoing, the following payments paid and/or incurred during the Subject Term shall not be included in Gross Earnings: (i) any recording costs, including studio, side musicians, producer and mixing fees and royalties, (ii) sound and light allocations paid to the Artist or on her behalf by any promoter or other third party, (iii) travel and/or accommodations and/or per diems allotments received from or paid on behalf of the Artist by any third parties in connection with travelling to and from an appearance or other professional activity, (iv) costs pertaining to production of videos; and (v) any other funds obtained from third parties for purposes of Artist's expenses in connection with Artist's Entertainment Activities.

(d) Following the Term, Artist shall pay Manager's Commission ("Post Term Commission") with respect to Artist's Gross Earnings, as and when collected, derived from Term Products, Term Services as follows:

POST-TERM YEARS	COMMISSION
1	10%
2	5%
3–4	2.5%
5+	0%

(e) In the event the Term does not continue beyond the Initial Term, in lieu of the terms provided for in subparagraph 4(d) above, the Post Term Commission with respect to Artist's Gross Earnings, as and when collected, derived from Term Products, Term Services and Pre-Term Products shall be as follows:

POST-TERM YEARS	COMMISSION
1	5%
2	2.5%
3+	0%

As used herein "Term Products" means creative works created, rendered and/or exploited by Artist during the Term including musical compositions. "Term Services" shall mean services of Artist rendered during or after the Term pursuant to agreements entered into during the Term, or substantially negotiated during the Term and/or entered into within three (3) months after the end of the Term (including, without limitation, those respecting endorsements and sponsorships opportunities). Notwithstanding anything to the contrary in the foregoing and for the avoidance of doubt, no earnings from live performances or respecting endorsements and sponsorships opportunities occurring after one year subsequent to the expiration of this Agreement shall be deemed to be Gross Earnings.

(f) If Artist forms a corporation or other entity for the purposes of furnishing and exploiting Artist's artistic talents, Artist agrees that such corporation or other entity is hereby deemed to have entered into this management agreement with Manager from the inception of the corporation or other entity identical in all respects to this Agreement (except as to the parties hereto). In such event the gross earnings of such corporation or other entity shall be included as part of the Gross Earnings.

5. EXPENSES.

In the event that Manager incurs any costs, fees or expenses in connection with Artist's professional career or with the performance of Management Services hereunder, Artist shall promptly reimburse Manager for such fees, costs and expenses. Notwithstanding the foregoing, (a) Artist shall not be obligated to reimburse Manager for general overhead expenses, and (b) Manager shall not, without the prior written approval of Artist, incur any singular expense; provided, if a particular expense is less than Two Hundred and Fifty Dollars ($250) and Artist fails to respond to Manager within twenty-four (24) hours after Manager requests Artist approval, such failure to response shall be deemed to be Artist approval as to the particular expense. Notwithstanding anything to the contrary in the foregoing, Manager shall not spend more than Five Hundred Dollars ($500) in any one four (4) week period without Artist's prior written approval. Travel expenses incurred by Manager which benefit multiple clients of Manager shall be pro-rated by Manager among the clients benefited. Upon Artist request, Manager shall provide Artist with itemized statements of all expenses incurred with respect to Manager's services rendered hereunder, together with supporting documentation evidencing such expenses. Artist shall reimburse Manager for such amounts within thirty (30) days of receipt of such statement.

6.   BOOKS AND RECORDS.

The parties hereunder agree that either Artist or a bona fide third party business manager approved by Artist and Manager shall be responsible for collecting Gross Earnings. Artist agrees to maintain and/or to cause all third parties collecting monies on Artist's behalf, during the Term and for so long thereafter as Manager's Commission (including Post Term Commissions) is payable hereunder, accurate books and records of all monies paid to or collected by Artist or by third parties on Artist's behalf. Such books and records may be inspected during regular business hours by a certified public accountant designated by Manager and at Manager's expense, at the place where same are regularly maintained, upon thirty (30) days' written notice to Artist; provided, however, that such examination shall not be permitted more than once per calendar year and further provided Manager may only examine and object to a particular statement within three (3) years after the applicable statement has been received by Manager. Manager will not have the right to sue Artist in connection with any accounting statement received, unless Manager commences suit within three (3) years and six (6) months after the applicable statement has been received by Manager. Artist will use good faith efforts to instruct all applicable parties to pay Manager monies and royalties payable hereunder.

7.   OTHER PARTIES.

If Artist is presently associated with one or more other performers in the performance of Artist's work or if during the Term of this Agreement Artist becomes associated with one or more such other performers, then the terms of this Agreement shall be and remain binding upon Artist without respect to the making or changing of any such association by Artist.

8. NOTICES.

All notices pursuant to this Agreement shall be in writing and shall be given by registered or certified mail, return receipt requested, or by recognized overnight courier (e.g., FedEx, UPS, etc.) at the respective addresses hereinabove set forth or such other address(es) as designated by either party. Such notices shall be deemed given when mailed, except that a notice of change of address shall be effective only from the date of its receipt. A copy of all notices sent to Manager hereunder shall be sent concurrently to _____, attn: _____, Esq., _____ and a copy of all notices sent to Artist hereunder shall be sent concurrently to _____, Esq., _____.

9. WARRANTIES AND REPRESENTATIONS.

(a) Artist warrants, represents and agrees that Artist is not under any disability, restriction or prohibition, either contractual, by force of any applicable law or otherwise, with respect to Artist's right to execute this Agreement or to perform fully all of its terms and conditions.

(b) Manager warrants, represents and agrees that Manager is not under any disability, restriction or prohibition, either contractual, by force of any applicable law or otherwise, with respect to Manager's right to execute this Agreement or to perform fully its terms and conditions.

(c) Excluded Services of Manager. Artist hereby acknowledges that Manager is not an employment agent, theatrical agent, or licensed artists' manager, and that Manager has not promised to procure employment or engagements for Artist, and that Manager shall not be obligated to procure or to attempt to procure any employment or engagements for Artist hereunder. Artist shall be solely responsible for payment of all necessary commissions to booking or similar agencies. Artist shall at all times engage reputable and competent licensed booking and theatrical agents or other employment agencies, which are acceptable to Manager, to obtain engagements and employment for Artist. Any compensation which Artist may be required to pay to such agents or agencies shall be at Artist's sole cost and expense.

10. INDEMNIFICATION.

Artist and Manager agree to indemnify, and hereby do indemnify, save and hold the other harmless from all actual loss, damage and expenses (including legal costs and reasonable attorney's fees) arising directly out of or connected with any claim by any third party which shall be inconsistent with any agreement, warranty or representation made by Artist or Manager in this Agreement. Artist and Manager each agree to reimburse the other, on demand, for any payment made at any time after the date hereof with respect to any liability to which the foregoing indemnity applies.

11. ASSIGNMENT AND KEY PERSON.

(a) Manager may not assign this Agreement except to a person or entity owning or acquiring a substantial portion of the stock or assets of Manager. Artist may not assign this Agreement or any of Artist's rights hereunder without Manager's prior written consent (except to a furnishing entity).

(b) Notwithstanding anything to the contrary above, _____ ("Key Person") shall have day to day supervision of Artist's account. During the Term, Key Person shall be primarily responsible for Manager's activities under this Agreement. Notwithstanding the foregoing, it is understood and agreed that Key Person may delegate day-to-day responsibilities to other employees of Manager provided Key Person remains primarily responsible for the activities and services provided by Manager. Notwithstanding anything to the contrary contained herein, in the event that the Key Person shall cease to be employed by Manager or shall cease to be primarily responsible for Manager's activities hereunder ("Key-Person Event"), Artist shall have the right to terminate the Term of this Agreement effective upon the date of Artist's notice to Manager of such Key-Person Event.

12. THE SIGNATURES OF MANAGER AND OF ARTIST BELOW INDICATE THAT EACH HAS SOUGHT LEGAL REPRESENTATION IN CONNECTION WITH THIS AGREEMENT OR HAS HAD THE OPPORTUNITY TO HAVE IT EXPLAINED TO THEM BY AN INDEPENDENT ATTORNEY OF THEIR CHOICE AND HAS KNOWINGLY AND WILLFULLY WAIVED THE RIGHT TO DO SO.

13. MISCELLANEOUS.

This Agreement, and all disputes arising between Artist and Manager, shall be governed by and construed in accordance with the laws of the State of New York. Unless expressly stated otherwise, the remedies specified herein are cumulative and in addition to any other remedies available at law or in equity. This Agreement constitutes the entire agreement between Artist and Manager respecting the subject matter hereof and supersedes all prior proposals, agreements, negotiations, representations, writings and all other communications, whether written or oral, between the parties. No modification or waiver of any provision of this Agreement shall be effective unless made in a writing signed by both parties. Artist may not assign this Agreement or any of Artist's rights hereunder without Manager's prior written consent. The prevailing party in any legal action brought by one party hereto against the other and arising out of any dispute between the parties shall be entitled, in addition to any other rights and remedies available to it at law or in equity, to seek reimbursement from the other party for its costs and expenses (including court costs and reasonable fees for attorneys) incurred with respect to bringing and maintaining any such action. This Agreement may be signed in counterparts and any signed copy of this Agreement delivered by facsimile transmission, shall for all purposes be treated as if it were delivered containing an original manual signature of the party whose signature appears in the facsimile and shall be binding upon such party in the same manner as though an originally signed copy had been delivered.

IN WITNESS WHEREOF, the parties hereto have executed this Agreement the day and year herein above the first written:

ARTIST: MANAGER:

By: _____   By: _____
                                           Authorized Signatory

PRODUCTION COMPANY DEALS (. . . AND THE CONTRACT FROM HELL WHICH NO ARTIST SHOULD SIGN)

INTRODUCTION: PRODUCTION COMPANIES SHOULD SHOP ARTISTS, NOT EXPLOIT THEM

This chapter will focus on production companies, what they do, and their relationships with artists. The next chapter will address artists' deals with record companies.

Production Companies Are Not Labels

Production companies usually consist of one or two individuals with limited resources who plan on making a few demos for an artist and shopping the artist to a record company. Unfortunately, more than occasionally, such a company will present an agreement that locks the artist into a long term deal, makes the company the artist's music publisher, takes a substantial cut of all the income that the artist makes in the entire entertainment business, and contains other unfair and overreaching provisions.

The first agreement we will examine in this chapter is typical of a contract offered to an artist by a production company masquerading as a "label." Be warned: this agreement is a terrible deal for artists. It presents all the negative terms typically contained in an exclusive recording agreement offered by a major label, including multiple options for additional albums that could extend the duration of the agreement indefinitely and 360 provisions designed to give the company a significant portion of the artist's income from any of her activities in the entertainment business. See the discussion of 360 deals below. But, this agreement offers none of the benefits that a major label deal contains, such as a recording budget or an advance.

There are many differences between a production company and a real label, but they have at least the following in common: both production companies and labels own or have access to recording studios and equipment, and they both have producers on payroll or relationships with indie producers who they can call on to make professional recordings. A real label, however, has the following additional assets:

- Staffers and/or freelancers who provide both traditional marketing and publicity as well as online social networking support;
- Staffers and/or freelancers who continually pitch records to terrestrial radio—still a crucial element in breaking a new artist, especially in pop, R&B, hip hop, rock, and country;
- A video department to produce, oversee, and pay for the production of promo videos and electronic press kits (EPKs);
- Relationships with popular TV shows such as *Saturday Night Live*, *The Tonight Show*, and *Last Call* to help the artist garner invaluable exposure;
- Relationships with leading digital services to promote an artist—for instance, by continually lobbying iTunes to feature the artist on its home page;
- Relationships with music supervisors and ad agencies to secure placements in TV shows, movies, and ad campaigns;
- Distribution channels through all the big-box chains, such as Walmart, Best Buy, and Target to sell physical copies of records;
- The ability to coordinate digital distribution to hundreds of digital music services throughout the world;
- The money necessary to pay staffers and freelancers to do the all the work above;
- International physical and digital distribution via affiliated companies or licensees; and
- Perhaps most importantly, the financial capacity to *pay the artist an advance* on top of production costs so she can quit her day gig.

First Agreement: Production Company Posing as Label

This form agreement came from an actual production company that presented an agreement that only a real label should offer. As we just discussed, a production company has almost none of the resources of a true record label. The production company should have offered a "shopping deal" under which they would have a limited time to find a suitable label deal for the artist. Instead, this agreement includes provisions that are completely unfair and unjustifiable. Here is an overview of the key provisions and how and why they should be changed:

Term

The term of this agreement is an initial period of 15 months followed by options for the "delivery" of four additional albums. Since delivery depends on when the company decides to record each album, the contract could continue indefinitely. The artist could hire a lawyer to try to get out of this contract, but at the end of the day, the production company could contend that the contract was valid, which could impede the artist from securing another deal.

If a company is merely a production company and not a real label, it should offer a shopping deal under which it has a limited amount of time to produce at least five or six tracks (sometimes referred to as "demos") that feature the artist's best work and shop those tracks to real labels to help the artist get to the next level. Generally, a production company has nine months to shop the demos. If the production company cannot secure such a deal, the artist should be free to terminate the agreement.

Album Options

A production company does not have the resources to help the artist as a real label could, and therefore, it should not try to trap an artist in a multiple-album deal. On the other hand, if the production company secures a good deal for the artist with a reputable label, they should share with the artist in monies the record label pays to the artist, including advances and royalties for the artist's exclusive recording services. A fair deal may provide that the company will share in such revenues for the first several albums released by the label.

Royalty

A reasonable royalty for producing demos and shopping them to get a deal with a label is 5% to 20%. The percentage should be based on what the label pays the artist, so if the artist's advance is $100,000, the production company would receive $5,000 to $20,000. If the artist's royalty was 15%, the production company would get 5% to 20% of that royalty, that is, .75% to 3%. The lower royalty of 5% would be appropriate for shopping an artist who has already produced records ready to shop, and the production company doesn't have to do anything except shop the artist. The higher royalty of 20% would be appropriate when the production company has to produce all new demos and perhaps even release tracks on social networks and possibly iTunes to get a buzz going for the artist. Yet, many production companies will try to take advantage of a naive artist and demand 40% or 50% or even more. The production company's royalty should also be limited to advances and royalties payable by the label. In a terrible deal for the artist, such as the first one analyzed in this chapter, the company will also try to secure a percentage of *any* income the artist receives in the entertainment business, including live performance, merchandise, and publishing.

It is fair, though, that a production company be compensated for expenses if it secures an acceptable label deal. But, the company's expenses should be reasonable, documented, and approved by the artist. Moreover, those expenses should be "taken off the top." This means if the company's expenses were $10,000, and a label is paying an advance of $100,000 for the artist's recording services, the $10,000 should be deducted from the $100,000, and the company should receive 20% of $90,000 ($18,000). The artist should receive 80% of $90,000 ($72,000). If the expenses are not taken off the top, the company would receive 20% of $100,000 plus the $10,000 for expenses, that is, $30,000. The artist would only receive 80% of the balance of $70,000, that is, $56,000.

360 Provisions

Since income from recorded music has drastically declined since 1999, labels have changed their standard deal to share in money from other income streams including merchandise (or "merch"), endorsements, live performances and touring, and even appearances in TV programs or movies. Because labels wish to share in all of the artist's income streams, these deals are known as "360." A major label that can provide the marketing muscle to make an artist a household name arguably deserves to share in those income streams, but a production company has not earned that. However, if the production company actually does something to help the artist make money from activities other than record sales, there is nothing wrong in rewarding them for that success. For instance, if the company finds a good paying gig playing at a private event, the company may deserve a percentage of the fee payable to the artist.

In the Introduction of the next chapter, we go into further detail about 360 deals and provide negotiating tips on how to make 360 provisions less harsh without killing the deal.

Second Agreement: A Fair Shopping Agreement

Unlike the first contract, this agreement is an example of a shopping deal that is fair to both sides. The second contract provides a 20% royalty to the production company, but it also provides significant protections for the artist. Unlike the first contract, the second contract (i) gives the artist the right to approve the choice of the "Distributor" (that is, the label), participate in the negotiation of the deal, and approve all the terms of that deal; (ii) limits the Term to nine months unless the Company find a suitable deal; and (iii) limits the company's royalty to income flowing from the label, and not from any other income that the artist may earn in the entertainment business.

THE CONTRACT FROM HELL THAT YOU SHOULD NEVER SIGN

_____ Records, Inc.

_____

Los Angeles, CA

Dated as of: _____ _____ , 2017

Mr. [Artist]

_____

Hoboken, NJ

Dear Mr. _____ ,

This agreement shall confirm and memorialize our discussions with reference to you and Company entering into an exclusive artist recording agreement regarding your perfor-mances as a musical recording artist. (You and Company are sometimes referred to herein as the "parties"). Although the parties contemplate the execution of a more formal long form recording agreement (the "Long Form Agreement"), this Letter Agreement, when signed by both you and Company, shall constitute a binding and enforceable agreement regardless of whether the Long Form Agreement is ultimately executed.

Following are the major terms and conditions which the parties agree shall form the basis of our contractual arrangement and which shall be incorporated in the Long Form Agreement (it being understood that such Long Form Agreement shall not be limited to these terms):

1.   ARTIST: _____

2.   TERRITORY: World

3.   TERM: The "Initial Contract Period" shall run for fifteen (15) months from the comple-tion and satisfactory delivery of the Initial Album hereunder. Each subsequent Contract Pe-riod, if any as provided for below, shall run for the longer of (i) 15 months from the completion and satisfactory delivery of the Masters to be delivered to Company during such Contract Period and (ii) 18 months from the commencement date of such respective Con-tract Period. At all times during the Term, you shall render your exclusive recording services to Company for the purpose of making Masters (as hereinafter defined) and for all other purposes as provided for herein.

As discussed in the introduction, most production companies consist of one or two individuals with some experience in the record business who may or may not be producers but own or have access to a professional recording studio. Their goal is to land a deal for the Artist with a real label to take the Artist to the next level by providing the money and staff to properly market, promote, and distribute records.

Generally, a production company has nine months to shop demos to secure a deal. An album is not necessary to shop an artist for a label deal. Note that, under the language in Paragraph 3, since delivery does not occur unless the Company records the Artist, delivery may never occur. Therefore this agreement could go on indefinitely.

This provision needs to be altered to give the Company a reasonable time to find a suitable label deal. If they do not find one within that time, the Artist should have the right to terminate.

---

4. <u>RECORDING COMMITMENT/FUTURE OPTIONS</u>: During the Initial Contract Period, you shall record up to three (3) previously unreleased "singles" (the "Initial Track(s)"), the first of such Initial Tracks to be commercially released not later than five (5) months after the satisfactory delivery thereof (unless otherwise agreed by you and Company). During the period ending not later than nine (9) months after the commercial release of the Initial Track, Company shall have the right and option, in its sole discretion, to require you to record a full-length album comprised of not less than 10 songs (the "Initial Album"). Thereafter, Company shall have an option(s), to be exercised by Company in its sole discretion, for up to four (4) consecutive additional Contract Periods, comprised of one (1) full-length album during each Contract Period, each such option to be exercised, if at all, not later than the expiration of the then current Contract Period, subject to a ninety (90) day written notice and cure period in the event Company fails to exercise any such option. (The Initial Album, all additional audio only masters recorded by you during the Term hereunder, all audio-visual products, and all other recordings or other formats now or hereafter known embodying your musical performances are sometimes referred to individually and collectively herein as the "Master(s)"). Selection of the Masters to be recorded hereunder shall be subject to the mutual cooperation and agreement of the parties, it being understood and agreed that Company shall have the final word with respect to selection of Masters and for all other creative matters, including, but not limited to, the selection of the songs to be recorded, producers of Masters and album artwork.

A good shopping deal for an artist makes a production company adhere to a firm deadline. If they do not find a deal within nine months, for instance, the Artist can walk away. On the other hand, the company should have the right to share in the Artist's success from a record deal that the production company helped the Artist secure. A typical provision to address this would read as follows:

"The term of this agreement ('Term') shall commence upon the date of this Deal Memorandum and continue until the commercial release by a Distributor in the United States of the fourth (4th) full-length, studio album containing Artist's featured performances and delivered to such Distributor in fulfillment the Artist's recording obligation to the Distributor. Notwithstanding the foregoing, if an agreement for Artist's exclusive recording services between the Company and a Distributor ('Distribution Agreement') has not been executed within nine (9) months from the date of completion of production of the Initial Masters hereunder ('Shopping Period'), the Artist may terminate the Agreement."

5.   <u>RECORDING COSTS/ADVANCES</u>: Company shall administer and pay all pre-approved recording costs in connection with the production of the Masters. All master recording costs, video production costs, independent marketing and promotion costs, all other sums paid by Company to you or on your behalf, (whether related to Other Music Activities or otherwise) and all other typically recoupable costs and expenses incurred by Company hereunder shall constitute "Advances", fully recoupable by Company from any royalties or other sums to be paid to you (or on your behalf) by us or any third party (excluding mechanical royalties) under this Agreement or any other agreement between you and Company.

> There are two things wrong with this provision. First, "all recording costs" should only be expenses that are reasonable, documented, and, if possible, approved by the Artist. Second, in a real recording agreement, the Artist should receive a real advance so they can quit their day gig and move out of their parents' house.

6.   <u>ROYALTIES</u>: As your sole and complete consideration of your services rendered hereunder, Company shall pay you a sum equal to thirty-five (35%) percent of the net revenues received by or credited to Company in connection with the exploitation of the Masters, after recoupment by Company of all Advances, recording costs and expenses and all other chargeable costs related to the distribution and/or exploitation of the Masters, including, but not limited to manufacturing costs, third party distribution fees and charges, and marketing and promotional expenses, it being understood that there shall be no so-called "double-dipping" and such recoupable expenses shall only be charged to your royalty account once. It is understood and agreed that Company's otherwise standard policies would apply to the calculation and payment of all royalties (e.g., free goods, program discounts, reserves, reductions, etc.). You acknowledge and agree that no royalties of any kind nor any other compensation (other than mechanical royalties, if any) shall be due to you except as provided in this paragraph. Company shall account and pay you any sums due not semi-annually, within ninety days after the end of each semi-annual period ending on June 29th and December 31st. Company shall be entitled to withhold any and all taxes as required by law with respect to any sums payable to you hereunder.

> If the Company were a real label, a 35% percent royalty payable to the Artist on record sales would not be unfair. But because the Company is only a production company, the goal is not to sell records but rather to secure a suitable label deal. When the production company achieves that, it should share in the revenues generated by the major label, but not 65%. The following clause should be added to the royalties section of the agreement:
>
> "Notwithstanding anything to the contrary above, If Company enters into Distribution Agreement, with your prior approval, the Company shall receive [5% to 20%] (see introduction) of any advances or royalties payable by the Distributor for the recording services of the Artist. The Artist shall receive the balance, that is, 80% of such Advances or royalties for the first four (4) Albums. Notwithstanding anything to the contrary above, Company shall have the right to deduct its actual documented approved recording costs that have not already been recouped by Company."

7.   NAME AND LIKENESS RIGHTS/WEBSITE: Company shall have the perpetual right, which such right shall be exclusive during the term and non-exclusive thereafter, without liability to any person, to use and to authorize other persons to use your name, likeness and biographical material for purposes of advertising, marketing, promotion and trade in connection with making and/or exploitation of Masters, recordings, audio-visual materials, and all other materials hereunder. You hereby grant to Company the exclusive right, during the Term (and the non-exclusive right thereafter, with respect to an alternate name), to establish and maintain all Artist-branded digital sites and social networking sites, including a website having the URL "_____.com" or any similar designation based on or containing your professional name. You shall make yourself available at Company's reasonable request and expense and upon reasonable notice to appear for photographs, posters, cover art, interviews with representatives of the media and publicity personnel and to perform other reasonable promotional functions.

This clause should be added:

"Notwithstanding, anything to the contrary above, (i) Artist shall have the right to continue his YouTube and Facebook pages; and (ii) all content in Artist branded sites shall be subject to Artist's approval."

---

8.   REPRESENTATION/WARRANTY/INDEMNITY: You warrant and represent that you have been, are and shall continue to be possessed of the full right to enter into this agreement and perform hereunder and that you're entering into this agreement and performing hereunder shall not infringe upon the rights of any person or entity. Upon the expiration or other termination of this Agreement, you agree not to re-record any composition embodied on a Master hereunder until the date that is the later of i) three years after the end of the Term and iii) five years from the completion of recording of such Master hereunder. You indemnify us against any losses or damage (including reasonable attorneys' fees) arising out of any claims by any third parties which are inconsistent with any warranty made by you herein or any condition contained herein. You shall promptly pay us on demand any sums for which you are liable under the proceeding sentence and, alternatively, Company shall be entitled to withhold any such sums from monies otherwise payable to you hereunder.

9.   OWNERSHIP: The Masters (including, but not limited to, any audio-visual recordings related thereto), all duplicates and derivatives thereof, all records made therefrom or duplicates or derivatives (including the copyright and renewal and/or extension of such copyright), and all artwork and other intellectual property created or obtained by Company, together with the performances embodied therein, all in any form, manner, or medium now or hereafter known, shall be exclusively and perpetually property of Company, free from any claim

whatsoever by you or any person deriving any rights from you. The Masters shall be deemed a work made for hire within the meanings of the United States Copyright Act. If the Masters are determined not to be a work made for hire, they will be deemed transferred to Company by this agreement, together with all rights in it. Accordingly, the Masters, together with yours and all the performances embodied on them, shall be the sole property of Company, its assignees and successors in perpetuity and throughout the world, free from any claims by you or any other person; and Company shall have the exclusive right to copyright the Master in its name as the author and owner thereof and to secure any and all renewals and extensions of such copyright throughout the world. You will execute and deliver to Company such instruments of transfer and other documents regarding the rights of Company in the Master as Company may reasonably request to carry out the purposes of this Agreement, and Company may sign such documents in your name and make appropriate disposition of them.

This paragraph states that all "Masters shall be deemed work for hire" for the Company. Work for hire means that all the copyrights in the recordings are owned by the Company, and that the Company will have the right to use them for any purpose after the termination of the agreement. In a pro-artist agreement, the copyrights in the master recordings would be owned jointly by the Artist and the Company. This means that if the Agreement terminates, neither the Artist nor the Company would have the right to exploit the master recordings without mutual approval.

Without limiting the generality of the foregoing, Company, or any person authorized by Company shall have the perpetual unlimited, exclusive right, throughout the world: (i) to manufacture records, video-records, and any derivatives thereof derived from the Master in any form, in any medium, and/or by any method now or hereafter known; (ii) to sell, transfer or otherwise deal in the same under any trademarks, trade names and labels; (iii) to reproduce, adapt, transmit, distribute, broadcast, perform, communicate and otherwise use the Master in any medium or in any manner, including but not limited to use in physical, digital, electronic, mobile and internet formats; (iv) to cause or permit the public performance of the Master, or derivatives thereof, through any and all media; (v) to add to, delete from, edit, mix and otherwise alter the Master without restriction; and (vi) to exploit the Master and derivatives therefrom through any and all means, whether now or hereafter known, all without payment of any compensation to you except the royalties as described in this Agreement. In the alternative, Company may, at its election, refrain from doing any or all of the foregoing.

10. <u>MECHANICAL LICENSE</u>: With respect to any musical compositions embodied in the Masters which are owned or controlled by you or your designees, you hereby grant to us and our designees the irrevocable non-exclusive right to reproduce the Song on records (including digitally delivered reproductions) and to distribute any of those records in the United States and Canada. Mechanical royalties shall be payable on a maximum of ten (10)

songs on each album, on net sales of such records at the following rates: (i) on such records sold in the United States, the rate shall be the United States mechanical rate. The "United States mechanical rate" shall mean the amount equal to seventy-five percent (75%) of the minimum statutory royalty rate (without regard to playing time) provided for in the United States Copyright Act which is applicable to the reproduction of musical compositions as of the date of initial release of the Master concerned; and (ii) on such records sold in Canada, the rate shall be the Canadian mechanical rate. The "Canadian mechanical rate" shall mean the amount equal to seventy-five percent (75%) of the minimum statutory royalty rate (without regard to playing time) provided for in the Canadian Copyright Act which is applicable to the reproduction of musical compositions as of the date of initial release of the Master concerned; (iii) the mechanical royalty rate for a Song contained on a mid-price record or budget record shall be three-fourths (3/4ths) of the United States mechanical rate or the Canadian mechanical rate, as applicable; and no mechanical royalties shall be payable on any phonograph records for which no royalties are payable by Company. If the copyright in a musical composition is owned or controlled by a person, firm or corporation other than you, you shall cause that person, firm or corporation to grant to us and our designees the same rights as you are required to grant to us and our designees hereunder. You hereby grant to us and our designees at no fee, royalty or other cost to us or our designees, the irrevocable, non-exclusive, worldwide right to reproduce and publicly perform each Song on audio-visual recordings, to distribute audio-visual records embodying those audio-visual recordings, and otherwise to exploit in any manner and through any media those audio-visual recordings. You grant to us and our designees, or shall cause to be granted to us, the irrevocable right to print and reproduce, at our election, the title and lyrics to the Song on the packaging of phonograph records embodying Masters throughout the world in perpetuity, without payment to you or any other person, firm or corporation of any monies or other consideration in connection therewith. Any assignment, license or other agreement made with respect to the Song shall be subject to the terms hereof.

This paragraph is known as the "Controlled Composition Clause." It provides that the Artist who writes his own songs does receive mechanical royalties from record sales by the Company, but the Company pays only ¾ of the statutory rate of 9.1 cents per song instead of the full rate. It is a standard clause in any major label or major indie deal and usually cannot be negotiated away unless the Artist has tremendous bargaining power.

---

11. <u>CO-PUBLISHING</u>: The parties agree that you (or your affiliated publishing company) and Company's designated publishing affiliate shall be co-publishers with respect to music and lyrics of all compositions written, owned and/or controlled by you during the Term. Accordingly, you (or your affiliated publishing company) hereby irrevocably and absolutely assign, convey and set over to Company (or its designee), or will cause Company (or its designee) to

receive an assignment, of fifty (50%) percent of all right, title and interest (including the world-wide copyright and all extensions and renewals thereof) in and to each and every controlled composition which is recorded hereunder. Upon request, you agree to execute and deliver to Company, or to cause to be executed and delivered to Company (or its designee) a separate Co-publishing Agreement with respect to each such controlled composition in accordance with standard forms of such agreements. If you shall fail to promptly execute such agreements, you hereby grant to Company the right to sign same on your behalf, though Company's failure to exercise the rights granted to use such authority shall not diminish Company's rights as set forth within this Agreement. Company shall be the exclusive administrator of 100% of all rights in and to such controlled compositions, and it (and/or its designees) shall be entitled to exercise any and all rights with respect to the control, exploitation and administration of such compositions including, without limitation, the sole right to grant licenses, collect all income and to use the name, likeness and biographical material of each composer, lyricist and songwriter hereunder in connection with such composition for the full term of copyright (including all renewals and extensions thereof) in and to such Composition. From all sums actually earned and received by Company in the United States of America from the exploitation of such Composition throughout the world (the "Gross Receipts"), Company shall: (i) deduct and/or retain all out-of-pocket costs incurred by Company in connection with the exploitation and protection of such Composition; (ii) deduct and pay royalties payable to the writers (including you) of the Composition (which you warrant and represent shall not exceed fifty (50%) percent of the Gross Receipts); and (iii) pay to you an amount equal to fifty (50%) percent of the balance remaining after deducting the aggregate sums set forth in subparagraphs (i), (ii) and (iii) above, and the remaining fifty (50%) percent thereof shall be retained by Company for its sole use and benefit. Accountings for such royalties shall be rendered semi-annually subject to all the terms and provisions of Paragraph 11 hereof.

Paragraph 11 should be completely deleted. A real music publishing company is equipped to represent, exploit and collect income from songs, both domestically, and all around the world. A production company does not have those resources.

---

12. OTHER MUSIC ACTIVITIES: You shall pay to Company a sum equal to thirty (30%) percent of all OMA Income ("the OMA Payment", provided that the OMA Payment in connection with your touring and other live musical performances shall be deemed to be twenty (20%) percent). You authorize Company to collect all OMA Income on your behalf but to the extent such is not collected by Company, within fifteen (15) days of the end of each calendar quarter of the Term, you will send Company a detailed written account of all OMA Income received by you or on your behalf during such accounting period and the amount of the OMA Payment accordingly payable to Company. On receipt of each such accounting statement, Company will elect either to deduct the OMA Payment from monies (including royalties) due

to you hereunder or to receive payment, in which case you shall pay the amounts shown to be due in each accounting statement within ten (10) days of the date of such statement. You agree to maintain complete and accurate books and records relating to OMA Income. At any time within two (2) years after any accounting statement is rendered to Company hereunder, Company shall have the right to inspect such books and records on reasonable notice but not more than once during each year. As used herein, "Other Music Activities" shall mean all of your professional activities connected to the entertainment industry including, without limitation, merchandising, advertising, sponsorship, endorsements and tie-ins, touring and all other live performances, and TV or film appearances (but specifically excluding music publishing, any fees or royalties you receive for acting as a "producer" of records for others, record royalties hereunder, and any other income payable to you which Company is otherwise participating in (i.e., there shall be no "double dipping" with respect to OMA Income). "OMA Income" shall mean all gross sums paid or payable to you with respect to your "Other Music Activities" during the Term or with respect to any and all agreements related thereto entered into during the Term and for a period of three months thereafter (whether received during the term or thereafter), after deduction of third party out-of-pocket expenses or deductions reasonably incurred in connection with the Other Music Activities, including booking agent commissions, monies payable to third party co-publishers and co-writers of musical compositions written by you and reimbursement for actual out-of-pocket expenses incurred by you in connection therewith (but which such deduction shall not apply to production, travel, musician, or other show related costs for your live performance activities or management commissions). Upon request by Company, you hereby agree to execute standard Letters of Direction authorizing and directing any third parties to pay any such OMA Payments directly to Company.

The Artist should delete this paragraph completely for the reasons discussed in the introduction to this chapter (see 360 Provisions). But, in fairness to the Company, if they do something to deserve ancillary revenues, there is nothing wrong with compensating them for their efforts. Here is an alternative to harsh 360 clauses compensating the Company if they actually help the Artist make money:

"Ancillary Rights.

(a)   Company may, from time to time, secure and coordinate 'synch' placements of any of the Artist's Songs in motion pictures, TV program, ad campaigns, video games etc. ('Company Synchs'). It is understood that Company is not a music publisher and shall not be required to procure any synchs for Artist. If Company does secure and coordinate any live personal appearance for the Artist, Company shall be entitled to collect all gross revenue from the Company Synchs. Company shall pay Artist seventy-five percent (75%) of gross revenue derived from such Company Synchs. Company shall make such payment to Artist within three (3) days of Company's receipt of such monies together with a comprehensive accounting statement. Notwithstanding anything to the contrary above, (i) Artist shall have the right to approve Company Synchs and the synch fee; (ii) Artist has no obligation to Company for any synch placement not secured by Company. Company shall have no other rights in Artist's songs except as set forth in this Subparagraph.

(b)   Company may, from time to time, secure and coordinate live personal appearances for Artist and shall negotiate the Artist's compensation in connection therewith for concerts or live performances

('Company Shows'). It is understood that Company is not an employment agency or a talent agent and shall not be required to procure any employment for Artist, and that Company has not represented that it will procure employment for Artist. Any live personal appearance that Company does secure and coordinate for the Artist shall be incidental to its role as a record company. Company shall pay Artist seventy-five percent (75%) of Net Revenue derived from such Company Show. 'Net Revenue' as used in this paragraph shall mean all gross revenue actually received by Company less documented reasonable expenses incurred by Company in connection with such Company Show such as lighting and sound. Company shall make such payment to Artist within three (3) days of Company's receipt of such Net Revenues together with a comprehensive accounting statement. Notwithstanding anything to the contrary above, (i) Artist shall have the right to pre-approve each Company Show and her performance fee; (ii) Artist has no obligation to Company in connection with any live performance not secured by Company."

13. <u>MISCELLANEOUS</u>: This agreement is the entire agreement between the parties with respect to the contents hereof, supersedes all prior agreements, understandings, negotiations and discussions, whether oral or written, of the parties, and shall not be modified, except by an instrument in writing, signed by each of the parties duly authorized to execute such modification. Company may assign its rights under this Agreement in whole or in part.

There is a great deal of boilerplate language here that may be legally necessary but is not more favorable to one party than the other. But there is one truly insidious sentence:

"Company may assign its rights under this Agreement in whole or in part."

This would mean that the Company could assign the agreement (together with the five albums that the Company is entitled to) to any other company or individual. In other words, the Company could literally sell the Agreement. This sentence should be modified to allow the Artist to approve any assignment of the Agreement to a third party.

You may not assign this agreement or your rights or responsibilities hereunder without the prior approval of Company, such approval not to unreasonably withheld with respect to a so-called "furnishing company" owned or controlled by you which is exclusively entitled to your recording services. A waiver by either party of any term or condition of this agreement shall not be deemed or construed as a waiver of such term or condition for the future, or of any subsequent breach thereof. All remedies, rights, undertakings, obligations, and agreements contained herein shall be cumulative and none of them shall be in limitation of any other remedy, right, undertaking, obligation or agreement of either party. No breach of this agreement by either party shall be deemed material, unless the non-breaching party shall have given the other party notice of such breach and such breaching party shall fail to cure such breach within 30 days after receipt of such notice. If any part of this agreement shall be determined to be invalid or unenforceable, the remainder of this agreement shall remain in full force and effect. This Agreement has been entered into in the State of California and the validity, interpretation and legal effect of this Agreement shall be governed by the laws of California applicable to contracts entered into and performed entirely within California, with respect to the determination of any claim, dispute or disagreement which may arise out of the interpretation, performance or breach of this Agreement. All claims, disputes or disagreements which may arise out of the interpretation, performance or breach of this Agreement shall be submitted exclusively to the jurisdiction of the appropriate court in California. You acknowledge that Company has given you the right and opportunity to have this Agreement reviewed by an attorney of your choice having competence in the music industry, and you have done so. You further acknowledge that said attorney has reviewed with you the terms of this Agreement and that he/she has advised you as to all legal ramifications and consequences of your entering into this Agreement. You acknowledge that your services hereunder are of a special, unique, unusual, extraordinary and intellectual character and in the event of a breach by you of any material term, condition, representation, warranty or covenant herein, Company will be caused irreparable injury and damage. You expressly agree that Company shall be entitled to the remedies of injunction and other equitable relief to prevent or remedy a breach, which relief shall be in addition to any other rights or remedies, for damages or otherwise, which Company may have.

Under the last sentence above, the Company could seek a court to enjoin the Artist from recording for another record label: meaning that a court could order the Artist not to record with another company.

If because of: an Act of God; inevitable accident; fire; lockout; strike or other labor dispute; riot or civil commotion; act of public enemy; enactment, rule, order or act of any government or governmental instrumentality (whether federal, state, local or foreign); failure or delay of transportation facilities; or other cause of a similar or different nature not reasonably within Company's control, Company is materially hampered in the recording, manufacture, distribution or sale of records, then, without limiting Company's rights, Company shall have the option by giving you notice to suspend the running of the then current Contract Period for the duration of any such contingency plus such additional time as is necessary so that Company shall have no less than sixty (60) days after the cessation of such contingency in which to exercise its option, if any, to extend the Term of this Agreement for the next following Option Period.

The parties agree that, upon both of our signatures below, this letter shall constitute a valid and binding agreement regarding the exclusive rights to your services. Notwithstanding the contemplation of the Long Form Agreement, all legal and equitable rights, obligations and remedies of both parties attach hereto with no limitation.

ACCEPTED AND AGREED TO:

_____ Records Inc.   Artist

_____   _____
An Authorized Signatory   SS#:

FAIR SHOPPING DEAL

_____ Productions, Inc.

c/o _____, Esq.

f/s/o _____ [Producer]

_____

New York, NY

As of _____, 2017

_____ Music, LLC

f/so _____ [Artist]

c/o _____, Esq. [Attorney]

Los Angeles, CA

Note that the Artist was represented by experienced counsel.

Re: Deal Memorandum

Ladies and Gentlemen:

The following sets forth the terms on which (i) _____ Inc. ("Company") f/s/o _____ and _____ Music LLC ("you") furnishing the services of _____ ("Artist") agree to form a California limited liability company (the "Venture") to furnish the exclusive services of Artist to a Distributor (as defined herein), (ii) Artist will furnish her exclusive recording services to the Venture, and (iii) Company will furnish the services of _____ ("Producer") to the Venture to produce the Venture Masters (defined below).

This agreement was essentially between two individuals: an artist and a producer who owned a production company. "Company" is the name of the producer's corporation. The Artist entered into this agreement through a "furnishing" company as well. By entering into the deal as companies rather than individuals, both parties secured "limited liability" and certain tax advantages. Limited liability means that even if a company consists of only one individual, the personal assets of that individual (such as their personal bank account, house, and car) are not be subject to liability.

As used herein, the term "Distributor" shall mean Sony Music, Universal Music and Warner Music, their wholly owned affiliated labels (collectively "Major Label"); a major independent record company, or an indie record label that is regularly distributed by a Major Label.

This agreement uses the word "Distributor" to refer to the record company with which the Company is trying to secure a deal. The definition of "Distributor" will vary, but it's in the interest of the Artist to narrow this definition to the three major labels—Warner, Sony, and Universal—and their wholly owned label affiliates such as Atlantic, Epic, Columbia, Republic, and Interscope, or a major independent such as Beggars Banquet (the Strokes), Big Machine (Taylor Swift), or Glassnote (Mumford and Sons). But the Company may want a broader definition embracing companies with national distribution such as RED, ADA, and Caroline, which are owned by the majors but are essentially distributors who seldom provide advances or marketing support.

The definition of "Distributor" is not as important in this agreement as it could otherwise be because, as set forth in Paragraph 2, the Distributor is subject to the prior written approval of the Artist.

1. <u>ORGANIZATION OF THE VENTURE.</u> Contemporaneously with the execution of this Deal Memorandum, Company and you will cause to be filed Articles of Organization in the State of New Jersey organizing a limited liability company called "_____ LLC," such name deemed approved by both Company and you hereunder (or, if such name is not available, another name mutually agreed upon by Company and Artist). The Venture shall be owned 20% by Company and 80% by you.

Note that the Artist will receive 80% of any income; the Company is limited to 20% compared to 65% for the production company in the first agreement discussed above.

2. <u>ARTIST OBLIGATIONS.</u> The term of this agreement ("Term") shall commence upon the date of this Deal Memorandum and continue until the commercial release by a Distributor in the United States of the fourth (4th) full-length, studio album containing Artist's featured performances and delivered to such Distributor in fulfillment the Venture's recording obligation to the Distributor. Notwithstanding the foregoing, if an agreement for Artist's exclusive recording services between the Venture and a Distributor (a "Distribution Agreement") has not been executed, or substantially negotiated, within nine (9) months from the date of completion of production of the Initial Masters hereunder (the "Shopping Period"), upon written notice, via registered mail, return receipt requested, by Artist given to Company, the parties' obligations hereunder shall terminate and Artist shall be released from any further obligations to the Venture.

The maximum duration of this Agreement is four albums. But, note that unless the Artist has approved a Distribution Agreement within nine months from the date of completion of production of the Initial Masters (six tracks), the Artist has the right to terminate the deal with the Company.

In such event, neither Company nor you shall have any right to exploit the Venture Masters without the express written permission of Company and you. All master recordings containing Artist's featured performances that are recorded during the Term, including without limitation the Initial Masters (defined below), shall be referred to as "Venture Masters" and shall be deemed "works made for hire" specially commissioned by the Venture.

> If the contract terminates, neither the Company nor the Artist has the right to exploit the Initial Masters without mutual approval. Again, this is very favorable for the Artist. In a pro-company agreement, the Company would exclusively own the copyrights in the recordings and be able to exploit and/or license any masters made during the term. In this agreement, the Venture (that is the Company and the Artist) jointly own the copyrights.

Notwithstanding the foregoing, if during the Shopping Period Venture receives a bona fide written offer from a Distributor to enter into a Distribution Agreement and the Distribution Agreement is not fully executed prior to the expiration of the Shopping Period, then Shopping Period shall automatically be extended for an additional ninety (90) days.

> The Company needs this provision in order to wrap up any negotiations that are ongoing as of the end of the nine month shopping period.

Further, notwithstanding anything to the contrary expressed in or implied by this Agreement, it is understood and agreed that the choice of the Distributor, as well as the terms and provisions of the Distribution Agreement, shall be subject to the prior written approval of Company and you, such approval not to be unreasonably withheld or delayed; further, Company and you agree that if you choose not to enter into a Distribution Agreement with a Distributor during the Shopping Period then you shall not directly or indirectly deal with such Distributor (or its affiliates) for a period of twelve (12) months following the expiration of the Shopping Period.

> Here, it is made clear that the Artist has the right to approve the terms of the Distribution Agreement as well as the Distributor. This is absolutely key. Without the right to approve the Distribution Agreement, the Company could enter into a deal that is bad for the Artist, and the Artist would be powerless to prevent it. The Company may argue that the Distributor will not finalize the deal if the Artist does not sign an "inducement" letter confirming his assent to the agreement. But without the right to approve the deal, if the Artist did not sign the inducement letter, the Artist would arguably be in breach of the agreement with the Company. The Artist should at least have approval of the major deal points including duration, number of options for additional albums, recording budget, advances, and royalties.

3.   COMPANY OBLIGATIONS. Company agrees as follows:

(a) Engagement. Promptly after the execution of this Deal memorandum, Company will cause Producer to record and deliver to the Venture six (6) Masters (the "Initial Masters"). In addition, provided that a Distribution Agreement is entered into or substantially negotiated during the Shopping Period, the Venture shall engage Company to, and Company will cause Producer to produce and deliver three (3) Venture Masters per album for potential inclusion on each of the first four (4) "commitment" albums to be delivered to the Distributor pursuant to the Distribution Agreement. For the purposes hereof, the Initial Masters and all other Venture Masters produced by Producer shall be referred to as "Produced Masters." The first four (4) "commitment" albums to be delivered to the Distributor pursuant to the Distribution Agreement are sometimes referred to as "First Album," "Second Album," "Third Album" and "Fourth Album," respectively.

In this agreement, the Company was furnishing the services of a top notch producer. In addition to shopping the Artist to labels, the agreement contemplates that the producer would also have a role in producing tracks for the Artist after he got signed.

(b) <u>Producer Advance; Costs</u>. In respect of the Initial Masters and any other Produced Masters on the First Album, the Venture shall pay, or cause the Distributor to pay, to Company, as advances, recoupable against the Producer's Royalty (the "Producer Advances"), $15,000.00 per Master payable as follows: (1) $7,500.00 payable promptly upon execution of the Distribution Agreement, and (2) the balance promptly following delivery and acceptance by the Distributor of technically satisfactory Masters. In addition, use of Company's studio in recording, edition and/or mixing any Produced Masters shall be billed in accordance with a budget that has been approved by both you and Company, which budget is attached hereto as Exhibit "A" (the "Approved Budget").

This provision and the next do not require the label to use the producer's tracks but does guarantee that the producer would receive advances and a royalty (also referred to as "points") on the first four albums.

(c) <u>Producer Royalty</u>. The Venture shall pay Company (or cause the Distributor to pay to Company) a producer's royalty (the "Producer's Royalty") of three percent (3%) of SRLP in respect of net sales of full-priced records through normal retail channels in the United States ("USNRC") embodying solely the Produced Masters. Notwithstanding the foregoing, in no event shall the Producer Royalty hereunder be lower than the royalty equivalent of three produced tracks per album, through the fourth album. Producer's Royalty on all other sales and exploitations shall be reduced, adjusted, calculated and paid in the same proportion, and at the same times, as is the Venture's basic "all in" royalty. As to records not consisting entirely of the Produced Masters, the royalty rate shall be prorated by multiplying such royalty rate by a fraction, the numerator of which is the number of Produced Masters embodied thereon and the denominator of which is the total number of royalty bearing masters (including the Produced Masters) embodied thereon. Producer's Royalty shall be paid retroactive to the first record sold or other exploitation after recoupment of the recoupable portion of all recording costs incurred in connection with the Album on which they are embodied at the net artist rate (i.e., the "all in" royalty payable to the Venture less the Producer's Royalty payable to Company and the royalties payable to all other producers, mixers and engineers of such Masters), subject, however, to recoupment of the unrecouped portion of the Producer Advance. There shall be no reduction in the Producer's Royalty due to; (i) amounts payable to mixers or executive producers, or (ii) after delivery and acceptance of any Master, amounts payable to any third party producer. In calculating "recording costs" for recoupment purposes, "recording costs" shall not include any "in pocket" advances payable to the Venture or Artist. Producer's Royalty shall be paid directly to Company by the Distributor pursuant to an irrevocable letter of direction.

3% to 5% is a normal producer royalty.

(d) <u>Credit</u>. The Venture shall instruct, and use reasonable efforts to cause, Distributor to accord Producer the following credit in all trade and consumer advertisements relating to any Produced Master of ½ page or larger, and in and on the outer packaging, label copy, liner notes and labels of all records embodying the Produced Master:

"Produced by _____"

The Venture shall instruct, and use its best efforts to cause, Distributor to include Company's logo (the "Company Logo") and Artist's Logo (the "Artist Logo") in all trade and consumer advertisements relating to any record embodying any Venture Master of ¼ page or larger, and in and on the outer packaging, label copy, liner notes and labels of all records (including promotional and commercial singles) embodying any Venture Master. Each such logo shall be no less prominent, and no smaller in size, than any other logos (including the other party's logo) included on such records or in such advertisements, including, without limitation, Distributor's logo. In the event that any Distributor will not agree to include both the Artist Logo and the Company Logo on such terms, Company and Artist shall negotiate in good faith to determine which logos, if any, will be so included.

(e) <u>Controlled Compositions</u>. Producer's interest in any compositions embodied on any Produced Masters shall be subject to any so-called "controlled composition" provisions contained in the Distribution Agreement between the Venture and Distributor.

See comments for Paragraph 10 in the first agreement.

---

4.   <u>MANAGEMENT, VOTING AND CONTROL.</u>

(a) The business and affairs of the Venture shall be managed by Company and you. Company and you will have joint decision making authority and all decisions made regarding the business and affairs of the Venture must be mutually approved by you and the Company, in writing, including, without limitation, those decisions relating to: (i) determining which Distributor(s) with which to enter into Distribution Agreement(s), and (ii) the release and/or exploitation of any Master(s). For the avoidance of doubt, the Venture shall not enter into any agreements or other undertakings regarding any Venture Master prior to the execution of a Distribution Agreement, including, without limitation, any license agreement or otherwise, without unanimous written consent of you and Company.

(b) Artist and Company further agree as follows: (i) Company's counsel and Artist's counsel and Artist shall jointly represent the Venture in connection with any Distribution Agreement(s) to be entered into by the Venture, and (ii) Artist's counsel shall represent Artist's interests in connection with any additional obligations that Artist may have to any Distributor (such as an obligation to deliver additional commitment albums). Company's counsel and Artist's counsel shall split any legal fees paid or reimbursed by any Distributor in connection with the Distribution Agreement and the Venture shall be responsible for paying, or shall make appropriate arrangements for discharging, all reasonable legal fees of Artist's counsel and Company's counsel in connection with any Distribution Agreement(s) that are not paid or reimbursed by the Distributor.

This is a very favorable provision for the Artist as it not only gives him approval, but lets his attorney actively engage in negotiations with the label.

---

5. ALLOCATIONS AND DISTRIBUTIONS.

(a) All advances and royalties (including audit settlements) received by the Venture, or credited to the Venture against an advance previously paid to the Venture, shall be distributed as follows:

(i) First, to the reimbursement of any actual out-of-pocket expenses incurred by the Venture, or by Artist or Company with the Venture's prior written approval, in connection with the Initial Masters, including the Approved Budget, and in soliciting or negotiating any Distribution Agreement (including, without limitation, legal fees incurred by the Venture pursuant to paragraph 4(b) above); and

(ii) Then, after payment of any Producer Advances, Producing Royalty (subject always to recoupment of recording costs and/or the Producer Advances on the terms set forth above) and/or the Approved Budget amount due to Company, 80% to you and 20% to Company.

(b) Company and Artist agree to require, as a condition of any Distribution Agreement, any Distributor to agree to account directly to: (i) Company for any Producer Royalties that may become payable, (ii) you for 80% of all royalties that may be payable to the Venture under any Distribution Agreement (net only of the Producer Royalties payable to Company, if any); and (iii) Company for 20% of all royalties that may be payable to Venture under any Distribution Agreement (net only of the Producer Royalties payable to Company, if any). For the avoidance of doubt, as between Company and Artist, subject to the payment of the Producer Advances due to Company pursuant to paragraph 3(b) above, 80% of all "in pocket" advances payable under any Distribution Agreement shall be payable to you.

Note that the Company's compensation is limited to monies payable by the label, not to any monies that the Artist may earn in the entertainment business. This is not a 360 deal, which is a good thing for the Artist.

(c) Except as expressly otherwise provided herein, each of you and Company shall be responsible for payment of its own attorney's fees, personal management commissions and/or business management commissions out of its share of distributions and/or payments by the Venture. Under no circumstances shall the Venture be responsible for payment of commissions in respect of personal managers, business managers or other advisors engaged by Artist, Producer or Company unless such person was retained expressly to represent the Venture with the prior written consent of both Artist and Company.

6.   OTHER.

(a) The Venture shall maintain accurate books and records of all monies paid to or collected by the Venture pursuant to any Distribution Agreement(s). The Venture's books and records relating thereto may be inspected during regular business hours by a certified public accountant or attorney at law designated by Company or you and at the inspecting party's expense, at the place where same are regularly maintained, upon thirty (30) days' written notice to the Venture; provided, however, that such examination shall not be permitted more than once a calendar year.

(b) Neither party may assign, convey, sell, transfer, give, liquidate, encumber, or in any way alienate ("Transfer") all or any part of his or its respective membership interest in the Venture without the prior written consent of the non-transferring party, which consent may be given or withheld in the sole discretion of such non-transferring party. Any attempted Transfer of all or any part of a membership interest without the necessary consent, or as otherwise permitted hereunder, shall be null and void and shall have no effect whatsoever.

Unlike in the first agreement, the Company is not trying to give itself the right to sell the contract.

---

7.   DEFINITIVE AGREEMENT. You and Company hereby acknowledge that it is the parties' mutual intent to enter into a more formal operating agreement (the "Operating Agreement"), as well as a long-form producer agreement (the "Producer Agreement") and a Furnishing

Agreement, at a later date. You and Company hereby agree to negotiate in good faith the terms of such agreements, provided that such agreements shall not contain any provision contrary to any material provision set forth herein, unless mutually agreed in writing by both parties. Until such time, this Deal Memorandum shall serve as the operating agreement between the parties regarding the Venture.

ACCEPTED AND AGREED TO:

_____ PRODUCTIONS, INC.

_____

_____ MUSIC, LLC

_____

CHAPTER 3

ARTIST RECORDING CONTRACTS WITH RECORD COMPANIES

INTRODUCTION: RECORDING CONTRACTS THAT AN ARTIST SHOULD SIGN

This chapter discusses deals between artists and production companies. As discussed, there is a huge difference between a production company and a legitimate label. A real record company can offer an artist marketing, publicity, video production, and support with social media, radio promotion, tours and worldwide physical and digital distribution. Artists should not allow production companies to corner them into an exclusive recording contract with options for multiple albums and 360 provisions that would entitle the companies to income from various income streams besides record sales. Instead, the production company should have a limited time to shop the artist to major labels and/or major indie record companies. Unfortunately, more often than not, production companies will present an agreement that would lock the artist into a long-term deal, make the company the artist's music publisher, and take a substantial cut of all of the artist's income from any endeavor in the entertainment business, as well as other horrors. This chapter is about artist agreements with real record companies, that is, companies with resources to promote, market and distribute as well as produce records.

The first part of this Introduction will summarize the three contracts republished at the end of this chapter. Each contract will also be annotated with comments. The second part of this chapter will analyze 360 deals and include tips on negotiating them.

The Three Contracts in This Chapter

Contract #1: License to Distribute a Single Album

The first contract (below) is between a label and an artist for an existing single album. It is a license deal in which the artist receives an advance of a certain sum of money and a royalty after recoupment. In exchange, the artist gives the label the exclusive right to distribute, license, or sell an album that the artist has already recorded for a limited period of time. It is a good deal for the artist, in this case a progressive electronic singer/songwriter, because she retains the copyrights in her records and songs and the right to sell or license the album after the limited term of 18 months. Another beneficial aspect of this contract is that the artist remains free to record and release records with another label or on her own. My annotations on this contract show how even a good deal for an artist may be improved.

Contract #2: Exclusive Recording Agreement

The second contract is a typical exclusive recording agreement with an indie label. Similar to the license deal, it offers the artist an advance against recording royalties, but it also provides that the label will pay production costs. In exchange, the artist grants the label options for additional albums. The advantage to the label is obvious: if the artist is successful, the label can order additional albums. The artist, however, will receive additional recording funds to produce these albums. The basic terms of this deal are as follows:

- The artist is exclusive to the label. In other words, he/she cannot record an album for another label or release an album on his/her own;
- The contract contains "work for hire" language, making the label the "author" of the record, and therefore the owner of the copyrights in the record;
- The label has options for up to two subsequent albums;
- The label pays the artist an advance, including a "signing bonus," which will provide the artist money to live on without having a day job;
- The label commits to a "recording budget" for the first album and each option album; the amount of the recording budget for each subsequent album is tied to the success of the prior album; the more money the prior album makes, the greater the recording budget for the next album. If the artist keeps production costs down, he can pocket the balance; this concept is usually implemented with a "min-max" formula that states that, notwithstanding the success or lack thereof of a prior album, there will be a floor and ceiling that the budget cannot dip below or exceed;
- The artist receives a recording royalty, the amount of which varies from contract to contract. In this contract, the artist receives 18% of the retail selling price of the record or the equivalent amount from monies received by the label from streaming services such as Spotify and YouTube;
- The label "recoups" the advances and any production and indie marketing costs from the artist's recording royalty. Recoupment occurs at the artist's royalty rate so that if, for example, the artist receives 15 cents from an iTunes download and recoupable advances are $100,000, the artist would need to sell 666,666 downloads just to break even;

- There is a provision, which is often included in indie label deals, which states that the label has the right to enter into an agreement with a major recording company;
- If the label enters into such a deal, commonly called a "label deal," the artist and the label share any advances or royalties to be paid by the major. That split is usually 50–50 between the label and the artist (though sometimes the artist receives somewhat more);[1]
- The artist grants the label the right to use any song written by the artist in exchange for a "mechanical royalty." That royalty is usually ¾ of "stat," that is, the statutory rate of 9.1 cents. The ¼ reduction is a traditional reduction based on the greater bargaining power of labels. An established artist may be able to negotiate a 100% rate;
- This agreement contains 360 provisions, but they are much fairer to the artist than the 360 provisions contained in the "Contract from Hell" discussed in Chapter 2;
- 360 deals, as noted in Chapter 2, usually give the label income participation in the artist's other income streams besides record sales, but the 360 provisions in this deal are based on how much the label contributes to the artist's success with regard to those other income streams. We discuss 360 deals in more detail below, including tips on making onerous 360 provisions less harsh.

Contract #3: Single Deal with a Major Label with an Option for a Second Single

As the recording business has declined about 70% since its height in 1999, the major labels have become far more cautious in investing in new acts. This contract is an example of how a major label takes a shot on a new artist without overspending. Similar to the first agreement, this contract is for a record the artist has already recorded. If the record is successful, the label can order an additional master and has the right to "match" any offer by a competing label for a long-term deal.

360 Deals

As previously noted, many 360 deals (such as the one in the prior chapter) present major disadvantages for artists because they have catch-all phrases which give the label a

---

[1] Examples of indie labels are Beggars Group (Radiohead, Bon Iver, others), Glassnote Records (Mumford & Sons, Childish Gambino, others), Big Machine Records (Taylor Swift, Tim McGraw, others), Shady Records (Eminem, Slaughterhouse, others) and 300 (Fetty Wap, T-Wayne, and others). Each of these indie labels have deals with the major record companies from which they receive international physical and digital distribution, and additional funding for studio time, producers, physical manufacturing, physical and digital packaging, photos, marketing publicity, music videos, radio promotion and other elements needed to make an indie label's artist a star.

financial interest in everything else that the artist does in the entertainment business. Below is a brief history of 360 deals and tips on how to negotiate for better terms.

History

The 360 deal is not new. The first reported one was English recording star Robbie Williams' deal with EMI in 2002. But in the last decade, 360 deals have become commonplace. New artists signing with a major label or their affiliates can expect it as a matter of course.

Income from sales of pre-recorded music reached its peak in 1999 at approximately $14.5 billion. By 2012, that amount had shrunk to approximately $7 billion and has remained relatively steady since that time. This is the reason labels have begun to pursue income from sources that were once sacrosanct.

Under the traditional paradigm, the label would pay the artist a small royalty, which was even smaller after all the deductions. The artist could expect to receive no recording royalty at all unless his album was a major commercial success, but he got to keep everything else: publishing, merch, touring, endorsements, etc.

These days, artists often generate more money from other activities than record sales. For instance, Lady Gaga's Monster Ball Tour grossed over $227 million dollars, and 50 Cent's deal with Vitamin Water turned to gold when he accepted shares in the company in exchange for authorizing the use of his professional name in "Formula 50." It is reported that his shares were worth over $100 million after Coca-Cola purchased Vitamin Water's parent, Glacéau, for $4.1 billion.

These developments have spurred the labels to seek to participate in all possible revenue streams generated by an artist. In my own practice, I have seen production companies get in on the act and insist that new artists sign 360 deals with them, even if they contribute little or no money into recording and make no promises in regards to marketing or promotion. This is the "Contract from Hell" reported in Chapter 2.

The Label's Argument

The labels argue that they make significant investments in an artist's career by putting up considerable sums for recording, including paying advances to A-level producers, getting the artist's music on commercial radio, securing invitations for the artists to perform on popular television shows, paying for one or more top quality videos for YouTube and other outlets, and providing tour support before the artist is popular enough to demand significant sums for live performances, among other things.

For emerging artists, a major label deal may be the path to becoming rich and famous. For instance, Lady Gaga was virtually unknown before Interscope spent a vast sum putting her on tour as an opening act for the New Kids on the Block, paying for marketing (particularly to the gay community), hiring wardrobe and makeup, and paying all her other expenses for over a year, not to mention using their clout to get her invited as a guest on almost every important radio station in the country. The labels argue that 360 deals are fair because monies generated from touring, merch, endorsements, and other streams would not exist at all without their efforts.

Many artists and their representatives would contend that it isn't their fault that the labels are making less money from their records. 360 deals, they would maintain, are just a cynical money grab by record companies who are facing dwindling income from recorded music because they have failed to react appropriately to the changing industry. Asking artists to foot the bill hardly seems fair. But the reality is that, since all the major labels and affiliates usually demand 360 terms, the artist may not have much choice. Given that reality, let's discuss how the artist's attorney can improve the deal.

How to Improve the Deal

The ability of the artist's attorney to improve a 360 deal depends on the artist's leverage as much as the lawyer's knowledge and negotiating skills. For instance, if there is a bidding war among two or more labels, the lawyer's ability to improve the deal increases immensely. If the artist is already making significant income from live shows, if not from record sales, this can also aid the lawyer in negotiating better terms, or at least carving out the areas where the artist is already earning money.

Carve-outs

If an artist is already earning revenues from a particular source, the lawyer should try to carve that stream out of the 360 deal. For instance, certain EDM artists are earning tens to hundreds of thousands of dollars playing large venues and festivals. If a label wants this kind of artist, it should be prepared to forego tapping into live performance income, as they had nothing to do with creating that income.

Get the Label to Work for the Money or At Least Pay Advances for Each Stream

In an interview about 360 deals with entertainment attorney Elliot Resnick, we discussed the splits in a form agreement that he received from one of the labels. The contract provided that the label's share for various streams was as follows:

- 50% Merch
- 25% Touring and live performance
- 25% of "digital products" such as ringtones and sales from the artist's fan site
- 25% Publishing
- 25% of Endorsements
- 25% of any other income from the entertainment business including appearances on TV and in movies, theaters, published books, etc.

While these percentages are typical, the actual amounts vary from deal to deal. Whatever the splits are, the artist's attorney should try to get the label to commit to doing something to deserve a share of each income stream. For instance, in return for 25% of the profits on merch, the label should commit to manufacture merch, sell it at retail via the Internet, and supply the artist with merch for sales on tour.

Points About Publishing

Regarding publishing, a 360 deal may include a "co-publishing" agreement in which the label has exclusive control of any songs that the artist writes during the term, and the label retains 25% of any monies generated from the songs. Or, the label may demand 100% of the "publisher's share" or 50% of all income generated by the artist's songs. In exchange for either of these arrangements, which are major gives, the label should have a dedicated staff committed to collecting monies generated by the artist's songs and pitching the songs to other artists for covers and music supervisors for placements in movies, television, video games, etc.

Aggressively Negotiating Advances

Regardless of whether the label is or is not equipped to provide support in respect to any income stream, the artist should try to exact advances for each stream. Ideally, as soon as the label recoups each advance for each income stream, the label's right to commission that income stream should terminate. For instance, if the label advances $25,000 against a 25% commission for branding and endorsements and the artist gets an endorsement deal for $100,000, the artist would pay $25,000 to the label (25% of $100,000), but thereafter the label would not be entitled to any more money from that income stream.

Avoid Cross-Collateralization

Just as important as negotiating for the label to commit to earn its keep for each stream and to pay advances for each stream, the artist's lawyer should make sure the label cannot cross-collateralize each stream. This means that the label should not be able to take money from one stream to pay for un-recouped balances for another. For instance, if the label pays $100,000 for recording costs and the artist's royalty after deductions is 50 cents for an album that sells at $12.00, the artist must sell 200,000 albums to break even.

Now, suppose the artist only sells 100,000 (still a considerable feat in today's market), and his income from touring is $50,000. If the contract allows the label to cross collateralize the various streams, the $50,000 will be applied to the "red balance" in his recording royalty account. This means the artist would receive nothing from touring—the monies would be applied to the unrecouped recording costs.

Net Versus Gross Profits

If the artist must shell out a percentage of his touring or merch or other income to the labels, his or her lawyer has to make certain that the percentage is based on net, not gross profits. For instance, if a tour earns the artist $25,000 but her expenses added up to $20,000 (for hotels, transportation, booking agent fees, sound and lighting, etc.), the label should only commission the $5,000 in profits, not the entire $25,000. Indeed, if the label's commission was 25% and that was based on gross, the amount due to the label would actually exceed the artist's profit.

In Summary

As I mentioned earlier, 360 deals generally suck for artists. However, it may be the only offer an emerging artist receives. But the artist's attorney should be innovative and seek to improve the deal as much as possible.

LICENSE FOR SINGLE ALBUM

From: _____ Limited
    London
    ("we"/"us"/"our")

To: _____
    _____
    Professionally known as "_____"
    ("you"/"your")

Date: _____ ____, 2017

Dear _____,

We set out below the terms upon which you have agreed to license to use the Recordings (as defined below).

1. The term of this agreement shall be a period commencing on signature of this agreement and continuing for nine (9) months from the date above or, if longer, until six (6) months after the initial release in the United Kingdom of the Album comprising the Minimum Commitment ("Term"). You shall not without our prior consent release or authorize any third party to release during the Term any other recordings under the artist name "_____."

2. You shall record and deliver to us within Eight (8) months of signature of this agreement:

2.1 a minimum of Eight (8), and a maximum of Eighteen (18) recordings, with a total running time of not less than thirty (30) minutes (unless otherwise agreed in writing between you and us), embodying your musical performances of previously unrecorded songs which are technically satisfactory to us (the "Minimum Commitment") provided that such Recordings shall be deemed satisfactory to us and accepted by us pursuant to this clause if we have not within ten (10) working days of delivery to us of such Recordings provided to you written reasons why such Recordings are not satisfactory to us; and

2.2 any Recordings made by you prior to the Term as listed in the schedule; the term "Recordings" hereunder shall mean recordings embodying your performances as a recording artist and/or musician (alone or with other artists) under the artist name "_____" and made prior to and during the Term.

3. The territory of this Agreement and the area in which we shall be exclusively entitled to exploit the Recordings (the "Territory") shall be the World and the Universe.

4. We shall have the exclusive right during the Term to make videos to promote the sale and exploitation of the Recordings ("Videos"). Subject to reasonable notice from us and subject to

your prior professional commitments, during the Term you agree to prepare conscientiously for, and to attend filming sessions at such times and places as we shall reasonably designate and to perform as a recording artist at such sessions for the purposes of making Videos. You and we shall mutually agree on the storyboard, director, producer and budget for Videos and other principal creative decisions. And if, after a reasonable period of good faith discussions, you and we are unable to agree on any such matter, we shall have the final say.

The Artist should try to delete "and if, after a reasonable period of good faith discussions, you and we are unable to agree on any such matter, we shall have the final say."

---

5. We shall use our reasonable endeavors to release or to procure the release for retail sale in the United Kingdom and in other countries of the Territory Records and by EMD embodying Recordings comprising the Minimum Commitment within six (6) months following delivery to, and acceptance in writing by us, of the Minimum Commitment. If we fail to release the Recordings within that period then you shall have right to serve a thirty (30) cure notice ("the Cure Notice"). If we fail to release before expiry of the Cure Notice then you shall have the right to terminate the license granted hereunder.

The Artist should try to add: "and retain any advance previously paid to you."

---

6. For the purposes of this agreement "Records" shall mean a physical carrier of sound recordings either alone or with audio visual material and "EMD" shall mean any transmission, distribution, dissemination or making available of Recordings (or their digitized content) by any means now or in the future known including but not limited to via telephone, satellite, broadcast, wireless, cable and/or the internet whether or not a direct or indirect charge is made including without limitation streams, limited downloads, permanent downloads and the use of Recordings in mobile applications, but excluding the manufacture, distribution and sale of Records.

7. We shall arrange and pay for such press and promotion to accompany the release by us of Records and/or EMD embodying the Minimum Commitment as we shall think fit in our good faith business judgment after consultation with you. You agree upon reasonable prior notice and in any event subject to your prior professional commitments and at our reasonable expense, to attend at such times and places as we shall reasonably designate for the purposes of attending interviews, promotional appearances and photographic sessions, to promote the sale and exploitation of such records and/or to publicize you as a recording artist. You shall not receive a fee for such activities but provided you obtain our prior approval for any expenses you incur in connection with such activities, we shall reimburse you, on a non-re-recoupable basis, for such reasonable out of pocket expenses incurred by you.

The Artist should try to add: "If you have to travel for such promotional event, we will cover the cost of round trip air fare, accommodations and reasonable per diem."

---

8.   We shall be entitled (but are not obliged) to enter into licensing arrangements with any one or more companies ("Third Party Agreements") for the purposes of the sale, distribution, promotion and marketing of Recordings.

9.   The period during which we shall be exclusively entitled to exploit the Recordings shall be the period commencing on date of this agreement and expiring six (6) years after the end of the Term ("License Period"). We shall have a six (6) month non-exclusive sell-off period after the end of the License Period.

The Artist should try to add: "Immediately following the License Period all rights in the Minimum Commitment will revert to you subject to the six (6) month non-exclusive sell-off period. For avoidance of doubt, (i) we shall pay you your normal royalty and mechanical for that sell-off period; (ii) you shall have the right to exploit the Minimum Recording commitment in any manner you wish; (iii) after the sell-off period, you shall have the exclusive right to exploit the Minimum Recording Commitment in any manner or media throughout the world without any obligation to us."

---

10. We shall pay you the following (non-returnable) advances, which shall be recoupable from your Royalty (but not any mechanical royalties and/or future advances):

10.1 For the Minimum Commitment Album, Eight Thousand (£8,000), payable as to:

(a) Four Thousand Pounds (£4,000) upon signature of this agreement;

(b)   Four thousand pounds (£4,000) upon delivery to us of the Minimum Commitment Album; and

(c)   Plus 100 complimentary cd and vinyl (50 each)

10.2 We shall pay you a royalty ("Royalty") equal to fifty percent (50%) of our Net Receipts from the exploitation of the Recordings under this Agreement.

10.3 "Net Receipts" shall mean gross income (including advances) actually received by us or credited to us (other than any credits against advances) and either (i) directly attributable to exploitation of Recordings and/or Videos made during the Term of this Agreement (ii) or the pro-rated share of monies received by us for licenses including other recordings less all of our reasonable and bona fide third party costs and expenses paid and/or incurred by us (or re-charged to us) directly in the creation and exploitation of such Recordings and/or Videos as listed below

(a)   recording costs;

> Delete this—the Artist already recorded the album.

(b) mastering costs;

> Add "actual, reasonable" to this as well as (c), (d), (e), and (f).

(c)   manufacturing costs;

(d)   artwork costs if we use a third party to create the artwork;

(e)   any and all distribution costs in relation to Records and EMD;

(f)   press, promotion and marketing costs;

(g)   producers' and/or remixers' fees, advances and royalties;

> Delete this—the Artist delivered a final master.

(h)   mechanical royalties;

> Delete this—mechanical should not be recouped from recording royalties.

(i)   any approved costs incurred in the making of Videos;

> Only 50% of videos costs should be recoupable.

(j)   any and all pre-agreed and reasonable traveling, subsistence and/or accommodation costs for you or us, incurred in connection with any promotional activities; and

(k)   our reasonable legal fees incurred in the licensing or other exploitation of the master recordings recorded hereunder (but not in relation to the protection of our rights therein and/or any legal fees incurred in relation this agreement); but specifically excluding any and all general office overheads ("Expenses").

> Add: "Such legal fees shall be pro-rated if such license includes records other than yours. For avoidance of doubt and by way of example, if we sub-license 5 different recordings, only one of which is yours, and our legal fees are $1,000 we shall only charge your account for $200."

10.4 In each accounting period, we shall be entitled to make a reasonable reserve from Net Receipts not exceeding 20% of Net Receipts. Such reserve (if any) shall be liquidated in the accounting period following the one in which the reserve was made.

10.5 We shall account to you for your Royalty no less frequently than twice within each twelve (12) month period and will provide a statement of account in reasonable detail and pay the sums due to you within ninety (90) days of the appropriate account date.

Change as follows: "We shall account to you for your Royalty no less frequently than twice within each twelve (12) month period beginning _____ ____, 2017, and will provide a comprehensible statement of account in reasonable detail (including number of units sold, format, territories in which such sales were made, and if an Internet sale, the name of the websites, such as iTunes) and pay the sums due to you simultaneously with the statement."

10.6 We shall be required to account to you for sales by our licensees only insofar as we have received payment from our licensees. We will use our reasonable endeavors to enforce the accounting obligations in our contracts with our licensees and we warrant that all arrangements with our licensees shall be on bona fide arms length commercial terms and shall not have the effect of artificially reducing the Royalty hereunder.

10.7 You shall be entitled upon providing a minimum thirty (30) days written notice to us to appoint a chartered accountant to audit our books and records relating to calculation of Net Receipts no more than once: (i) in any twelve (12) month period and (ii) in respect of any accounting statement issued to you. If any such audit reveals an agreed underpayment to you of: (i) five thousand pounds (£5,000); or (ii) five per cent (5%) of the total amount due to you for the period covered by the audit; then we shall pay your reasonable costs of such audit up to a maximum of two thousand pounds (£2,000) (excluding travel, accommodation and subsistence).

10.8 The advances specified in clause 10.1 and all other sums paid to or on behalf of you (other than your Royalties and any mechanical royalties) constitute advances against and to be first deducted from any Royalties and fees payable under this agreement (other than mechanical royalties and any future advances).

11. In consideration of the payment to you of the advances and Royalties set out in this agreement, you:

11.1 grant to us during the License Period and throughout the Territory an exclusive license to exploit the Recordings and/or Videos by any and all means and in any and all media whatsoever whether now existing or invented in the future, including, without limitation, the right to remix, edit or otherwise alter the Recordings and/or Videos;

11.2 grant us all consents required under the Copyright Designs and Patents Act 1988 (as amended) and/or any similar legislation throughout the world to exploit the recordings and Videos to the fullest extent possible and grant to us the exclusive lending and rental rights in the recordings and Videos;

11.3 irrevocably and unconditionally waive (and shall procure that all performers whose performances are embodied on Recordings shall) and (where waiver is permitted by law) agree not to assert against us, our permitted assigns and licensees, any and all moral and like rights that you have in Recordings and/or Videos and in your performances and Controlled Compositions embodied in Recordings and Videos; and

11.4 acknowledge and agree that the advances and Royalties payable to you under this agreement constitute fair and equitable remuneration for the services (and the products and results of the services) to be rendered and rights granted by you under this agreement including but not limited to all rental and lending rights.

12. You will not for a period of two (2) years from the end of the Term record or re-record any composition or any part thereof recorded and commercially exploited hereunder for a third party with the intention of releasing and commercially exploiting such recording.

12.1 During the Term and subject to the provisions of this agreement, we shall seek your approval in respect of the following:

(a)   the licensing of any Recordings hereunder for synchronization with any visual images other than those embodying solely the Artist's performances;

Add to 12.1(a): "With regard to the foregoing sentence, we shall pay you fifty percent (50%) of any monies that we receive for an approved license of any Recording and one hundred percent (100%) of any monies that we receive for the licensing of the underlying musical composition."

(b)   any third party license of a Recording for inclusion in any multi-artist compilation record.

Add to 12.1(b): "With regard to the foregoing sentence, we shall pay you your pro-rated share of any monies that we receive. For avoidance of doubt and by way of example, if there are 5 different tracks, only one of which is yours, we will pay you, or credit to your account if you are unrecouped, 50% of 20% of any monies that we receive."

(c)   approval of commissioned remixes or re-edits of the master recordings if applicable.

12.2 We agree to obtain and procure that our licensees shall obtain mechanical licenses in respect of musical compositions embodied on Recordings and Videos released pursuant to this agreement.

12.3 You warrant that you will either grant to us or will procure that we are granted mechanical licenses, which shall be paid for by us, in all musical compositions if (and to the extent only) written or controlled by you ("Controlled Composition"), which such grant constitutes a provisional copyright license enabling us and/or our licensees to release Records and/or Videos embodying such Controlled Compositions and/or to exploit such Controlled Compositions by EMD:

(a)   in the case of Records and Videos manufactured and EMD sold in the United Kingdom, at the applicable rate in accordance with any licensing scheme currently in effect between the BPI and the MCPS (or, if such licensing scheme expires and is not re-negotiated during the Term, at the rates in the last licensing scheme then in effect provided that such scheme was generally adopted by the record industry);

(b)   in the case of Records manufactured and EMD sold in the United States of America and/or Canada, at seventy-five per cent (75%) of the then current minimum statutory or industry agreed rate per Controlled Composition (that is, 9.1 cents per song) regardless of playing time on all Records and EMD sold less returns, subject to a total payment:

(i)   per Album Record of ten (10) times, or

(ii)   per so-called "single" Record two (2) times, or

(iii)   per so-called "EP" four (4) times,

the above mentioned seventy-five per cent (75%) rate;

Add: "We shall account and pay to you the above mechanical royalties on the same date as Record Royalties are due together with a comprehensive accounting statement. For the avoidance of doubt, such mechanical royalties shall be payable from the first unit sold and not subject to recoupment of any of our Expenses."

(c)   in the case of Videos manufactured for sale in the United States of America and/or Canada, at a rate not exceeding the lesser of six (6) cents per title or six percent (6.5%) of the published dealer price of each Video;

(d)   in the case of:

(i)   Videos manufactured and EMD sold in any country outside the United Kingdom, the United States of America and/or Canada; and

(ii)   Videos manufactured and EMD sold in any country outside the United Kingdom, the United States of America and/or Canada;

at the current minimum statutory rate in that country or, if no such statutory rate exists, at the then customary rate in the country.

12.4 You will either grant to us or will procure that we are granted a synchronization license for free in respect of any Video incorporating any Recording exploited under this agreement that incorporates a Controlled Composition.

12.5 You will use your reasonable endeavors to procure that we are granted a synchronization license at the rate specified in the current BPI/MCPS agreement in respect of any Video incorporating any Recording made and exploited under this agreement that incorporates a composition that is not a Controlled Composition.

12.6 You shall grant or procure that we are granted mechanical licenses, which shall be paid for by us, in all musical compositions embodied in the Recordings that are not Controlled

Compositions, which such grant constitutes a provisional copyright license enabling us and/or our licenses to release Records and/or Videos embodying such compositions and/or to exploit such compositions by EMD at the current minimum statutory rate in each country of the Territory or, if no such statutory rate exists, at the then customary rate in each such country.

12.7 We reserve the right not to accept a Recording of any composition that is not a Controlled Composition. Any copyright royalties paid by us or our licensees in excess of the amounts specified in this clause 12 are to be deducted from any other monies (including mechanical royalties) payable to you and/or in respect of Controlled Compositions.

12.8 You must issue (or cause the music publishing companies having the right to do so to issue), to us at no cost for the use of all compositions embodied on Records: (i) worldwide, perpetual synchronization license in connection with Videos, so-called electronic press kits and any websites that we may set up and/or host in respect of you and your recording services, and (ii) worldwide, perpetual licenses for public performance in connection with any such websites.

12.9 No later than delivery to and acceptance by us of the Recordings you shall notify us in writing of any so called "samples" of sound recordings ("Samples") embodied in the Recordings. You shall provide all reasonable assistance requested by us in obtaining any necessary clearances for Samples. We reserve the right not to accept a Recording that contains a Sample which has not been cleared.

12.10 Any costs incurred by us in clearing any Samples in accordance with this agreement shall be treated as recording costs and deductible as an Expense from any and all gross income received by or credited to us under this agreement.

13.   You hereby grant to us the right (which is exclusive during the Term and non-exclusive after the Term) to use and allow others to use (alone or with other matter) your professional name, approved likenesses, approved photographs, approved biographical material, approved images, approved voices and approved signatures (or representations of them) in connection with recordings, Videos, websites, mobile applications your career and/or institutional advertising.

14.   You hereby (and shall procure that all performers whose performances are embodied on Recordings delivered to us under this agreement shall) irrevocably and unconditionally waive and (where waiver is not permitted by law) agree not to assert against us, our permitted assigns and licensees, any and all moral and like rights that you have in Recordings delivered to us under this agreement and in Videos and in your performances and Controlled Compositions embodied in Recordings and Videos.

15.   We shall mutually agree with you the concept, design and preparation of artwork, including physical album artwork, digital artwork for exploitation of the Records in any

digital platform, and any artwork intended for promotional use, and we shall pay the costs incurred in connection with artwork.

16.   You warrant that:

16.1 you are at least eighteen years old;

16.2 you have full right, power and authority to enter into, grant the rights contained in and perform the terms of this agreement;

16.3 save to the extent of Samples previously disclosed to us, all materials furnished by you to us (including, without limitation, any master recordings, compositions or performances embodied thereon) do not now nor will they infringe the rights, (including, without limitation, copyright and rights of privacy) of any third party and shall not be criminally obscene or defamatory of any person;

16.4 you have not entered and/or will not enter into any agreement(s) of any kind which may interfere with the performance of your obligations under this agreement;

16.5 you have not performed and will not perform any acts which could in any way impair or materially deprive us of any of our rights or benefits under this agreement; and we have advised you to seek, and you have obtained, independent advice from a lawyer specializing in the music industry to enable you fully to understand this agreement.

17.   You shall indemnify us from and against any costs, loss or damage (including reasonable out of house legal fees) caused by your breach of this Agreement and/or any warranty or undertaking herein PROVIDED THAT such costs, loss, or damage has been adjudicated by a court of competent jurisdiction or settled with your prior written consent (not to be unreasonably withheld or delayed). You shall be notified of any such claim, action or demand and shall have the right at your own expense, to participate in the defense thereof with counsel of your choice.

18.   This agreement replaces and supersedes all previous arrangements, understandings, representations or agreements between the parties either oral or written with respect to the subject matter hereof and expresses and constitutes the entire agreement between you and us and no variation of this agreement shall be effective unless and until it is agreed in writing and signed by you and us.

19.   Wherever in accordance with the terms of this Agreement we are to procure your consent or approval such consent or approval shall not be unreasonably withheld or delayed and in the event that you have not given us written notice of you withholding such consent or approval within five (5) working days of your receipt of our written request your consent or approval shall be deemed given.

20. All notices given pursuant to this agreement shall be in writing and shall be served upon the other party personally or by prepaid first-class post at its address as set out above or by electronic mail and, if served personally or by electronic mail, shall be deemed served on the date of service or sending of such electronic mail and, if served by post, shall be deemed served on the date forty-eight (48) hours after the date of posting. The parties' email addresses for purposes of this agreement are as follows:

You: _____@___.com:

Us: _____@___.com:

21. The headings to the clauses of this agreement are for reference purposes only and do not form part of and shall not be read into the construction of this agreement.

22. No waiver of any term or condition of this agreement or any breach of this agreement or any part of it shall be deemed a waiver of any other terms or conditions of this agreement or of any later breach of this agreement or any part of it.

No person other than the parties hereto and their permitted assigns (and your lawful successors) are intended to derive any benefit or have any right, entitlement or claim in relation to this agreement by virtue of the Contracts (Rights of Third Parties) Act 1999 save as otherwise expressly stated herein.

23. We shall not have the right to assign this agreement and any of our rights and obligations under it to any third party. You shall not assign this agreement without our prior written consent.

24. The illegality and un-enforceability of any part or parts of this agreement shall not affect the legality or enforceability of the balance of this agreement.

25. Nothing contained in this agreement shall be deemed to have given rise to the relationship of a partnership between the parties hereto.

26. This agreement shall be governed by and construed in accordance with the laws of England and Wales, whose courts shall have exclusive jurisdiction.

If the above correctly reflects your understanding of the agreement between us then please sign this letter and return it to us.

Yours sincerely

_____

For and on behalf of
_____ Limited

Read and Agreed

_____

EXCLUSIVE ARTIST AGREEMENT WITH INDIE LABEL

AGREEMENT made as of _____ ___, 2017, by and between _____ Records Inc. with offices at _____, New York, NY _____ (hereinafter referred to as "Company") and the artist known as_____ p/k/a "_____" residing at _____, _____ (hereinafter referred to as "you," "your" or "Artist").

The parties hereby agree as follows:

1.   TERM.

(a) The term hereof (the "Term") shall consist of an initial period (the "First Contract Period") plus the additional "Contract Periods," if any, by which such Term may be extended by Company's exercise of one or more of the options granted to Company below (unless otherwise extended or suspended as provided herein).

(b) You hereby irrevocably grant to Company two (2) separate consecutive options to extend the Term for additional Contract Periods. Company shall exercise its options, if at all, by written notice to you prior to or on the date upon which the Term would otherwise expire. Notwithstanding anything to the contrary contained herein, if Company has not exercised its option for a subsequent Contract Period as of the date upon which the then-current Contract Period would otherwise expire, you shall send Company written notice that such option has not yet been exercised and Company shall have fifteen (15) days from the date of its receipt of such notice to exercise the option. If Company fails to exercise its option within said fifteen (15) day period or if it notifies you in writing that it does not wish to exercise its option, then the Term shall expire.

This agreement gives the right to the label to order two additional albums. An alternative goal for this indie label is to find a major label that will invest in the Artist and provide additional funds and marketing muscle to make the Artist a star. Paragraph 20 provides that the label has the right to enter into such an agreement, usually referred to as a "label" deal. That deal could be for just this Artist or other artists signed to the indie label. For instance, the label run by Sean Combs (a/k/a P. Diddy), Bad Boy Records (whose artists include French Montana and Machine Gun Kelly), has a label deal with Sony Music. See my notes on Paragraph 20 for more details.

(c) The First Contract Period shall commence on the date hereof and shall continue until the earlier of (i) the date that Company exercises its option a subsequent Contract Period or (ii) the date twelve (12) months after the initial commercial release in the United States of the Minimum Recording Commitment. The subsequent Contract Periods, if any, shall commence on the date following the date of expiration of the immediately preceding Contract Period and shall continue until the earlier of (i) the date that Company exercises its option for the subsequent Contract Period or (ii) the date twelve (12) months after the initial commercial release of the Minimum Recording Commitment for such Contract Period. The final contract period shall end six (6) months after release of the last Album released hereunder provided that Artist shall not be entitled to release any music recording for any third party prior to one (1) year after release by Company or the Distributor of the last Album.

(d) Notwithstanding anything to the contrary contained herein, you shall have the right to terminate the Term of this Agreement by giving written notice thereof to Company within thirty (30) days following ninety (90) days from the date of Delivery of the any Album (as hereafter defined) unless the Company has commercially released the Album.

> This provision requires the label to release each album within one year of delivery. The Artists should try to negotiate for a definition of "commercial release" to include national physical and digital distribution. Otherwise, simply putting a record up on iTunes could be deemed to be a commercial release.

2. RECORDING SERVICES.

During the Term of this Agreement, you shall render to Company your exclusive services as a recording artist for the purpose of making Master Recordings and as otherwise set forth herein.

> This clause makes the Artist exclusive to the label.

3. RECORDING COMMITMENT.

During each Contract Period, you shall render your services to Company, in accordance with the terms and conditions hereof, in connection with recording a minimum number of Masters (the "Minimum Recording Commitment"). The Minimum Recording Commitment for the First Contract Period shall be one (1) Album. The Minimum Recording Commitment for the subsequent Contract Period of this Agreement shall be one (1) Album.

4. RECORDING PROCEDURE.

(a) In connection with Master Recordings to be made hereunder, Company shall consult with you concerning the following matters and any other matters or issues arising during the recording process, provided that in the event of a disagreement between you and Company and after good faith consultation, Company's decision shall be final:

> The label usually has final say about creative decisions, but the parties usually jointly agree and sometimes pre-agree on the selection of one or more producers.

(i) Selection of the producer(s);

(ii) Selection of material to be recorded, including, without limitation, the identity and number of Compositions to be recorded; and

(iii) Selection of dates of recording and studio where recording is to take place, including the cost of recording therein. The scheduling and booking of all studio time will be done by Company or the Distributor.

(iv) Selection of any side artist(s), other featured artist(s), engineer(s), and any other creative personnel.

(b) Each Master Recording made hereunder shall be subject to Company's and/or the Distributor's approval as commercially satisfactory for the manufacture and sale of Records.

5.   RECORDING COSTS.

(a) Company and/or the Distributor will pay all specifically approved Recording Costs in connection with Master Recordings made hereunder. The recording budgets for Albums Delivered hereunder shall be determined by the Company, provided that the recording budget for the first Album to be produced hereunder shall be no less than fifteen thousand dollars ($15,000). Said recording budget, and any other Recording Costs, shall be treated as an Advance fully recoupable from any royalties payable to you below or under the Addendum to this Agreement. Company shall inform Artist of any additional recoupable Recording Costs and shall make reasonable efforts to avoid excesses to the recording budget. Notwithstanding anything to the contrary in the foregoing, you shall be solely responsible for paying any Recording Costs incurred by Company or the Distributor which are in excess of the recording budget approved by Company and the Distributor and which are due solely on account of Artist's actions or omissions. You shall reimburse Company for any such costs or, at Company's discretion, Company may deduct an amount equal to such excess costs from your share of monies payable to you hereunder. You shall not incur any Recording Costs without Company's prior written approval.

(b) The recording budget for the option Albums, if any, shall be equal to sixty-six and two-thirds percent (66-2/3%) of the amount of net royalties credited to your royalty account hereunder in respect of USNRC Net Sales of the prior Album, subject to a minimum of Twenty-five Thousand Dollars ($25,000) and a maximum of One Hundred Thousand Dollars ($100,000). For the purposes of making the computations pursuant to this subparagraph, Company shall refer to accounting statements rendered to you from the initial United States release of the prior Album through the end of the accounting period immediately prior to your Delivery of the option Album (or 12 months following Company's initial release in the United States of the prior Album, if earlier); and (ii) solely for the purposes of making said computation, Company shall make a good faith estimate of so-called "pipeline" royalties earned by you hereunder in the United States, which estimate shall be based on the most current information reasonably ascertainable by Company. As used in the preceding sentence, "pipeline" royalties means royalties for USNRC Net Sales of the Records concerned which have been earned by you but have not yet been reported by Company on accounting statements rendered to you hereunder.

This is a "Min-Max" formula, which rewards the Artist with a greater recording budget if the prior album does well.

(c) Nothing contained in this Agreement shall obligate Company to permit the continuation of any recording session to be held in connection with Master Recordings hereunder, if Company anticipates that the Master Recordings being recorded will not be satisfactory, or that the Recording Costs will exceed the budget therefore.

6. ADVANCES & ROYALTIES.

(a) Company shall pay you a signing advance of thirty thousand ($30,000) payable as follows: fifteen thousand ($15,000) upon execution of this Agreement, and the balance of fifteen thousand ($15,000) payable in installments of two thousand five hundred $2,500 commencing at the end of February 2015 and at the end of the next six (6) months thereafter. This payment shall be treated as an Advance fully recoupable from any royalties payable to you below or under the Addendum to this Agreement attached hereto as Schedule A.

This agreement provides for a relatively small advance for the Artist and an installment payment so that the Artist can quit his day job and focus on music.

(b) All monies paid to you, or on your behalf, pursuant to or in connection with this Agreement other than royalties paid pursuant to this paragraph, paragraph 19 and under the Addendum Agreement shall constitute Advances unless otherwise expressly agreed in writing by an authorized officer of Company and shall be recoupable from Artist's royalties hereunder.

(c) Conditioned upon your full and faithful performance of all of the terms and conditions hereof, Company shall pay to you with respect to the Minimum Recording Commitment recorded during each contract period an Advance equal to fifty percent (50%) of the net advance actually received and retained by Company from any Distributor. "Net advance" as used in this paragraph means the gross advances actually received by the Company in connection with Company's Minimum Recording Commitment under the Distribution Agreement for the Contract Period concerned less all actual expenses incurred by the Company and Distributor in connection therewith, including without limitation, all Recording Costs, video production costs, promotional costs, payments to third parties in connection with the exploitation of Records, and any other out of pocket cost or expense incurred by the Company and Distributor in connection with the Masters hereunder.

This subparagraph (c) as well as (d) contemplates a 50-50 split if the label enters into a distribution deal with a major label. See Paragraph 20.

(d) Conditioned upon your full and faithful performance of all of the terms and conditions hereof, Company shall pay to you with respect to the exploitation of Records hereunder fifty (50%) percent in each successive Contract Period of the net royalties actually received by Company from the Distributor. "Net royalties" shall mean the gross royalties actually received by Company from the Distributor after recoupment of all monies recoupable under the Distribution Agreement and this Agreement less all royalties payable to others, including, without limitation, producers and mixers.

(e) With respect to any Record embodying the Artist's performance together with the performance by another artist or artists with respect to whom Company or the Distributor is obligated to pay royalties, the royalty rate to be used in determining the royalties payable to you hereunder shall be computed by multiplying the royalty rate otherwise applicable thereto by a fraction, the numerator of which shall be one (1) and the denominator of which shall be the total number of royalty artists whose performances are embodied on such Record.

7. PRIOR MASTER RECORDINGS. Intentionally deleted.

In this case the label was not interested in acquiring any prior recordings made by the Artist.

8. GRANT OF RIGHTS.

(a) All Master Recordings recorded hereunder, from the inception of recording thereof, and all Records manufactured there from, together with the performances embodied thereon, shall be the sole property of Company (or if Company so designates, the Distributor) throughout the universe, free from any claims whatsoever by you or any other Person; and Company (or the Distributor) shall have the exclusive right to copyright such Master Recordings in its name as the owner and author thereof and to secure any and all renewals and extensions of such copyrights. The product of all Persons rendering services in connection with the recording of such Master Recordings, including you, shall be deemed "work made for hire" for Company (or the Distributor). If such product is determined not to be a "work made for hire" then you hereby assign all rights, including without limitation the copyright in the Master Recordings, to Company.

Almost all exclusive recording agreements are "work for hire." Under the Copyright Act, any assignment of copyright reverts to the grantor after 35 years, except for works for hire. So, under this clause, the Artist is not entitled to reacquire the copyrights in the records recorded under this agreement.
    However, it is not clear whether this work for hire clause is enforceable. Under the definition of work for hire in the 1976 Copyright Act, only two types work can be works for hire. The first is works

by an employee. Artists are not employees because, among other reasons, they are not on payroll, don't receive a salary, and most recording agreements actually state (including Paragraph 22(b) of this contract) that they are not employees. The second kind of work for hire is a work specially ordered or commissioned under a written contract that needs to fall under one of the following categories: (1) as a contribution to a collective work, (2) as a part of a motion picture or other audiovisual work, (3) as a translation, (4) as a supplementary work, (5) as a compilation, (6) as an instructional text, (7) as a test, (8) as answer material for a test, or (9) as an atlas.

It is not clear that a recording artist's agreement fits into any of these categories although the labels would argue that an "album" is a compilation (see #5 above). However, as of the time this book is written, no court has ruled on the matter. The labels have quietly settled any claims by artists demanding their copyrights back and have no interest in litigating the matter for fear of an adverse judicial opinion.

(b) Without limiting the generality of the foregoing, Company and any Person authorized by Company shall have the unlimited exclusive right, throughout the universe, to manufacture Records by any method now or hereafter known, derived from the Master Recordings made hereunder, and to sell, market, transfer or otherwise deal in the same under any trademarks, trade names and labels, or to refrain from such manufacture, sale and dealing. Such rights shall exist for the duration of the copyrights in such Records.

(c) Company and any Person authorized by Company each shall have the exclusive right throughout the universe, and may grant to others the right, to reproduce, print, publish, or disseminate in any medium your name, portraits, pictures, likenesses and biographical material concerning you, as news or information, or for the purposes of trade, or for advertising purposes in connection with Records hereunder. During the Term of this Agreement, you shall not authorize any Party other than Company to use your name or likeness in connection with the advertising or sale of Records. As used in this Agreement, "name" shall include, without limitation, any professional names.

(d) Company and any Person authorized by Company each shall have the exclusive right throughout the universe, and may grant to others the right, to create, maintain and host any and all websites relating to the Artist, including MySpace and other social networking sites, and to register and use the Artist's name, each member's professional or stage name, and any variations thereof as Uniform Resource Locators (or "URL's"), addresses or domain names for each website created by Company in respect of the Artist. All such websites and all rights thereto and derived there from shall be Company's property.

9. ROYALTY ACCOUNTINGS.

This Paragraph sets forth standard accounting and audit provisions.

(a) Company shall compute and pay royalties due you hereunder within thirty (30) days after Company has received accountings and payments from the Distributor. Company shall not be obligated to pay any share of recording funds or recording advances until thirty (30) days after Delivery by Company and acceptance by the Distributor of the applicable Masters. Company may deduct from any royalty or other payment due to you under this Agreement any Advance against royalties, any charges or other sums recoupable hereunder from royalties, and any amount You may owe Company under this Agreement or otherwise.

(b) If Company is unable, for reasons beyond its control, to receive payment for foreign sales in United States Dollars in the United States of America, royalties therefore shall not be credited to your account during the continuance of such inability; if any accounting rendered to you hereunder during the continuance of such inability requires the payment of royalties to you, Company will, at your request and if Company is able to do so, deposit such royalties to your credit in such foreign currency in a foreign depository, at your expense.

(c) At any time within two (2) years after any royalty statement is rendered to you hereunder, you shall have the right to give Company written notice of your intention to examine Company's books and records with respect to such statement. Such examination shall be commenced within three (3) months after the date of such notice, at your sole cost and expense, by any certified public accountant designated by you, provided he is not then engaged in an outstanding examination of Company's books and records on behalf of a person other than You. Such examination shall be made during Company's usual business hours at the place where Company maintains the books and records which relate to you and which are necessary to verify the accuracy of the statement or statements specified in your notice to Company and your examination shall be limited to the foregoing. Your right to inspect Company's books and records shall be only as set forth in this paragraph 9(c) and Company shall have no obligation to produce such books and records more than once with respect to each statement rendered to you.

> Successful artists may be able to get interest and accountant's fees if the audit reveals that the labels failed to pay the artists more than a certain percentage of actual payments. This is important, as audits are expensive and often do reveal that the label has underpaid the Artist.

(d) Unless notice shall have been given to Company as provided in paragraph 9(c) hereof, each royalty statement rendered to you shall be final, conclusive and binding on you and shall constitute an account stated. You shall be foreclosed from maintaining any action, claim or proceeding against Company in any forum or tribunal with respect to any statement or accounting rendered hereunder unless such action, claim or proceeding is commenced against Company in a court of competent jurisdiction within three (1) year after the date such statement or accounting is rendered.

(e) You acknowledge that Company's books and records contain confidential trade information. Neither you nor your representatives will communicate to others or use on behalf of any other person any facts or information obtained as a result of such examination of Company's books and records, except as may be required by law.

10. WARRANTY AND INDEMNIFICATION.

(a) You warrant and represent that:

(i)   You are under no disability, restriction or prohibition, whether contractual or otherwise, with respect to (A) your right to enter into this Agreement, and (B) your right to grant the rights granted to Company hereunder, to perform each and every term and provision hereof, and to record each and every Composition hereunder;

(ii) Company shall not be required to make any payments of any nature for, or in connection with, the acquisition, exercise or exploitation of rights by Company pursuant to this Agreement, except as specifically provided in this Agreement;

(iii) You are or will become and will remain to the extent necessary to enable the performance of this Agreement, a member in good standing of all labor unions or guilds, membership in which may be lawfully required for the performance of your services hereunder;

(iv) Neither the "Materials" nor any use of the Materials by Company will violate or infringe upon the rights of any Person. "Materials" as used in this subparagraph means any musical, artistic and literary materials, ideas and other intellectual properties furnished by Artist, contained in or used in connection with any Recordings made hereunder or the packaging, sale, distribution, advertising, publicizing or other exploitation thereof, which have not been supplied by the Company;

This provision makes the Artist responsible for the use of samples. In practice, while the label expects the Artist to inform them of the presence in any track of any samples, the label usually pays for the sample clearance and deducts that cost from record royalties, or if the Artist is unrecouped, the label adds that cost to the Artist's unrecouped or "red" balance.

(v) All of your representations and warranties shall be true and correct upon execution hereof and upon Delivery of each Master Recording hereunder, and shall remain in effect in perpetuity. Company's acceptance of Master Recordings or other materials hereunder shall not constitute a waiver of any of your representations, warranties or agreements in respect thereof.

(b) (i) During the Term of this Agreement, you will not enter into any agreement or engage, or fail to engage, in any action which would interfere with the full and prompt performance of your obligations hereunder, and You will not perform or render any services for the purpose of making Records or Master Recordings for any person other than Company. After the expiration of the Term of this Agreement, for any reason whatsoever, you will not perform any Composition which shall have been recorded hereunder for any person other than Company for the purpose of making Records or Master Recordings prior to the date three (3) years subsequent to the date of Delivery of the Master containing such Composition or two (2) years subsequent to the expiration date of the Term of this Agreement, whichever is later; and

---

The last sentence of this Paragraph is known as the "Re-recording restriction" and is designed to prevent the Artist from re-recording songs that the label has previously released for a period of time.

(ii) You will not at any time record, manufacture, distribute or sell, or authorize or knowingly permit your performances to be recorded by any party for any purpose without an express written agreement prohibiting the use of such Recording on Records in violation of the foregoing restrictions.

(c) In the event that you shall become aware of any unauthorized recording, manufacture, distribution or sale by any third party contrary to the foregoing re-recording restrictions, You shall notify Company thereof and shall cooperate with Company in the event that Company commences any action or proceeding against such third party.

(d) You will at all times indemnify and hold harmless Company and any Licensee of Company from and against any and all claims, damages, liabilities, costs and expenses, including legal expenses and reasonable counsel fees, arising out of any alleged breach or breach by you of any warranty, representation or agreement made by you herein. You will reimburse Company and/or its Licensees on demand for any payment made at any time after the date hereof in respect of any liability or claim in respect of which Company or its Licensees are entitled to be indemnified. Upon the making or filing of any such claim, action or demand, Company shall be entitled to withhold from any amounts payable under this Agreement such amounts as are reasonably related to the potential liability in issue provided, however, that Company shall not continue to withhold such monies for more than one (1) year if no action has been taken. You shall be notified of any such claim, action or demand and shall have the right, at your own expense, to participate in the defense thereof with counsel of your own choosing; provided, however, that Company's decision in connection with the defense of any such claim, action or demand shall be final.

(e) You shall comply with all of the terms and conditions of this Agreement and the Distribution Agreement to enable Company to fulfill all of its obligations under the Distribution Agreement.

(f) Company warrants and represents that:

(i) Company is under no disability, restriction or prohibition, whether contractual or otherwise, with respect to its right to enter into this Agreement, and to perform each and every term and provision hereof, and to record each and every Composition hereunder;

(ii) Neither the "Materials" nor any use of the Materials by Company will violate or infringe upon the rights of any Person. "Materials" as used in this subparagraph means any musical, artistic and literary materials, ideas and other intellectual properties furnished by Company, contained in or used in connection with any Recordings made hereunder or the packaging, sale, distribution, advertising, publicizing or other exploitation thereof, which have been supplied by the Company;

(iii) All of Company's representations and warranties shall be true and correct upon execution hereof and upon Delivery of each Master Recording hereunder, and shall remain in effect in perpetuity.

11. DEFINITIONS.

As used in this Agreement, the following terms shall have the meanings set forth below:

(a) "Advance"—amount recoupable by Company from royalties to be paid to you or on your behalf pursuant to this Agreement including Recording Costs. This Agreement shall include the Addendum attached hereto as Schedule A.

(b) "Album"—one (1) long-playing Record, in any configuration, of at least forty (40) minutes in playing time.

(c) "Composition"—a single musical composition or medley, irrespective of length, including all spoken words and bridging passages.

(d) "Controlled Composition"—a Composition embodied in a Master Recording recorded or released hereunder, which Composition (i) is written or composed, in whole or in part, by you or (ii) is owned or controlled, in whole or in part, directly or indirectly, by you or by any Person in which you have a direct or indirect interest.

(e) "Delivered" or "Delivery"—the actual receipt by Company and Distributor of fully mixed, edited and mastered Master Recordings commercially satisfactory to Company and Distributor and ready for the manufacture of Records, along with all necessary licenses, consents, approvals and forms necessary for the lawful exploitation of Records.

(f) "Distributor"—a company which is a parent or subsidiary of, or is affiliated with one of the major label distribution networks (that is, Sony, Universal, or Warner, or their successors) or nationally distributed major independent label distribution networks in the United States such as 300, Big Machine, Glassnote, etc. Notwithstanding the foregoing, Distribution Agreement as defined below shall not include a "P&D" deal as defined in the Addendum Agreement whether or not the other company is a major record company or distributed through a major record company.

> Note that the last sentence means that if the indie label enters into a P&D deal, the Addendum Agreement attached to this agreement would apply.

(g) "Distribution Agreement"—agreement between Company and a Distributor pursuant to which such Distributor shall have the right to distribute in the United States Records embodying Master Recordings produced hereunder, and in addition, the major label provides production marketing and promotion including such items as additional funding for recording, producer fees, packaging, photography, music videos and radio promotion.

(h) "EP"—any Record which is not either and Album or a Single.

(i) "Licensees"—includes, without limitation, any Distributor and all subsidiaries, wholly or partly owned, and other divisions of Company and any of Company's licensees.

(j) "Master Recordings" or "Masters"—each and every Recording of sound, whether or not coupled with a visual image, by any method and on any other substance or material, whether now or hereafter known, which is used in the recording, production, transmission, communication, and/or manufacture of Records.

(k) "Person" and "Party"—any individual, corporation, partnership, association or other organized group of persons or legal successors or representatives of the foregoing.

(l) "Record"—all forms of reproductions, now or hereafter known, manufactured, transmitted, communicated or distributed primarily for home use, school use, juke box use, or use in means of transportation, embodying (i) sound alone; or (ii) sound coupled with visual images.

(m) "Recording Costs"—all costs incurred with respect to vocalists, musicians, arrangers, conductors, orchestrates, producers, copyists, and other Persons, including without limitation you, in connection with the recording of the Master Recordings made under this Agreement and/or the Addendum attached as Schedule A, including, without limitation, union scale payments, payroll taxes, payments to labor organizations or designee thereof, advances and/or fees to producers, mixers or remixers, the cost of cartage and rental of instruments, studio costs, transportation, hotel and living expenses, tape and other recording media, editing, mixing, mastering and all other costs customarily recognized as recording costs in the entertainment industry.

(n) "Single"—a Record embodying thereon not more than three (3) Master Recordings of different Compositions.

In the event of any inconsistency between the aforesaid definitions and the definitions contained in the Distribution Agreement, the provisions of the Distribution Agreement shall control. Any terms defined in the Distribution Agreement which are not defined herein shall have the same meaning as in the Distribution Agreement.

12. SUSPENSION AND TERMINATION.

(a) If your voice or your ability to perform as an artist becomes materially impaired, or if you fail, refuse, neglect or are unable to comply with any of your material obligations hereunder (including, without limitation, failure to timely fulfill your recording commitment) then, in addition to any other rights or remedies which Company may have, Company shall have the right, exercisable at any time by notice to you: (i) to terminate this Agreement without further obligation to you as to unrecorded Master Recordings, or (ii) to extend the then current Contract Period of the Term for the period of such default plus such additional time as is necessary so that Company shall have no less than ninety (90) days after completion of your recording commitment or the fulfillment of any other material obligation within which to exercise its option, if any, for the next following Contract Period. Company's obligations hereunder shall be suspended for the duration of any such default.

This provision is especially important in cases in which the Artist is prone to substance abuse or trouble with the law. If, for instance, the Artist commits a crime and goes to jail, the label can terminate the deal or suspend it while the Artist serves his time.

(b) If, because of an act of God, inevitable accident, fire, lockout, strike or other labor dispute, riot or civil commotion, act of public enemy, enactment, rule, order or act of any government or governmental instrumentality (whether federal, state, local or foreign), failure of technical facilities, failure or delay of transportation facilities, illness or incapacity of any performer or producer, or other cause of a similar or different nature not reasonably within Distributor's or Company's control, Company or Distributor is materially hampered in the recording, manufacture, distribution or sale of Records, or Distributor's or Company's normal business operations become commercially impractical, then, without limiting Company's rights, Company shall have the option by giving you notice to suspend the Term of this Agreement for the duration of any such contingency plus such additional time as is necessary so that Company shall have no less than thirty (30) days after the cessation of such contingency in which to exercise its option, if any, for the next following option period. Any such extension of the then current Contract Period due to any cause set forth in this subparagraph which involves only Company shall be limited to a period of one (1) year.

13. LEGAL & EQUITABLE RELIEF.

You acknowledge that your services hereunder, as well as the Master Recordings recorded and the rights and privileges granted to Company under the terms hereof, are of a special unique, unusual, extraordinary and intellectual character which gives them a peculiar value, and that, in the event of a breach by you of any material term, condition, representation, warranty or covenant contained herein, Company will be caused irreparable injury and damage. You expressly agree that Company shall be entitled to the remedies of injunction and other equitable relief to prevent or remedy a breach of this Agreement, which relief shall be in addition to any other rights or remedies, for damages or otherwise, which Company may have.

Contractual slavery is illegal in this country, so a label cannot use a contract to force an Artist to record music, but the label can legally prohibit the Artist from recording with another label and get a court to "enjoin" (or prevent) the Artist from doing so.

---

14. ASSIGNMENT.

Company may assign this Agreement and/or any rights acquired pursuant to this Agreement, in whole or in part, to the Distributor or to any third party, or to any subsidiary, affiliated or controlling corporation or to any Person owning or acquiring a substantial portion of the stock or assets of Company. Company may also assign its rights hereunder to any of its Licensees to the extent necessary or advisable in Company's sole discretion to implement the license granted. You may not assign this Agreement or any of your rights hereunder and any such purported assignment shall be void ab initio.

"Ab initio" is a Latin term meaning retroactively.

---

15. NOTICES.

Except as otherwise specifically provided herein, all notices hereunder shall be in writing and shall be given by e-mail, fax, registered or certified mail, at the e-mail address and fax numbers to be supplied by the parties, or the respective addresses herein above set forth, or such other address or addresses as may be designated by either party. Such notices shall be deemed given when transmitted by e-mail, faxed, or mailed, except that notice of change of address shall be effective only from the date of its receipt.

16. FAILURE OF PERFORMANCE.

The failure by Company to perform any of its obligations hereunder shall not be deemed a breach of this Agreement unless the Artist gives the Company written notice of such failure to perform and such failure is not corrected within thirty (30) days from and after Company's receipt of such notice, or, if such breach is not reasonably capable of being cured within such thirty (30) day period, the Company does not commence to cure such breach within such thirty (30) day period and proceed with reasonable diligence to complete the curing of such breach thereafter.

17. ANCILLARY RIGHTS.

Following below are 360 provisions that, like all 360 terms, entitle the label to tap into other income streams besides record sales. However, these 360 provisions are much more fair than those contained in the "Contract from Hell" analyzed in Chapter 2. In that contract, the Artist basically had to pay 30% across the board for any income the Artist received from any income stream, except 20% for live performances, and the production company did not have to do anything to deserve such payment. In this agreement, the Artist only owes the label money if the label provides services or support to help the Artist generate additional income.

(a) You hereby grant to Company and its Licensees the exclusive right, throughout the world, to use and authorize the use of your name, including, without limitation any professional name, portraits, pictures, likenesses, biographical material and any other identifying materials, either alone or in conjunction with other elements, in connection with the sale, lease, licensing or other disposition of merchandise and merchandising rights, as well as for commercial endorsements and other commercial purposes. You shall fully cooperate with Company and its Licensees in connection with the rights granted hereunder. Company shall be responsible for all costs of manufacturing, shipping, licensing fees and any other costs associated with exploiting its rights hereunder. For the rights granted by you to Company in this subparagraph, Company shall pay to you a royalty of seventy-five (75%) percent of Company's net royalty receipts derived from the exploitation of such rights, after deducting all actual out of pocket costs and third party payments relating thereto. Such royalties shall be accounted to You separately from any recording royalties, and no Advances or Recording Costs shall be deductible from monies payable to you hereunder.

This provision contemplates that the label has a deal with a national merch company and that the label will pay for expenses associated with the manufacture and shipping of physical merch. Note that the last sentence of subparagraph (a) above provides that advances and recording costs for records shall not be "crossed" against monies payable to the Artist for merch sales. This is key, as artists are often "unrecouped," that is, they haven't sold enough records to pay the label back for advances and recording costs.

(b) Company may, from time to time, secure and coordinate live personal appearances for Artist and shall negotiate the Artist's compensation in connection therewith for concerts or live performances ("Company Shows"). It is understood that Company is not an employment agency or a talent agent and shall not be required to procure any employment for Artist, and that Company has not represented that it will procure employment for Artist. Any live personal appearance that Company does secure and coordinate for the Artist shall be incidental to its role as a record company. Company shall pay Artist seventy-five percent (75%) of Net Revenue derived from such Company Show. "Net Revenue" as used in this paragraph shall mean all gross revenue actually received by Company less documented reasonable expenses incurred by Company in connection with such Company Show such as lighting and sound. Company shall make such payment to Artist within three (3) days of Company's receipt of such Net Revenues together with a comprehensive accounting statement. Notwithstanding anything to the contrary above, (i) Artist shall have the right to pre-approve each Company show and her performance fee; (ii) Artist has no obligation to Company in connection with any live performance not secured by Company. This Net Revenue shall be accounted to You separately from any recording royalties, and no Advances or Recording Costs shall be deductible from monies payable to you hereunder.

(c) Company may, from time to time, secure and coordinate "synch" placements of any of the Artist's Songs in motion pictures, TV program, ad campaigns, video games etc. ("Company Synchs"). It is understood that Company is not a music publisher and shall not be required to procure any synchs for Artist. If Company does secure and coordinate a placement, Company shall be entitled to collect all gross revenue from the Company Synchs. Company shall pay Artist seventy-five percent (75%) of gross revenue derived from such Company Synchs. Company shall make such payment to Artist within three (3) days of Company's receipt of such monies together with a comprehensive accounting statement. Notwithstanding anything to the contrary above, (i) Artist shall have the right to approve Company Synchs and the synch fee; (ii) Artist has no obligation to Company for any synch placement not secured by Company. Company shall have no other rights in Artist's songs except as set forth in this subparagraph. Any monies payable under this subparagraph shall be accounted to You separately from any recording royalties, and no Advances or Recording Costs shall be deductible from monies payable to you hereunder

18. <u>VIDEOS.</u>

(a) Company shall have the right to require you to perform at such times and places as Company reasonably designates for the production of films, videotapes, or other visual media now known or hereafter discovered featuring your performances of Compositions embodied on Master Recordings recorded hereunder (hereinafter "Videos"). Company shall be the exclusive owner throughout the universe and in perpetuity of such Videos and all rights therein, including all copyrights and renewal of copyrights, and shall have all of the rights with respect thereto which are set forth in paragraph 8 above, including without limitation, the right (but not the obligation) to use and exploit such Videos in any and all forms.

(b) All sums paid by Company in connection with the production of Videos shall constitute Advances to you which are recoupable from royalties payable to you pursuant to this Agreement and/or the Addendum attached hereto as Schedule A. All sums paid by Company's Distributor in connection with the production of Videos which are recoupable from sums under the Distribution Agreement shall be recoupable hereunder on the same basis.

The Artist can usually negotiate that if the label spends more than a certain amount of money on a video such as $125,000 the label cannot recoup the overage. The argument supporting this is that the label is in control of spending and the Artist should not suffer if the label decides to put in an enormous amount of money for a video.

(c) As to the exploitation of the Videos by Company's licensees, Company shall credit your account with fifty (50%) percent of Company's net receipts attributable to the Videos. "Net receipts" shall mean all amounts received by Company less any amount which Company pays in connection with the exploitation of the Videos, including payments to publishers, labor organizations, shipping and duplication costs, and distribution fees. Your share of Company's net receipts shall be inclusive of any compensation for the use of any Controlled Compositions contained in the Videos.

19. <u>CONTROLLED COMPOSITIONS</u>.

(a) Artist represents and warrants that the Controlled Compositions are original and do not infringe upon or violate the rights of any other person and that Artist has the full and unencumbered right, power and authority to grant to Company all of the rights herein granted to Company. Artist hereby indemnifies Company against any loss, damage or expense (including reasonable attorneys' fees) in respect of any third party claims, demands, liens or encumbrances. Company shall have the benefit of all warranties and representations given by the writer of the Controlled Compositions.

(b) Artist shall promptly provide Company with a copy of Artist's songwriter agreement with the writer of each Controlled Composition or such other agreement evidencing Artist's rights in and to such Controlled Composition, and Artist shall provide Company with copies of such agreements with respect to Controlled Compositions not yet created promptly after their creation.

(c) Artist hereby grants to Company the right to distribute any Record embodying a Controlled Composition. Company shall pay Artist a mechanical royalty of three quarters (¾) of the current statutory royalty rate in effect at the time of release of the Record embodying the Controlled Composition at issue (currently 9.1 cents) for inclusion of any Controlled Composition in any audio Record released and sold hereunder or the Addendum to this Agreement attached hereto as Schedule A. Notwithstanding the foregoing, Company shall pass through to Artist any more favorable royalty provisions pursuant to the Distribution Agreement.

Note that while many would argue that a ¼ reduction to the Artist's mechanical royalty is unfair, at least in this agreement, the label is not trying to become the Artist's publisher and taking 25% of publishing income. See, by way of contrast, the "Contract from Hell" in the prior chapter (Paragraph 11) in which the production company seeks to become the Artist's publisher as well as record company.

20. DISTRIBUTION AGREEMENT.

In the event that at any time during the Term Company shall enter into a Distribution Agreement, then, notwithstanding anything to the contrary contained in this Agreement:

(a) Company shall have the right, at Company's election, to extend any Contract Period(s) to be co-extensive with the then-current period of the Distribution Agreement;

> This clause significantly impacts an Artist's rights, as it can have the effect of extending a major label deal for more than 6 albums, thus tying up an Artist's career for a very long time.

(b) From time to time, Company shall have the unrestricted right (but not the obligation), at Company's election, to conform any provision (e.g., reserves, free goods, etc.) of this Agreement to the provision of the Distribution Agreement which comprehends the same subject matter, including, without limitation, the Term, number of additional Albums and number of options for additional Albums, the Minimum Recording Commitment; and

(c) You hereby agree to duly execute any letters of inducement that may be required pursuant to the Distribution Agreement. In the event that you shall fail or refuse to execute any such letter of inducement promptly following Company's request therefore, you hereby appoint Company as your true and lawful attorney-in-fact to execute such letter of inducement in your name and on your behalf. Such power of attorney is irrevocable and is coupled with an interest.

> The Artist should try very hard to radically change this provision by: (i) making any Distribution Agreement subject to the Artist's consent, or at least all major deal points including advances, royalties, term and 360 provisions, (ii) entitling the Artist's attorney the right to take part or at least be consulted in the negotiations with the major or major indie label. As Paragraph 20 reads now, the label could enter into any kind of deal it wanted with the major label tying up the Artist for many years in an agreement that could be very unfavorable to the Artist.

---

21. APPROVALS.

Wherever in this Agreement your or Company's approval or consent is required, such approval or consent shall not be unreasonably withheld. Company may require you to formally give or withhold such approval or consent by giving you written notice requesting same and by furnishing you with the information or material in respect of which such approval or consent is sought. You shall give Company written notice of approval or disapproval within five (5) days after such notice. You shall not hinder nor delay the scheduled release of any record hereunder. In the event of disapproval or no consent, the reasons therefore shall be stated. Failure to give such notice to Company as aforesaid shall be deemed to be consent or approval.

22. <u>MISCELLANEOUS</u>.

(a) This Agreement contains the entire understanding of the parties hereto relating to the subject matter hereof and cannot be changed or terminated except by an instrument signed by the parties. A waiver by either party of any term or condition of this Agreement in any instance shall not be deemed or construed as a waiver of such term or condition for the future, or of any subsequent breach thereof. All remedies, rights, undertakings, obligations, and agreements contained in this Agreement shall be cumulative and none of them shall be in limitation of any other remedy, right, undertaking, obligation or agreement of either party. The headings of the paragraphs hereof are for convenience only and shall not be deemed to limit or in any way affect the scope, meaning or intent of this Agreement or any portion thereof.

(b) It is understood and agreed that in entering into this Agreement, and in rendering services pursuant thereto, you have, and shall have, the status of an independent contractor and nothing herein contained shall contemplate or constitute you as Company's employee or agent.

(c) Those provisions of any applicable collective bargaining agreement between Company and any labor organization which are required, by the terms of such agreement, to be included in this Agreement shall be deemed incorporated herein.

(d) The validity, interpretation and legal effect of this Agreement shall be governed by the laws of the State of New York applicable to contracts entered into and performed entirely within the State of New York. The New York courts, only, will have jurisdiction over any controversies regarding this Agreement; and, any action or other proceeding which involves such a controversy will be brought in the courts located within the State of New York, and not elsewhere. Any process in any action or proceeding commenced in the courts of the State of New York arising out of any such claim, dispute or disagreement, may, among other methods, be served upon You by delivering or mailing the same, via registered or certified mail, addressed to You at the address first above written or such other address as You may designate pursuant to paragraph 15 hereof. Any such delivery or mail service shall be deemed to have the same force and effect as personal service within the State of New York.

Note the record company is based in New York. See the first paragraph of this agreement. The label will almost want to the right to litigate and dispute in the state in which it has its headquarters. Artists can rarely change that.

(e) You warrant and represent that you have been advised with respect to the negotiation and execution of this Agreement to seek counsel from an independent attorney of your own choice and have done so.

(f)   If any part of this Agreement shall be determined to be invalid or unenforceable by a court of competent jurisdiction or by any other legally constituted body having jurisdiction to make such determination, the remainder of this Agreement shall remain in full force and effect.

ACCEPTED AND AGREED as of the date entered above.

_____ RECORDS, INC.

Authorized Signatory

ARTIST

_____

Name:

SSN:

This Addendum Agreement would govern any record that the indie label distributes without entering a Distribution Agreement. It basically provides a recording royalty of 18% for the Artist.

SCHEDULE "A"

ADDENDUM to Agreement between _____ Records, Inc. and the Artist _____

p/k/a "_____" ("Artist") Dated as of _____ ____, 2017 (The "Agreement")

Notwithstanding anything to the contrary in the Agreement to which this Addendum is attached, the terms set forth in this Addendum shall apply if Company releases any Master Recordings by itself. Company will be deemed to release Master Recording by itself with respect to Master Recordings that Company does not distribute pursuant to a Distribution Agreement. This shall include, without limitation, Company selling direct to retail, or using a regional distributor, or any form of digital distribution such as iTunes or through an aggregator such as CD Baby. Company will also be deemed to have released Master Recordings by itself if it enters into a pressing and distribution (P&D) deal (that is, a deal in which the other company agrees to manufacture records and then distributes them for a distribution fee) whether or not the other company is a major record company or a Distributor as defined in Paragraph 11(f) of the Agreement.

ARTIST'S ROYALTY

1.   COMPANY SHALL PAY ARTIST A ROYALTY of eighteen percent (18%) of the applicable Royalty Base Price in respect of Net Sales of Records consisting entirely of Master Recordings to be recorded under the Agreement, and sold by Company or its Licensees through Normal Retail Channels in the United States after deducting there from any Advances, or other monies then unrecouped or otherwise due from the Artist to Company.

2. <u>THE ROYALTY RATE</u> with respect to the following Records shall be one-half (1/2) of the rate otherwise applicable in Paragraph 1 above:

(a) Those sold to consumers and paid for by them through any mail order or record club or similar operation:

(b) Those sold to educational institutions or libraries or to armed forces or post exchanges;

(c) Those sold by Company or its Licensees for distribution outside the United States and Canada; and

(d) Those bearing a special label or a suggested retail price which is at least three dollars ($3.00) less than the suggested retail list price used for the top line Records released by Company or its Licensees in any territory.

3. <u>MISCELLANEOUS ROYALTIES</u>

The following shall apply to the computation of royalties, if any, payable pursuant to Paragraphs 1 and 2:

(a) With respect to Records embodying Master Recordings made hereunder together with other master recordings, the royalty rate shall be computed by multiplying the royalty rate otherwise applicable by a fraction, the numerator of which is the number of Sides contained thereon embodying Master Recordings made hereunder and the denominator of which is the total number of Sides contained on such Records;

(b) With respect to Records embodying Master Recordings hereunder which embody Artist's performances, together with the performances of another artist(s) to whom Company is obligated to pay royalties in respect of the sale of Records derived from such Master Recordings, the royalty rate to be used in determining the royalties payable to Artist shall be computed by multiplying the royalty rate otherwise applicable thereto by a fraction, the numerator of which shall be one and the denominator of which shall be the total number of recording artists whose performances are embodied in such Master Recording.

(c) No royalties shall be payable to Artist in respect of Records sold by Company or its Licensees until payment for such Record has been received by Company, or for Records sold as cut-outs after listing of such Records has been deleted from the catalogue of Company or particular Licensee, or for scrap at a salvage or close-out price, or less than fifty (50%) percent of Company's or its Licensee's regular wholesale price for such records, or in respect of Records distributed for promotional purposes or Records sold or distributed to radio stations, or for use on transportation carriers and facilities to promote or stimulate the sale of Records, or in respect of Records sold or distributed as "free" or "no-charge" or "bonus" records (whether or not intended for resale).

4.   COMPANY SHALL ALSO PAY ARTIST fifteen percent (15%) of any monies that Company actually receives from licenses to third parties for the use of any of the Master Recordings in movies, television, video games, and any and all other exploitation of the Master Recordings or Prior Recordings besides sales of Records, after deducting there from any Advances, or other monies then unrecouped or otherwise due from the Artist to Company.

5.   ROYALTY ACCOUNTING

The following shall apply to accounting for royalties, if any, payable pursuant to this Addendum:

(a) Company shall compute royalties payable to Artist hereunder as of June 30th and December 31st for each preceding six (6) month period during which Records for which royalties are payable hereunder are sold, and will render a statement and pay such royalties, less any unrecouped Advances and any of the permissible offsets, prior to each succeeding October 31st and April 30th respectively. Company may deduct from any royalty or other payment due to Artist under this Addendum any amount Artist may owe Company under the Agreement, this Addendum, or any other agreement between Artist and Company or its affiliates;

(b) Royalties for Records sold for distribution outside the United States ("Foreign Sales") shall be computed in the national currency in which Company is paid by its Licensees and shall be paid to Artist at the same rate of exchange at which Company is paid. For accounting purposes, Foreign Sales shall be deemed to occur in the same semi-annual accounting period in which Company's Licensees account to Company therefore. If Company is unable, for reasons beyond its control, to receive payment for such sales in the United States Dollars in the United States, royalties therefore shall not be credited to Artist's account during the continuance of such liability; if accounting rendered to Artist hereunder during the continuance of such inability requires the payment of royalties to Artist, Company will, at Artist's request and if Company is able to do so, deposit such royalties to Artist's credit in such foreign currency in a foreign depository, at Artist's expense.

6.   DEFINITIONS

All the definitions in the Agreement shall apply to this Addendum, except as used in this Addendum Agreement the following terms shall have the meaning set forth below:

(a) "Retail Selling Price"—with respect to records sold for distribution in the United States of America, the suggested retail selling price or suggested retail list price or suggested retail list price, as the case may be, and with respect to Records sold for distribution outside of the United States of America, the suggested retail list price of such Records, at Company's election, the country of manufacture, the United States of America or the country of sale;

(b) "Royalty Base Price"—One Hundred Percent (100%) of the applicable suggested Retail Selling Price of Records less all taxes and less the applicable Container Charge;

(c) "Container Charge"—(i) with respect to Records in any disc format including CD Records, twenty-five (25%) percent of the applicable Retail Selling Price of such Records; and (ii) with respect to Records in any non-disc configurations, twenty (20%) percent of the applicable Retail Selling Price of such Records;

(d) "Net Sales"—gross sales of Records less returns and credits of any nature;

(e) "Advance"—amount recoupable by Company from royalties to be paid to Artist or on Artist's behalf pursuant to the Agreement, this Addendum or any other agreement between Artist and Company or its affiliates. Advance shall include all actual out of pocket expenses incurred by the Company including without limitation, Recording Costs, the $30,000 advance payable to the artist under the Agreement, video production costs, promotional costs, payments to third parties in connection with the exploitation of Records, and any other out of pocket cost or expense incurred by the Company in connection with the Masters hereunder.

(f) "Side"—One Master Recording of one Composition;

(g) Sales "through Normal Retail Channels in the United States"—sales other than as described in Paragraph 2 of this Addendum;

(h) "Licensee"—includes, without limitation, subsidiaries, wholly or partly owned, and other divisions of Company and any of Company's licensees;

7. ALL OTHER TERMS

Except as set forth above, all other terms in the Agreement shall apply to the Addendum including transfer of copyrights in the Master Recordings to Company, recording procedures, representations and warranties, etc.

ACCEPTED AND AGREED as of the date entered above.

_____ RECORDS, INC.

Authorized Signatory

ARTIST

_____

Name:

SSN:

SINGLE DEAL WITH MAJOR LABEL WITH AN OPTION FOR SECOND SINGLE

I recently negotiated this deal for a single record that the Artist had already recorded with an option for an additional single and a "matching right" for the label, i.e., the label secured the right to "match" any offer by a competing label for a long-term deal. As stated in the Introduction, this is a method of giving an Artist a chance to succeed while limiting the label's upfront investment, and it is becoming more prevalent. I was pleased that there were no 360 provisions. The Artist wrote the song in the single, and another good thing about this deal was that the label offered to pay 100% of full stat mechanical royalty instead of a ¾ rate. Since the contract was essentially fair, there was no need for major changes. I inserted the few changes that I requested in the contract below. The label agreed to make all these changes and sent a revised version of the agreement for execution by the Artist.

<u>AGREEMENT</u>

Dated as of _____ ____, 2017

Between

_____ p/k/a "_____"

c/o Steve Gordon, Esq.
STEVEGORDONLAW
355 South End Avenue, Apt. 34G
New York, NY 10280

(collectively, "<u>you</u>" or "<u>Artist</u>")

– and –

_____ Records

_____

_____

("<u>Company</u>")

1. <u>ARTIST</u>: _____ p/k/a "_____." (All references in this agreement to "<u>you</u>," "<u>Artist</u>," "you and Artist," "<u>you or Artist</u>," and their possessive forms and the like shall be understood to refer to you alone.)

2. <u>TERM</u>:

(a) The term of this agreement (the "Term") shall commence on the date hereof and shall continue for an initial period (the "Initial Period") ending on the last day of the twelfth complete month following the date of the initial United States commercial release of the First Master. You hereby irrevocably grant to Company one (1) option to extend the Term for a further period (the "<u>Option Period</u>") upon the same terms and conditions applicable to the Initial Period, except as otherwise specifically set forth herein. If Company exercises its option therefor, the Option Period shall commence upon the expiration of the Initial Period and shall continue until the last day of the twelfth complete month following the date of the initial United States commercial release of the Option Master. The option shall be exercised, if at all, by notice to you at any time prior to the date the Term would otherwise expire. As used herein, the term "Contract Period" shall mean the Initial Period or the Option Period of the Term, as such may be suspended or extended as provided herein.

(b) Notwithstanding anything to the contrary contained in paragraph 2(a), if, as of the date when the then-current Contract Period would otherwise have expired, Company has not exercised its option to extend the Term for a further Contract Period, then: (i) you shall immediately send a notice to Company specifically referencing this paragraph 2(b) and stating that Company's option has not yet been exercised (an "Option Warning Notice"); (ii) Company shall be entitled to exercise its option at any time before receiving the Option Warning Notice or within ten (10) Business Days thereafter; and (iii) the current Contract Period shall be deemed to have continued until Company exercises its option or until the end of such ten (10) Business Day period (whichever shall occur first).

3.   DELIVERY COMMITMENT:

(a) Prior to or simultaneously with your execution of this agreement, you shall Deliver the Existing Recording. The "Existing Recording" shall mean each Recording of the performances by Artist of the Composition currently entitled "_____," from the inception of the recording thereof, including all edits, mixes and remixes thereof, if any, and all Videos relating thereto, whether now existing or hereafter coming into existence. The Existing Recording from the inception of recording includes all rehearsal recordings, "outtakes," and other preliminary versions of the Existing Recording with unfinished vocals which were created during the production of the Existing Recording.

(b) Within thirty (30) days following the commencement of the Term, you shall Deliver the First Master. The First Master will be derived from the Existing Recording (i.e., as same may be remixed or otherwise modified).

> Label should acknowledge prior delivery and acceptance of the Master. The whole reason the label signed this Artist was on the basis of a track he previously recorded, and he delivered the record prior to the receipt of this contract.

(c) Within three (3) months following the first day of the Option Period, if any, you shall Deliver one (1) additional Master (the "Option Master"). (The Existing Recording, the First Master and the Option Master are sometimes referred to collectively as the "Committed Masters.")

(d) Notwithstanding the foregoing, if you submit a Master after the First Master and prior to Company's exercise of its option for the Option Period (the "Early Option Master"), Company shall have the right to accept such Master as the Option Master hereunder.

4.   EXISTING RECORDING:

You hereby irrevocably sell, transfer and assign to Company all right, title and interest in and to the Existing Recording (including all copyrights and extensions and renewals of copyright therein), and the Existing Recording shall be the property of Company for the Territory free from any claims whatsoever by you or Artist or any other Person deriving rights from you or Artist. Company and you agree that the Existing Recording shall be deemed: (a) to be a Committed Master made under and as defined in this agreement for the purposes of the grant of rights, representations, warranties and other provisions of this agreement; (b) to have been recorded in the Initial Period; and (c) to be a "Material" under and as defined in this agreement.

5.   RIGHTS GRANTED:

(a) The Committed Masters from the inception of the recording thereof, and all reproductions derived therefrom, together with the performances embodied thereon, shall be the property of Company in perpetuity for the Territory free from any claims whatsoever by you, Artist or any other Person. Company shall have the exclusive right throughout the Territory to copyright the Committed Masters in Company's name as the author and owner of them and to secure any and all renewals and extensions of copyright throughout the Territory. Each of the Committed Masters shall be considered a "work made for hire" for Company; if for any reason any one (1) or more of those Recordings is determined not to be a "work made for hire," then you and Artist hereby irrevocably grant, transfer, convey and assign to Company the entirety of the rights, titles and interests throughout the Territory in and to all of those Recordings, including the copyright, any and all renewals and extensions of copyright, and the right to secure copyright registrations therefor. You and Artist hereby irrevocably and unconditionally waive any and all so-called droit moral and like rights that you and Artist have in the Committed Masters and in the performances embodied thereon and hereby agree not to make any claim against Company or any Person authorized by Company to exploit those Committed Masters based on such moral or like rights.

(b) Company and each Person authorized by Company shall have the perpetual right, for the Territory, without cost or any other liability to you or any other Person, to use and to authorize other Persons to use the Identification Materials relating to Artist, each producer, and each other Person performing services in connection with the Committed Masters, on and in the packaging of Records derived therefrom, and for purposes of advertising, promotion and trade and in connection with the marketing and exploitation of such Committed Masters and Records and general goodwill advertising, without payment of additional compensation to you, Artist or any other Person.

6.   ADVANCES:

(a) Upon receipt of invoices therefor, Company shall pay directly all Recording Costs actually incurred in the production of Committed Masters, provided such costs have been incurred in accordance with the Authorized Budget. Such Recording Costs shall be recoupable from royalties otherwise payable under paragraph 8 and shall be deducted from, and shall not exceed, the applicable Advances for Committed Masters set forth below (the "Recording Funds").

(b) The Recording Fund for the First Master shall be Ten Thousand Dollars ($10,000), payable following the full execution of this agreement and your Delivery to Company of the Existing Recording and the First Master.

(c) The Recording Fund for the Option Master, if any, shall be equal to sixty-six and two-thirds percent (66-2/3%) of the amount of net royalties credited to your royalty account hereunder in respect of USNRC Net Sales of the First Master, subject to a minimum of Ten Thousand Dollars ($10,000) and a maximum of Twenty Thousand Dollars ($20,000). For the purposes of making the computations pursuant to this paragraph 6(c), Company shall refer to accounting statements rendered to you from the initial United States release of the First Master through the end of the accounting period immediately prior to your Delivery of the Option Master (or 12 months following Company's initial release in the United States of the First Master, if earlier); and (ii) solely for the purposes of making said computation, Company shall make a good faith estimate of so-called "pipeline" royalties earned by you hereunder in the United States, which estimate shall be based on the most current information reasonably ascertainable by Company. As used in the preceding sentence, "pipeline" royalties means royalties for USNRC Net Sales of the Records concerned which have been earned by you but have not yet been reported by Company on accounting statements rendered to you hereunder.

I suggested making the maximum Recording Fund (the "max") for the second master $30,000. The thought being that if the Artist earns the max, the label will have made more money too. See the Introduction to this chapter for an explanation of min-max formulas.

---

7.   DISCRETIONARY MARKETING: For the First Master, Company shall establish a fund in the amount of Five Thousand Dollars ($5,000) to be expended on Marketing Activities to be determined by you in consultation with Company. All amounts expended from such fund shall be deemed an Advance hereunder. As used herein, "Marketing Activities" means any and all of the following activities, wherever performed throughout the Territory: advertising (including customer advertising), promotional activities, publicity material, promotional videos, trailers, touring, point of purchase, sales and positioning activities and inducements,

contests, giveaways and all other types of marketing efforts, advertising efforts and promotional efforts in connection with the First Master.

8. ROYALTIES: For top-line, full-priced units of Records sold through normal retail channels in the United States, a PPD-based royalty of eighteen percent (18%), pro-rated by the number of Recordings on the Record concerned and otherwise reduced, computed, adjusted and paid in accordance with the Exhibit attached hereto and made a part hereof. All monies paid to or on behalf of you, Artist or any Person representing you or Artist, other than royalties payable under paragraphs 8 and 11 herein and the Exhibit attached hereto, shall constitute Advances, unless Company shall otherwise consent in writing.

I urged that if the first Master was successful (specifically 100,000 downloads or one million streams) the label should increase the royalty for the second single to 22%. The label agreed to 20%.

---

9. ACCOUNTINGS/AUDITS: As set forth in the Exhibit.

10. RELEASE COMMITMENT:

(a) Provided you timely Deliver the First Master, Company will commercially release such Master in the United States within ninety (90) days following Delivery thereof ("First Master Release Deadline Period"). If Company fails to so release the First Master in the United States, you shall have the right to notify Company of its failure and stating your desire to terminate the Term if Company does not, within sixty (60) days after Company receives such notice ("First Master Cure Period"), commercially release the First Master in the United States. If Company then fails to release the First Master in the United States by the last day of the First Master Cure Period, notwithstanding anything to the contrary contained herein, Company shall have no liability whatsoever to you or Artist, and your only remedy shall be to terminate the Term by notice to Company at any time prior to Company's initial commercial release of the First Master.

In the unlikely event that the label failed to comply with the release commitment, I had them make it clear that the Artist would get all rights in the Master back if we refunded the Recording Fund.

(b) Provided you timely Deliver the Option Master, Company will commercially release such Master in the United States within one hundred and twenty (120) days following Delivery thereof ("Option Master Release Deadline Period"). If Company fails to so release such Master in the United States, you shall have the right to notify Company of its failure and stating your desire to terminate the Term if Company does not, within sixty (60) days after Company receives such notice ("Option Master Cure Period"), commercially release the Option Master in the United States. If Company then fails to release the Option Master in the United States during the Option Master Cure Period, notwithstanding anything to the contrary contained herein, Company shall have no liability whatsoever to you or Artist, and your only remedy shall be to terminate the Term by notice to Company at any time prior to Company's initial commercial release of the Master concerned. Notwithstanding the foregoing provisions of this paragraph 10(b), the last day of the Option Master Release Deadline Period with respect to the Early Option Master shall not occur prior to nine (9) months after the initial commercial release of the First Master.

(c) For purposes of calculating the First Master Release Deadline Period, the Option Master Release Deadline Period, the First Master Cure Period and the Option Master Cure Period, the number of days during any such period which fall during the period from October 15 to and including the following January 15 shall not be counted.

11. <u>MECHANICAL LICENSE</u>: Controlled Compositions shall be and are hereby irrevocably licensed to Company and its licensees: (i) for the United States, at a royalty per Controlled Composition equal to one hundred percent (100%) of the United States minimum statutory rate applicable to the use of compositions on phonorecords under the United States Copyright Law (without regard to playing time) in effect as of the initial release of the Master (the "<u>Effective Date</u>"), or, if there is no statutory rate in the United States on the Effective Date, the per composition rate (without regard to playing time) then generally utilized by major record companies in the United States; and (ii) for Canada, at a royalty per Controlled Composition equal to one hundred percent (100%) of the Canadian statutory per composition rate (without regard to playing time) in effect as of Effective Date, or, if there is no statutory rate in Canada as of such date, the per composition rate (without regard to playing time) generally utilized by major record companies in Canada as of the Effective Date. Mechanical royalties shall be paid on one hundred percent (100%) of Publishing Net Sales. Mechanical royalties payable in respect of Controlled Compositions for Publishing Net Sales other than from top-line, full-priced sales through normal retail channels shall be seventy-five percent (75%) of the rates set forth above.

12. <u>REPRESENTATIONS & WARRANTIES</u>:

(a) You warrant, represent and agree that:

(i) You and Artist have the right and legal capacity to enter into, execute and implement this agreement, and you and Artist are not subject to any prior obligations or agreements, whether as a party or otherwise, which would restrict or interfere in any way with the full and prompt performance of your obligations hereunder. You and Artist shall fulfill all of your obligations under this agreement in a timely manner;

(ii) (A) None of you, Artist or any other Person has sold or assigned to any other Person or otherwise disposed of any right, title or interest in or to the Existing Recording;

(B) No uses of the Existing Recording have been made by you, Artist or any other Person other than YouTube and SoundCloud. Prior to or simultaneously with the full execution of this agreement, you and Artist shall cause all exploitations of the Existing Recording specified in the immediately preceding sentence or otherwise to cease. Without limiting the generality of the foregoing provisions of this paragraph 12(a)(ii)(B), except as specified in this paragraph, neither you nor Artist has: (I) distributed, marketed and/or sold, and neither you nor Artist shall distribute, market and/or sell, any Records derived from the Existing Recording; or (II) authorized or permitted any Person other than Company to exploit in any manner or medium any Existing Recordings (including on Records or in connection with motion picture soundtracks);

(C) There are no claims or threats of claims of litigation involving the Existing Recording;

(D) Artist has not performed the Compositions performed in the Existing Recording for the making of any other Recording;

(E) Each Person who rendered any service in connection with, or who otherwise contributed in any way to the making of the Existing Recording, or who granted to you or Artist any of the rights referred to in this agreement, has the full, right, power and authority to do so, and was not bound by any agreement which would restrict such Person from rendering such services or granting such rights;

(F) All Recording Costs and expenses incurred in the creation and production of the Existing Recording have been paid in full;

(G) The Existing Recording was made in accordance with the rules and regulations of all unions having jurisdiction; and

(H) All necessary licenses for the recording of the Compositions performed in the Existing Recording have been obtained from the copyright owners, and all monies payable under such licenses or otherwise by reason of such recording have been paid;

(iii) Company shall not be required to make any payments of any nature for or in connection with the acquisition, exercise or exploitation of any of Company's rights hereunder, except as otherwise specifically set forth in this agreement;

(iv) The Materials or any use thereof shall not violate any law or infringe upon or violate the rights of any Person (including contractual rights, copyrights, rights of publicity and rights of privacy); and each track-by-track list identifying the performers on and timings of (and titles, writers and publishers of each Composition embodied on) each Master hereunder and describing their performances which you furnish to Company is and shall be true, accurate and complete. "Materials" as used in this paragraph 12(a)(iv) means: Recordings hereunder (including the Committed Masters and any Samples embodied therein); all Compositions; each name used by Artist, individually or as a group, in connection with Recordings hereunder; all photographs and likenesses of Artist; and all other musical, dramatic, artistic and literary materials, ideas and other intellectual properties contained in or used in connection with any Recordings hereunder or their packaging, sale, distribution, advertising, publicizing or other exploitation. Company's acceptance and/or utilization of Recordings, Materials or track-by-track lists hereunder shall not constitute a waiver of your representations, warranties or agreements in respect thereof or a waiver of any of Company's rights or remedies;

(v) Neither you nor Artist shall, during the Term, assign or otherwise permit Artist's professional name set forth on page 1 (the "Artist Name"), or any other professional name(s) utilized by Artist, to be used by any other individual or group of individuals without Company's prior written consent, and any attempt to do so shall be null and void and shall convey no right or title. You hereby warrant and represent that: (A) Artist is and shall be the sole owner of the Artist Name and all other professional names used by Artist in connection with Recordings hereunder; (B) no Person other than Company has, or shall have, the right to use such names and Artist's likenesses or to permit such names and Artist's likenesses to be used in connection with Records or Recordings at any time during the Term; (C) you and Artist have the authority to and hereby grant Company the exclusive right to use such names in the Territory in accordance with all of the terms and conditions of this agreement; and (D) you will not permit Artist to use (and Artist shall not use) any professional name other than the Artist Name during the Term without Company's prior written consent, which may be withheld for any reason. If any Person challenges Artist's right to use a professional name (including the Artist Name) or if Company determines in its reasonable good faith discretion that any such professional name (including the Artist Name) is not available for use by Company hereunder in any portion of the Territory or that its availability in any portion of the Territory is in question, then you and Artist shall, at Company's request, promptly designate another professional name to be used by Artist, such other professional name to be subject to Company's prior written consent; upon Company's written consent of any such professional name, such name shall be deemed to be the Artist Name for purposes of this agreement. Notwithstanding anything to the contrary contained in this paragraph 12(a)(v), Company's failure to object to Artist's use of any professional name (including the Artist Name) or Company's approval of Artist's use of any such name, shall not constitute a waiver by Company of any of your or Artist's warranties and representations hereunder;

(vi) Artist shall not perform for the purpose of recording any Composition, or any adaptation of any Composition, embodied on any Committed Master for any Person other than Company for use in the Territory on Records (including in radio or television commercials or otherwise for synchronization with visual images), before the later of: (A) five (5) years after the date of Delivery of all Recordings made hereunder as the last Delivered Recording of the restricted Composition concerned or adaptation thereof; or (B) two (2) years after the expiration or other termination of the Term (the "Re-recording Restriction");

(vii) You will submit all Masters embodying the performances of Artist to Company until Company accepts a Master as the Option Master (or, if Company does not exercise its option for the Option Period, until the last day of the ten (10) Business Day period referred to in paragraph 2(b) above);

(viii) All Persons rendering services in connection with Masters or Videos shall fully comply with the provisions of the Immigration Reform Control Act of 1986; and

(ix) Artist is a United States citizen and is at least eighteen (18) years of age.

(b) You shall and do hereby indemnify, save and hold Company and its parent, affiliates, divisions, successors, licensees and assigns and/or the officers, directors and employees of any of the foregoing (collectively, the "Company Indemnitees") harmless from any and all loss, damage and liability (including court costs and reasonable attorneys' fees) arising out of, connected with or as a result of: (i) any act or omission by you or Artist (or any of your respective agents) or (ii) any inconsistency with, failure of or breach or threatened breach by you of any warranty, representation, agreement, undertaking or covenant contained in this agreement including any claim, demand or action by any third party in connection with the foregoing, which has resulted in a judgment or which has been settled with your consent. Notwithstanding the preceding sentence, (i) Company shall have the right to settle without your consent any claim involving sums of Ten Thousand Dollars ($10,000) or less, and this indemnity shall apply in full to any claim so settled, and (ii) if you do not consent to any settlement proposed by Company for an amount in excess of Ten Thousand Dollars ($10,000), Company shall have the right to settle such claim without your consent, and this indemnity shall apply in full to any claim so settled, unless you obtain a surety bond from a surety acceptable to Company in its sole discretion, with Company as a beneficiary, and such surety agrees unconditionally, in writing, to pay all costs, expenses, losses, damages, etc. (including court costs and reasonable attorneys' fees) incurred by the Company Indemnitees by reason of such claim. In addition to any other rights or remedies Company may have by reason of any such inconsistency, failure, breach, threatened breach or claim, Company may obtain reimbursement from you, on demand, for any payment made by the Company Indemnitees at any time after the date hereof with respect to any loss, damage or liability (including anticipated and actual court costs and reasonable attorneys' fees) resulting therefrom. Such amounts may also be deducted from all monies becoming payable under this agreement or any other agreement to the extent to which they have not been reimbursed to Company by you. If the amount of any such claim or loss has not been determined, Company may withhold from monies otherwise payable under this agreement or any other agreement an amount consistent with such claim or loss pending such determination unless you post a bond in a form and from a bonding company acceptable to Company in an amount equal to Company's estimate of the amount of the claim, demand or action. If no action is filed within one (1) year following the date on which such claim was first received by Company and/or its licensees, Company shall release all sums withheld in connection with such claim, unless Company, in its reasonable business judgment, believes that such an action may be instituted notwithstanding the passage of such time. Notwithstanding the foregoing, if after such release by Company of sums withheld in connection with a particular claim such claim is reasserted, then Company's rights under this paragraph 12(b) shall apply in full force and effect. Company shall give you notice of any third-party claim, demand or action to which the foregoing indemnity applies and you shall have the right to participate in the defense of any such claim, demand or action through counsel of your own choice and at your expense; provided that, Company shall have the right at all times, in its sole discretion, to retain or resume control of the conduct thereof.

13. NOTICES: All notices under this agreement shall be in writing and shall be given by courier or other personal delivery, by overnight delivery by an established overnight delivery service (e.g., Federal Express, Airborne Express, UPS, etc.), or by registered or certified mail (return receipt requested) at the appropriate address set forth above, or at a substitute address designated in a notice (made in accordance with this paragraph) sent by the party concerned to the other party hereto, provided that all notices to Company shall be sent to the attention of its Executive Vice President, Business & Legal Affairs. Notices shall be deemed given when mailed or deposited into the custody of an overnight delivery service for overnight delivery, or, if personally delivered, when so delivered, except that a notice of change of address shall be effective only from the date of its receipt. Company may send royalty statements and payments to Company by first class mail.

14. APPROVALS: Except as otherwise specifically set forth in this agreement, as to all matters designated herein to be determined by mutual agreement or selection, or as to which any approval or consent is required, such agreement, selection, approval or consent shall not be unreasonably withheld. You agree that any approvals (including creative or marketing approvals) to be exercised by you and/or Artist hereunder shall apply only during the Term, except as otherwise expressly provided herein. Your agreement, selection, approval or consent, whenever required (including your written agreement, selection, approval or consent), shall be deemed to have been given unless you notify Company otherwise within five (5) Business Days following the date of Company's request to you. You shall not hinder or delay

the scheduled release of any Record subject to this agreement. In the event of your disapproval or no consent, the reasons therefor shall be stated. Each of your then-current attorney and manager is hereby deemed an authorized agent to give approval on your behalf.

15. <u>BREACH</u>: No breach of this agreement by Company shall be deemed material unless within thirty (30) days after you learn of such breach, you serve notice thereof on Company specifying the nature thereof and Company fails to cure such breach, if any, within thirty (30) days after receipt of such notice. You shall not be deemed to be in default or breach of this agreement unless you are given notice thereof and same is not cured within thirty (30) days after receipt of such notice; provided that the foregoing shall not be applicable to any breach, alleged breach or threatened breach of the exclusivity provisions of this agreement, to your or Artist's failure to timely Deliver the Existing Recording or the Committed Masters, to the provisions of paragraph 12(a)(vi) of this agreement or to any breach, alleged breach or threatened breach for which a cure period is already provided in this agreement.

16. <u>GOVERNING LAW</u>: This agreement has been entered into in the State of New York and its validity, construction, performance and breach shall be governed by the laws of the State of New York applicable to agreements made and to be wholly performed therein. The New York courts (State and Federal), only, will have jurisdiction of any controversies regarding this agreement; any action or other proceeding which involves such a controversy will be brought in those courts, in New York County, and not elsewhere. The parties waive any and all objections to venue in those courts.

17. <u>MATCHING RIGHT</u>: You shall have the right to negotiate with third parties with respect to each of the Applicable Rights (as defined below), subject to the remainder of this paragraph 17. Until the date occurring twelve (12) months after the last day of the Term, you shall not have the right to enter into an agreement with a third party for any of the Applicable Rights unless you notify Company in writing of the material terms of the Applicable Third-Party Proposal (the "Notification") and offer Company the right to enter into an agreement with you upon the same terms and conditions contained in such Applicable Third-Party Proposal; provided that Company shall not be required, as a condition of accepting any offer made to it pursuant to this paragraph 17, to agree to any terms or conditions which cannot be fulfilled by Company as readily as by any other Person or to waive any of Company's rights under this agreement or any other agreement. If Company does not advise you that it wishes to accept such offer within forty-five (45) days after its receipt of the Notification, you shall have the right to enter into the agreement with the third party identified in the Applicable Third-Party Proposal, but only on terms and conditions no less favorable to you than those contained in the Notification. If you desire to accept an offer less favorable to you than that set forth in the

Notification, you shall be obligated to submit such less favorable terms and conditions to Company by notice and Company shall have forty-five (45) days from receipt thereof to exercise its rights as provided in this paragraph 17. As used herein, the term "Applicable Rights" means the right to enter into a term agreement for (a) Artist's Recordings and recording services, (b) the right to participate financially in Artist's touring, endorsements, sponsorships and other collateral entertainment activities, (c) the right to exploit merchandising relating to Artist, and (d) the right to Artist's fan club and VIP ticketing, and the term "Applicable Third-Party Proposal" means a bona fide proposal for an agreement with a legitimate third-party company regarding the Applicable Rights described in paragraph 17(a), either alone or together with any one or more of the rights described in paragraphs 17(b), 17(c) and 17(d).

18. DEFINITIONS: For the purposes of this agreement, the following definitions shall apply:

(a) "Advance"—a prepayment of royalties; Company may recoup Advances from royalties to be paid or accrued to you pursuant to this or any other agreement;

(b) "Album"—a Record having no less than forty (40) minutes of playing time and which embodies at least eleven (11) Masters each containing a different Composition sold in a single package;

(c) "Business Day"—any day other than a Saturday, a Sunday, a day on which banks in New York City or Los Angeles are authorized or obligated by law to close or a day on which Company's headquarters is officially closed;

(d) "Composition"—a musical composition or medley consisting of words and/or music, or any dramatic material and bridging passages, whether in the form of instrumental and/or vocal music, prose or otherwise, irrespective of length;

(e) "Controlled Composition" shall mean any composition or material embodied in a Master which, in whole or in part, is written, composed, owned and/or controlled, directly or indirectly, by you, Artist, any producer of the Master and/or anyone associated or affiliated with you, Artist or any such producer;

(f) "Delivery" shall mean your delivery to Company of a two track stereo master file containing the Master concerned, fully edited, mixed, equalized and otherwise in the proper form for the production of the parts necessary for the manufacture of commercial Records, together with an amended version suitable for radio, the unmixed multitracks, inclusive of all session files and alternate mix passes inclusive of an instrumental mix, TV track mix, a cappella mix and mix stems (and, for any video, an HD-Cam and HD QUICKTIME 1280x720, with uncompressed audio and otherwise in accordance with Company's specifications) and all materials, consents, approvals, licenses and permissions necessary or advisable for Company to exercise its rights hereunder. Each Master shall be subject to Company's approval as technically and commercially satisfactory, and shall not be deemed Delivered unless and until such approval is given. Without limiting the preceding sentence, no Master shall be deemed Delivered if, in Company's reasonable, good faith opinion, such Master or material embodied in such Master would constitute an invasion of any Person's rights (including copyright infringement, libel or slander) or would violate Company's standards of decency or any applicable rules, regulations, statutes or laws. Upon the request of Company, you shall cause Artist to re-record any Composition until a technically and commercially satisfactory Master shall have been obtained. Only Masters Delivered in full compliance with the provisions of this agreement shall be applied in fulfillment of the Delivery Commitment and no payments shall be required to be made to you in connection with any Masters which are not in full compliance. Any payments made by Company following the physical delivery of Masters herein but prior to Delivery shall not constitute a waiver of your Delivery obligations hereunder or of Company's right to approve Masters as technically and commercially satisfactory;

(g) "Identification Materials"—the name(s) (including any professional names, sobriquets and group name(s) heretofore and hereafter adopted), characters, symbols, emblems, logos, designs, artwork, voice and likenesses (including photographs, portraits, caricatures and stills from any artwork or Videos), visual representations, autographs (including facsimile signatures), biographical material, service marks and/or trademarks, whether or not current;

(h) "Master"—a Recording: (i) containing newly-recorded studio performances of a previously unrecorded Composition made specifically for the applicable recording project; (ii) embodying performances featuring only Artist; (iii) having a playing time of not less than three minutes; (iv) not embodying solely an instrumental performance; (v) embodying solely Artist's featured performances of a single Composition which is not a medley; and (vi) not containing any Composition designed to appeal to a specialized or limited audience (e.g., gospel, opera, Christmas or children's music);

(i) "Person"—any natural person, legal entity or other organized group of persons or entities. All pronouns, whether personal or impersonal, which refer to Persons include natural persons and other Persons;

(j) "Principal Licensee"—Company's licensee for the majority (or plurality) of Records sold on behalf of Company in the territory concerned including Company's affiliates and non-affiliated Persons

(k) "Recording" shall mean any recording of sound or data used in the production of sound, whether or not coupled with a visual image, by any method and on any substance or material, whether now or hereafter known, which is used or useful in the recording, production and/or manufacture of Records or for any other exploitation of sound;

(l) "Record"—any form of reproduction, distribution, transmission or communication of, or facilitation of access to, Recordings (whether or not in physical form) now or hereafter known (including reproductions of sound alone or together with visual images) which is manufactured, distributed, transmitted or communicated primarily for personal use, home use, institutional (e.g., library or school) use, jukebox use, or use in means of transportation, including any computer-assisted media or technology (e.g., CD-ROM, DVD Audio, CD Extra, Enhanced CD, player application, widget) or use as a so-called "ringtone" in any form (e.g., as so-called "master ringtones," "polyphonic ringtones" and "MIDI ringtones");

(m) "Recording Costs"—wages, fees, advances and payments of any nature to or in respect of all musicians, vocalists, conductors, arrangers, orchestrators, engineers, producers, copyists, etc.; payments to a trustee or fund based on wages to the extent required by any agreement between Company and any labor organization or trustee; union session scale payable to Artist; all studio, tape, editing, mixing, re mixing, mastering and engineering costs; artist development costs including physical training, vocal conditioning, cosmetic enhancement and other similar costs, authoring costs; all costs of travel, per diems, rehearsal halls, non studio facilities and equipment, dubdown, rental and transportation of instruments; all costs occasioned by the cancellation of any scheduled recording session; all amounts paid in connection with the production, conversion, authoring, mastering and delivery of audiovisual materials prepared for or embodied on Records; all expenses of clearing and licensing any Samples embodied on Recordings hereunder; and all other costs and expenses incurred in the production, but not the manufacture, of Recordings and Records hereunder or otherwise made in connection with Artist, which are then customarily recognized as recording costs in the recording industry. If Company furnishes any of its own facilities, materials, services or equipment for which Company has a standard rate, the amount of such standard rate (or if there is no standard rate, the market value for the services or thing furnished) shall be deemed Recording Costs. Payments to the American Federation of Musicians' Special Payments Fund and the Music Performance Trust Fund based upon Record sales (so-called "per-record royalties") shall not constitute a Recording Cost and shall not be recoupable from your royalties or reimbursable by you;

(n) "Sample"—any copyrightable work which is owned or controlled by any Person other than you, embodied on a Recording hereunder, but not Artist's newly recorded performance hereunder of an entire Composition previously recorded by other recording artist(s) and theretofore released;

(o) "Territory"—the universe;

(p) "Streaming"—the digital transmission of a Recording to an end user, other than as a physical Record or permanent download, whereby such transmission is contemporaneous with the performance of the Recording embodied therein via a receiving device, and which transmission is not intended to be or capable of being stored on the receiving device (other than any temporary copies used solely for so-called "caching" or "buffering");

(q) "Streaming Usage"—Streaming of Recordings including via Subscription, embedded media players, and as so-called "ringback tones";

(r) "Subscription"—transmission of Records other than physical Records to consumers, either by Company or through its distributors, its Principal Licensees or their distributors or another Person, in return for a subscription or other fee paid by the consumer to obtain access to such Recordings for a limited period of time and/or a limited number of uses or any other method of exploitation commonly recognized as a subscription service;

(s) "Video"—a Recording embodying an audiovisual work primarily featuring the audio soundtrack of one (1) or more Masters hereunder.

If the foregoing is in accordance with your agreement with us, please so indicate by signing in the appropriate place below.

Very truly yours,

_____ RECORDS

By: _____

An Authorized Signatory

ACCEPTED AND AGREED TO:

_____

_____ p/k/a "_____"

EXHIBIT

Capitalized terms used but not defined in this exhibit ("Exhibit") shall have the meanings set forth in the agreement to which this Exhibit is attached.

(a) Calculation of Royalties: Except as set forth in paragraph (b) below, for top-line, full-priced net sales of Records sold by or on behalf of Company through normal retail channels in the United States, whether in the form of physical Records or permanent digital downloads (including ringtones), Company will credit your royalty account with a royalty of 18%. The royalty rates provided for in the preceding sentence and in the rest of this Exhibit will be applied against the royalty base price for Records sold, paid for and not returned. (As used herein, "net sales" means gross royalty bearing sales, less returns, credits and reserves against anticipated returns and credits, "royalty base price" means the PPD for the Record concerned less program discounts, excise taxes, duties and other applicable taxes and deductions pursuant to any law, government ruling or restriction affecting the amount of the payments any foreign licensee can remit to Company, and "PPD" means the published price to dealers utilized by Company or its distributors, as applicable, in the United States and by Company, Company's regular foreign licensee or its distributors in each country outside the United States. Company's principal distributors in the United States and Company's regular foreign licensee in Canada both currently refer to the published price to dealers as the "Base Price"). In computing sales, Company shall have the right to deduct all returns made at any time and for any reason.

(b) <u>Physical Singles, Maxi-Singles and EPs/ Audiovisual Records</u>: For top-line, full priced net sales of physical singles, maxi-singles and extended play Records sold by Company through normal retail channels in the United States, Company will credit your royalty account with a royalty of 14%. For top-line, full-priced net sales of audiovisual Records sold by Company through normal retail channels in the United States, Company will credit your royalty account with a royalty of 15%.

(c) <u>Foreign Rate Reductions</u>: The royalty rates for full-priced net sales of Records through normal retail channels outside the United States will be 85% of the applicable basic U.S. rate in Canada, 80% of such rate in the United Kingdom, 75% of such rate in France, Germany, Scandinavia, Benelux, Australia, New Zealand and Japan, and 50% of such rate in the rest of the world.

(d) <u>Packaging Deductions</u>: None.

(e) <u>Mid-priced/ Budget Records/ Development Records</u>: With respect to mid priced Records and development Records, the royalty rate shall be 75% of the otherwise applicable royalty rate. With respect to budget Records, the royalty rate shall be 50% of the otherwise applicable royalty rate. (As used herein, a "mid priced Record" is a Record which is sold by Company or its licensee(s) at a price which is below Company's or the applicable licensee's then prevailing top-line royalty base price, which price is consistently applied by Company to such Records and which Records are sold by Company or its licensee(s) as mid-priced Records. A "budget Record" is a Record which is sold by Company or its licensee(s) at a price which is below Company's or the applicable licensee's then prevailing top-line royalty base price, which price is consistently applied by Company to such Records and which Records are sold by Company or its licensee(s) as budget Records. A "development Record" is a Record which is sold by Company or its licensee(s) at a price which is below Company's or the applicable licensee's then prevailing top-line royalty base price, which price is consistently applied by Company to such Records and which Records are sold by Company or its licensee(s) as development Records or in some like-denominated sales category).

(f) <u>Direct Mail/ Mail Order/ Major TV or Radio Advertising Campaign</u>: The royalty rate on any Record described in sections (i) and (ii) of this sentence shall be 50% of the royalty rate that would otherwise apply if the Record concerned was sold through normal retail channels: (i) any Record sold by Company or its regular foreign distributors through any direct mail or mail order distribution method other than the methods described in paragraph (g)(i) below, and (ii) any Record sold in conjunction with a major television or radio advertising campaign, during the accounting period in which that campaign begins and the next two such periods.

(g) Licensing:

(i) Club Operations: With respect to Records licensed by Company for sale through any club operation, Company will credit your royalty account with an amount equal to 50% of Company's net receipts solely attributable to the Master. No royalties shall be payable with respect to Records received by members of any club operation in an introductory offer in connection with joining it or as a result of the purchase of a required number of Records including, without limitation, Records distributed as "bonus" or "free" Records, or Records for which the club operation is not paid.

(ii) Streaming Usages: The royalty rate for any streaming usages hereunder shall be the basic U.S. rate set forth in paragraph (a) above applied to Company's net receipts. (As used herein, the term "Streaming Usages" means the "Streaming" of recordings, including via subscription services, embedded media players, and so-called ringback tones, and the term "Streaming" means the digital transmission of a recording to an end user, other than as a physical Record or permanent download, whereby such transmission is contemporaneous with the performance of the recording embodied therein via a receiving device, and which transmission is not intended to be or capable of being stored on the receiving device (other than any temporary copies used solely for so-called "caching" or "buffering").

I made the label clarify that if it received an advance from a company such as Spotify, that my client would be credited with a proportionate amount of that advance based on the number of streams for his Masters.

(iii) Other Licensing. The royalty rate for any Master licensed by Company or any of its regular foreign licensees for use in the distribution of Records (other than for Streaming Usages) shall be 50% of Company's net receipts. The royalty rate for any Master licensed by Company or any of its regular foreign licensees for use in synchronization with motion pictures, television programs or any form of commercials shall be 50% of Company's net receipts.

As used in this Exhibit, the term "net receipts" means all monies actually received by Company in the United States from its customers, licensees and distributors (including affiliated distributors such as WEA and WEA International Inc.) which are directly and identifiably attributable to the exploitation of the Master concerned after deduction by Company of all direct expenses, third-party payments, taxes and adjustments related thereto.

(h) Program Discounts: No royalties shall be payable in respect of discounts given by way of price breaks or so-called "free goods" to "one-stops," rack jobbers, distributors or dealers, whether or not affiliated with Company, which are not reflected in the PPD. No royalties shall be payable for Records sold as scrap, salvage, overstock, cutouts, or below cost.

(i) Promotional Records: No royalties will be payable for Records given away or sold at below stated wholesale prices for promotional purposes to disc jockeys, Record reviewers, radio and television stations and networks, motion picture companies, music publishers, Company's employees, you, Artist or other customary recipients of promotional Records or for use on transportation facilities. Company shall have the right to include or to license others to include any one or more of the Masters in promotional Records on which such Masters and other recordings are included, which promotional Records are designed for sale at a substantially lower price than the regular price of Company's albums. No royalties shall be payable on sales of such promotional Records.

(j) Records Sold to the U.S. Government, Educational Institutions and Libraries: Your royalty rate will be 50% of the otherwise applicable basic U.S. royalty rate (based upon the retail list price of such Records).

(k) Premiums: Your royalty rate will be 50% of the otherwise applicable basic royalty rate (applied to Company's actual sales price).

(l) Pro-Ration: For Records not consisting entirely of Masters hereunder, the royalty otherwise payable shall be prorated on the basis of the number of Masters hereunder compared to the total number of Recordings on such Records.

(m) All-In Royalties: The royalties payable pursuant to this Exhibit and the agreement to which this Exhibit is attached include all royalties payable to you, Artist and each artist, producer and other Person rendering services in connection with the Master concerned (as well as each Record label or production company entitled to the services of any of the foregoing).

(n) Intentionally omitted.

(o) Records Sold for Distribution Outside of the United States: Royalties will be computed in the same national currency as Company is accounted to by its licensees and shall be paid to you at the same rate of exchange as Company is paid. Such royalties will not be due and payable until payment thereof has been received by Company in the United States in United States Dollars. If any law, any government ruling, or any other restriction affects the amount of the payments which a licensee can remit to Company, Company may deduct from your royalties an amount proportionate to the reduction in such licensee's remittances to Company. In the event Company is unable to receive payment in United States Dollars in the United States due to governmental regulations, royalties therefor shall not be credited to your account during the continuance of such inability.

(p) Legislative Payments, Blanket Licenses: Notwithstanding anything to the contrary expressed or implied in this Exhibit or the agreement to which this Exhibit is attached, neither you nor Artist shall be entitled to royalties in respect of (i) any payments received by Company pursuant to any statute or other legislation (including, without limitation, payments for the public performance of recordings or royalties payable for the sale of blank cassettes or for the sale of recording equipment) or (ii) any so-called "blanket licenses" (including, without limitation, performance licenses) between Company and a licensee under which the licensee is granted access to all or a significant portion of Company's catalogue of recordings.

(q) <u>Public Performance</u>: If: (i) legislation or a collective bargaining agreement or industry agreement applicable to Company requiring the payment of copyright royalties for the public performance of sound recordings is or has been enacted in any country of the Territory; (ii) such legislation or collective bargaining agreement apportions such royalties into a recording artist share and a Record company share; (iii) Artist does not receive or waives the right to receive (e.g., fail to make a timely application to receive) the applicable recording artist share of such royalties; and (iv) Company actually receives in the United States a recording artist share of royalties attributable to Artist; then Company shall credit your royalty account hereunder with such recording artist share of royalties directly attributable to the Master.

(r) <u>Accountings</u>: Statements as to royalties payable hereunder shall be sent by Company to you within 90 days after the expiration of each six-month period ending June 30 or December 31. Concurrently with the rendition of each statement, Company shall pay you all royalties shown to be due by such statement after deducting all recoupable advances and charges paid prior to the rendition of the statement. No statements need be rendered by Company for any such period for which there are no sales of Records subject to the agreement to which this Exhibit is attached. Company shall be entitled to maintain a single account with respect to all Masters. Company may withhold a reasonable reserve against returns of physical Records, exchanges, refunds, credits and the like with respect to physical Records, such reserve to be established by Company in its reasonable discretion, based on, among other factors, Artist's sales experience, which reserves shall not be in excess of 25% of royalties otherwise credited to your account hereunder for shipments of physical Records in any particular royalty period (unless Company anticipates in its reasonable, good faith judgment, returns, exchanges, refunds, credits and the like which justify the establishment of a larger reserve) and each such reserve shall be fully liquidated no later than with the rendition of statement rendered two years following the statement with respect to which such reserve was originally maintained. You shall be deemed to have consented to all accountings rendered by Company hereunder and said accountings shall be binding upon you and not subject to any objection by you for any reason unless specific objection, in writing, stating the basis thereof, is given to Company within two years after the date Company is deemed to have rendered the applicable statement, and unless suit is instituted within three years after the date Company is deemed to have rendered the applicable statement. Company shall be deemed conclusively to have rendered each statement on the date prescribed in this paragraph unless you notify Company otherwise with respect to any particular statement within 120 days after that date.

(s) <u>Audits</u>: You shall have the right at your sole cost and expense to appoint a certified public accountant who is not then currently engaged in an outstanding audit of Company to examine Company's books and Records as the same pertain to sales of Records subject to the agreement to which this Exhibit is attached as to which royalties are payable to you, provided that any such examination shall be for a reasonable duration, shall take place at Company's offices during normal business hours on reasonable prior written notice and shall not occur more than once in any calendar year.

CHAPTER 4

A SIMPLE GUIDE TO SYNC DEALS

INTRODUCTION: SIGNING THE BEST SYNC DEAL POSSIBLE

This chapter focuses on the use of music in audiovisual works such as movies, television, TV commercials, and video games. I will provide examples of the amount of money you can expect to make, explain the role of Performing Rights Organizations in collecting additional income on behalf of songwriters, discuss the key provisions in standard licenses, and describe the role of publishers, sync reps, and other licensing agents.

This chapter also provides comprehensive comments on the following three licenses: (1) MTV's "Music Submission Form," (2) a license for use of music in a TV commercial, and (3) a license for music in a television movie. If you get a similar deal, you will know what to look out for, how to make the deal fairer, and how to decide if it's still worth it if the company that wants to use your music won't negotiate.

Two Types of Copyrights: Sound Recordings and Musical Works

"Sync" licenses are agreements for the use of music in audiovisual projects. In its strictest sense, a sync license refers to the use of a musical composition in an audiovisual work. The term "master use" license is sometimes used to refer to the use of a sound recording (sometimes referred to as a "master") in an audiovisual work. While sync licenses can only make money for songwriters, master use licenses can make money for both songwriters and recording artists. It is possible for a license to include both a grant of rights in a song and a master if the same person wrote the song and produced the master.

Copyright law protects "musical works," such as songs and accompanying words as well as orchestral works, librettos and other musical compositions. Copyright also protects "sound recordings"; that is, recordings of musical compositions. Indie artists/songwriters who record their own songs generally own the copyrights of both their songs and masters. But once that artist/songwriter enters into a music publishing agreement, she generally transfers the copyright in her songs to the publisher, and the publisher pays her a royalty from the commercial exploitation of the songs, including "syncs." If the same artist/songwriter enters into a standard recording contract, any record in which she performs during the term of the agreement is usually a "work for hire" for the record company. In that case, as explained in further detail below, the record company owns the copyright for the recordings, and pays royalties to the artist for both record sales and master use licenses.

However, in this chapter, we are going to look at sync and master use licenses from the point of view of songwriters and artists who have not entered into any exclusive publishing or recording agreements. Since an indie artist/songwriter does not have a publisher or label to negotiate sync and master licenses for her, she should have her own lawyer, or at least possess enough knowledge to avoid unfavorable contracts. Whether you are an indie artist, songwriter or producer, in this chapter, you will learn what questions to ask, what you can do to make the contract that you receive fairer, and when you should just walk away.

Indie Producers and Copyrights in the Musical Compositions Contained in their Masters

Before the genesis of hip hop in the early 1970s and the emergence of producers like Kool Herc, the role of producers was not to create music, but to help artists record their music and make it as professional as possible. However, that has all changed. In pop, R&B, and especially hip hop, producers do create new music by providing beats or even complete music floors over which an artist sings. In that case, the producer is creating two copyrights: 100% of the sound recording and a part of the musical composition. Therefore, producers often sign publishing deals. The producer will generally have to transfer the copyright in any part of the musical composition that they contributed, such as the beat.

Sync and Master Use Fees

Companies that wish to use an indie musician's music for a movie, commercial, TV show, or video game often will offer an up-front, one-time payment generally called a "sync" fee (even if the songwriter is transferring rights in both the song and the master). The amount of the fee, if any, will depend on a variety of factors including:

- *The professional standing of the musician*: If an ad agency regularly turns to certain producers to create music for a client's ads, it probably will have worked out a standard fee with that producer.
- *The nature of audiovisual work for which the music is sought and whether the song was a hit*: A major motion picture will usually pay from $10,000 to $25,000 for a song or master by an indie writer, artist or producer. However, the exact amount depends on

how many times the song is played and if it will be used in the beginning or end credits (there is also often an additional fee if the song is used in the trailer). But, an indie filmmaker may only be able to afford $5,000 or less for any song or master. Don't be surprised if they offer you no more than a credit. At the beginning of your career, a credit on the movie and on IMDB (an online database of information related to films, television programs, and video games, including cast, production crew such as music composers and musicians, biographies, plot summaries, trivia, and reviews) could be valuable. In contrast, a pop hit in major studio movie can easily fetch $100,000 or more.

- *The type of TV commercial*: In the case of a TV spot, the biggest factor is whether the commercial is national (which may pay from several thousand to over $10,000 for an indie song or master) or will only play in one or several markets (which often pays less). But, for a hit song, the fee could well be in the six figure range and even more for a hit by a superstar artist.
- *The type of TV program*: Here, the most important factor is whether the program is network or basic cable. Usually, but not always, network shows will pay better than shows on basic cable. The money for an indie songwriter or producer could range from no more than the royalty payable to the songwriter by his Performance Rights Organization (see below) to $2,500 to more than $10,000 depending on how much the production company or network wants the music.
- *Who owns what*: If the master and the song are owned by different parties—for instance, if you wrote the song but your producer owns the track—a license will be needed with each of you.

Additional Income for Public Performance

A songwriter may earn "public performance" income from the songwriter's Performance Rights Organization or "PRO" (i.e., ASCAP, BMI, SESAC, or the recently organized Global Music Rights or GMR) when her music is "publicly performed." For instance, a songwriter can receive money when her music is broadcast as part of a television show or played on a computer game. This income may be the only income that an indie songwriter receives, or could be in addition to the up-front sync fee.

Each PRO has rules that determine the amount of money that should be paid for a performance in an audiovisual work. The public performance income from a song in an audiovisual work can be substantial in some situations. For instance, if music is used in a national TV commercial that airs on network TV, the PRO royalty can exceed the sync fee. In contrast, when a small amount of a song is used in the background of a single scene in a basic cable program, the public performance income can be very small.

When the public performance income will be substantial, you may decide to accept a lower sync fee rather than potentially losing the deal altogether. Note that we are only discussing the public performance income payable for the musical composition. The same considerations do not apply to the owner of the master recording—i.e., an artist or a producer. Under U.S. copyright law, the owners of master recordings, unlike the owners of the underlying songs, are not entitled to public performance income for the broadcast of their recordings except via digital transmission such as Spotify, YouTube and Pandora, etc. If a commercial is intended to play on network TV, the commissioning company will generally try to get Internet rights for little or no additional compensation (see Media below). Sound-Exchange, similar to the PRO's for compositions, collects income for the public performance of music recordings, but only for audio-only Internet Radio services such as Pandora. The situation is different in most foreign countries, where artists can earn performing rights royalties for the "public performances" of their master recordings on television as well as standard broadcast radio.

In short, the owner of the master recording's only source of U.S. income from the master use license will be the up-front master use fee which she receives from the company for a TV commercial, movie, or TV show. If the owner of the master is not the songwriter, he will not be receiving any public performance income from the PRO's (or SoundExchange), so he may feel more of a need than the songwriter to negotiate the highest possible up-front fee.

Proper Registration of the Song with the PRO is Crucial

Each PRO has requirements that make writers responsible for properly registering their songs and for notifying the PROs of any audiovisual projects that may generate performance income. I spent a year trying to get one PRO to pay for the theme song of a cable talk show because the writer did not provide a "cue sheet" before the broadcast of the series. A cue sheet is a schedule of the music contained in a film or television program or any other audiovisual work and is essential for the PRO to distribute royalties for musical performances in audiovisual media. It is typically prepared by the production company, but the writer will not get paid unless the production company actually files it in a proper and timely manner. See below for an example of a cue sheet.

Some licenses require a songwriter to yield all rights in a song to the company. In that case, the writer has no right to receive any PRO royalties. However, there are cases in which the company requires the transfer of the copyright in the song, but allows the writer to receive the "writer's share" of performance rights income (that is, 50% of the total amount payable by the PRO). In that case, the writer has to make sure the company is properly registering the song, providing cue sheets to the PRO, and complying with any other forms that have to be completed.

Work for Hire vs. Non-Exclusive License

An issue sometimes even more important than money is whether a license is "work for hire." In a work for hire agreement, the songwriter, artist or producer loses all rights in her music, including the copyright and the right to use the music again for any purpose. If, on the other hand, the grant of rights to the company is a non-exclusive license, the creator keeps the copyright in her music, and retains the right to distribute it as a record and make other deals. Here is a typical work for hire clause:

> WORK FOR HIRE: Artist [Songwriter and/or Producer] agrees that all of the results and pro-ceeds of his services shall be deemed a "work made for hire" for the Company under the U.S. Copyright Law. Accordingly, the Artist further acknowledges and agrees that Company is and shall be deemed to be the author and/or exclusive owner of all of the Recordings and Musical Compositions contained therein for all purposes and the exclusive owner throughout the world of all the rights of any kind comprised in the copyright(s) thereof and any renewal or extension rights in connection therewith, and of any and all other rights thereto, and that Company shall have the right to exploit any or all of the Recordings in any and all media, now known or hereafter devised, throughout the universe, in perpetuity, in all configurations as Record Company determines, including without limitation [name of movie, TV show, TV commercial, etc.] In connection therewith Artist hereby grants to Company the right as attorney-in-fact to execute, acknowledge, deliver and record in the U.S. Copyright Office or elsewhere any and all such documents pertaining to the Recordings if he shall fail to execute same within five (5) days after so requested by Company.

It's always better that the artist, songwriter, and producer retain their copyrights. However, sometimes the work for hire clause will be non-negotiable, and then the creator must ask herself whether the up-front money (and in the case of a songwriter who retains the writer's share, the potential PRO royalties) adequately compensates for the loss of the right to use the music.

Other Basic Contract Terms

Here are a few other important terms in sync and master use licenses that are not work for hire:

- Duration (or "Term"): The company will usually want the right to exploit the following durations of use:
  - **Theatrical Films**: Generally for the "life of the copyright." In other words, the company's right to use your music will last as long as the song is protected by copyright law, which is as long as you're alive plus 70 years.
  - **Television**: Generally, the same as above.
  - **Commercials**: Typically an initial term of one year, often with the option for the company to renew for another equal term upon payment of an additional

licensing fee (which is usually the same as the original term, although you can try to negotiate for a higher fee, for instance 125% of the original fee.)

o **Computer Games**: Could be "life of the copyright," or a briefer term such as 3 to 5 years. There are few games which will have a life span of more than a year or two, so in most instances, the Company won't consider it all that important to obtain a long term license.

- Media: The company will want the right to exploit the audiovisual work as follows:
  o **Theatrical Films**: Generally, a movie producer, production company, or studio will want the right to use a song or master in festivals for one year, with an option to exploit the movie, including your music, in all media ("broad rights").
  o **Television**: Generally, the network or cable service will want all media rights because a TV show can be recycled in any number of platforms such as streaming, downloading, home video, etc. Talent should, however, try to negotiate a separate fee for home video including downloading.
  o **Commercials**: Typically limited to TV and Internet, but the songwriter/artist/producer can try to secure an additional fee for use of the commercial on radio.
  o **Computer Games**: Generally all media now or hereinafter developed.
- Territory: The Company will want the right to exploit the audiovisual work as follows:
  o **Theatrical Films**: Typically "worldwide."
  o **Television**: The creator may be able to negotiate an additional fee for foreign use.
  o **Commercials**: Local, multiple U.S. markets, national or worldwide.
  o **Computer Games**: Worldwide.

The Role of Music Publishers and Labels

Once you enter into an exclusive recording and/or publisher deal, your label and publisher will negotiate sync and master use licenses on your behalf. The split is generally 50% payable to the label and 25% to 50% payable to the publisher after recoupment of any advances (including, in the case of a label, recording costs) that they paid you.

Reps and Licensing Agents

If you are familiar with the "sync business" you know that there are many companies, such as Pump Audio that may be willing to represent your music for sync placements. Some are more selective than others, and some are more proactive in shopping your music than others. For instance, music libraries such as APM Music (Associated Production Music Inc.) have steady clients such as cable networks and ad agencies that continually scan the library's collection for interstitial or background music. The reps' fees vary from 65% in the case of Pump Audio all the way down to 20% or less if a rep really loves your music.

The biggest controversy in the sync licensing business is the exclusive vs. non-exclusive issue. The best argument to let a rep have exclusive rights is that they may be more motivated to shop your music. The best argument in support of non-exclusive rights is an exclusive rep may lose interest in your music and let it sit on a shelf for the duration of the agreement. The primary differences between a rep and a publisher are: reps rarely pay you an advance, but rep deals are usually limited to the song or tracks you wish them to present. Standard publishing agreements cover any songs you create during the term of the agreement.

MTV MUSIC SUBMISSION FORM: A TERRIBLE DEAL FOR ARTISTS, SONGWRITERS, AND PRODUCERS

MTV's submission agreement represents almost the worst possible deal for any creator. It basically allows MTV or its sister networks, such as BET and VH1, to use your music or video in its many reality shows, promos or websites or any other conceivable purpose without paying you a penny. Note that the form is part of MTV's terms of use, which hardly anyone reads.

This contract basically provides that you grant MTV the right to use your content "worldwide . . . perpetual and royalty free." In other words, they can use your music for any purpose without paying you anything forever. Moreover, they don't have to even give you a credit, can make "derivative works" (such as remixes) without your permission, and can grant all these rights to any third party!

MTV doesn't even allow you to receive royalties from your PRO when they use your music. Instead, they can register the song with their PRO as both the writer and the publisher and collect 100% of the public performance royalty. That means they can use your music in the background of a reality show—so deep in the background that nobody notices—send their PRO a cue sheet and get paid for using your music, all while you don't make a dime.

For our purposes it is not necessary to republish the entire submission agreement, but you can read it in full at www.mtv.com/legal/user-content.

USER CONTENT SUBMISSION AGREEMENT

Terms of Use

Privacy Policy

Copyright

Last Modified: December 02, 2011

Please read this User Content Submission Agreement carefully because it is a part of the Terms of Use Agreement and represents your legally binding agreement with us ("Submission Agreement") regarding your submission (and our display and distribution) of content to the Site via certain technology, functionality and/or features we make available to you so you can upload and post such content for display via the Site (collectively, the "User Content Submission Features"), and this Submission Agreement applies regardless of what type of Device you use to submit content to the Site. Unless defined separately, terms used in this Submission Agreement are defined in our Terms of Use Agreement.

As the form states at the outset, you should read it carefully so you can learn just how horrible it is.

When you submit User Content, or by using or attempting to use the User Content Submission Features, you are signifying your agreement with and acceptance of all terms and conditions of this Submission Agreement as well as the terms and conditions contained in the Terms of Use Agreement that govern your legal and contractual relationship with MTV.

> This means that whether you read this agreement or not, by simply uploading music to the site, you are agreeing to all the terms in the agreement. They are not even asking you to sign it.

We have the right to change the terms and conditions of this Submission Agreement at any time as described in our Terms of Use Agreement. If you do not agree with all the terms and conditions of this Submission Agreement at any time, including, without limitation, those times when we make changes, do not use, do not attempt to use, and immediately discontinue your use of, the User Content Submission Features, because if you do any of these things you are agreeing to be bound by all of the terms and conditions of this Submission Agreement, including, without limitation, any changes we have made.

. . .

1.   SUBMITTING USER CONTENT.

The term "User Content" means and refers to any and all content, media and materials you submit for posting on the Site using the User Content Submission Features, including, without limitation, still photographs, writings, spoken statements, music, audio, video, video recordings, audio-visual works and recordings, slides, portraits, animated and/or motion pictures, caricatures, likenesses, vocal or other sounds, sound recordings, voices, voice reproductions, computer graphics and visual effects, as well as any accompanying documentation, packaging or other materials, tangible or intangible, and to all derivative works, translations, adaptations or variations of same, regardless of the tangible medium, broadcast medium, format or form, now known or hereinafter developed or discovered, and regardless of where produced, on location, in a studio or elsewhere, in black-and-white or in color, alone or in conjunction with other work, characters, real or imaginary, in any part of the world. User Content is also considered a "Posting", as such term defined in the Terms of Use Agreement, and therefore, all terms and conditions contained within the section of the Terms of Use Agreement entitled "Postings" shall apply to all User Content you submit pursuant to the terms and conditions of this Submission Agreement for Posting to the Site.

> This means any material of whatever nature that you upload including videos, sound-only or even pictures will be covered by this form agreement.

Each time you upload or submit User Content (or if you attempt to do so) you will be confirming your acceptance of, and agreement to be bound by, all the terms and conditions of this Submission Agreement.

. . .

3. USER CONTENT STANDARDS; UNAUTHORIZED CONTENT.

This paragraph basically allows MTV to delete your content and makes you exclusively liable for any claims that may arise in connection with your content, such as copyright infringement.

You are solely responsible and liable for your communications and submissions (and the consequences) made under your name, user name, email address, password and your registration and profile information, if any. User Content does not reflect the views of MTV, and neither MTV, nor any of the Parent Companies or the Affiliates, represents or guarantees the truthfulness, accuracy, or reliability of any User Content, or endorses or supports any opinions expressed in any User Content. In no event shall MTV, the Parent Companies or the Affiliates have or be construed to have any responsibility or liability for or in connection with any User Content. If we determine, in our sole discretion, you have not met the Age Requirements (see Section 2 above) or if, in our judgment, you or any User Content you submit violates this Submission Agreement, we reserve the right, at any time, without notice and without limiting any and all other rights we may have under this Submission Agreement, at law or in equity, to (a) refuse to allow you to submit further User Content, (b) remove and delete your User Content, (c) revoke your registration and right to use the User Content Submission Features and (d) use any technological, legal, operational or other means available to enforce the terms of this Submission Agreement, including, without limitation, blocking specific IP addresses or deactivating your registration, access using your e-mail address, your user name and password.

. . .

5. RIGHTS GRANTED TO MTV.

As discussed before, this paragraph states that you grant MTV the right to use your content "worldwide . . . perpetual and royalty free," meaning they can use your music for any purpose without paying you anything, forever. Moreover, they don't even have to give you a credit. And they can make "derivative works," such as re-mixes without your permission. Plus they can grant all these rights to any third party.

In connection with all User Content you submit using the User Content Submission Features, you grant to MTV, the Parent Companies and the Affiliates, the unqualified, unrestricted, unconditional, unlimited, worldwide, irrevocable, perpetual and royalty free right, license, authorization and permission, in any form or format, on or through any media or medium and with any technology or devices now known or hereafter developed or discovered, in whole or in part, to host, cache, store, maintain, use, reproduce, distribute, display, exhibit, perform, publish, broadcast, transmit, modify, prepare derivative works of, adapt, reformat, translate, and otherwise exploit all or any portion of your User Content on the Site (regardless of the Device through which the Site may be accessed) and any other channels, services, and other distribution platforms, whether currently existing or existing or developed in the future, of MTV, the Parent Companies and the Affiliates (collectively, the "Platforms"), for any purpose whatsoever (including, without limitation, for any promotional purposes) without accounting, notification, credit or other obligation to you, and the right to license and sub-license and authorize others to exercise any of the rights granted hereunder to MTV, the Parent Companies and Affiliates, in our sole discretion. For the avoidance of doubt, without limiting the generality of the rights granted to MTV, the Parent Companies and the Affiliates, these rights include, without limitation, the right to distribute and synchronize all or any portion of your User Content in timed relation to any other visual elements; to web cast, pod cast, re-publish, re-broadcast, re-platform, port, syndicate, route, and link to and from all or any portion of your User Content; to encrypt, encode and decode, and compress and decompress all or any portion of your User Content; to edit, mix, combine, merge, distort, superimpose, create or add special effects, illusions and/or other material to or of all or any portion of your User Content; to create composite, stunt, comic or unusual photographs, videos, animations, motion pictures and/or voice reproductions from all or a portion of your User Content; and to excerpt and/or extract portions of your User Content in order to host, store, index, categorize and display your User Content on or through the Platforms.

By submitting User Content, in addition to the rights, licenses and privileges referred to above, you are also granting MTV, the Parent Companies and the Affiliates, the unqualified, unrestricted, unconditional, unlimited, worldwide, irrevocable, perpetual and royalty free right, license, authorization and permission to use and refer to your name, logo, marks, image, characteristic or other distinctive identification in presentations, marketing materials, customer lists and financial reports, to do, perform, take advantage of and exploit any and all of the rights set forth herein in connection with the marketing, advertising and promotion of the Platforms, and any products, goods, features, functions, capabilities and/or services associated with MTV, the Parent Companies and Affiliates and to use and otherwise exploit any ideas, concepts, content, material, expression or form of expression, in whole or in part, contained in your User Content, for any purpose whatsoever, without any credit, compensation or accounting to you, in products or services developed by MTV, the Parent Companies and the Affiliates, without limitation or restriction whatsoever.

The rights, licenses and privileges described in this Submission Agreement and granted to MTV, the Parent Companies and the Affiliates, shall commence immediately upon submission of your User Content to or through the User Content Submission Features and continue thereafter perpetually and indefinitely, regardless of whether you continue or remain a registered user or not, unless and until terminated, in whole or in part, by MTV on notice to you. Notwithstanding the foregoing, you acknowledge and agree that neither MTV, nor the Parent

Companies or the Affiliates, shall be required or have any obligation to host, index, display, accept or use any submitted User Content (or take advantage of any or all of the particular rights and authorities granted or otherwise available) and MTV may, in its sole discretion, remove or refuse to host, index, display, accept, use or do anything at all with respect to any User Content. Once you submit or attempt to submit User Content you shall have no right to prohibit, restrict, revoke or terminate any of the rights granted to MTV or the Parent Companies or the Affiliates. You are not entitled to and you will not receive any compensation or other consideration for your User Content or any use made of your User Content once submitted. You also understand and agree that neither all or any portion of your User Content, nor any commercial, advertisement, promotional, marketing or other material associated with your User Content, need to be submitted for approval prior to use.

You hereby release MTV, the Parent Companies and the Affiliates from any and all claims of any rights, encumbrances, liens, claims, demands, actions or suits which you may or can have in connection with your User Content, including, without limitation, any and all liability for any use or nonuse of the your User Content, claims for defamation, libel, slander, invasion of privacy, right of publicity, emotional distress or economic loss. MTV, and the Parent Companies and the Affiliates, have the right to assign, transfer, convey, license, sub-license and otherwise transfer, sub-contract, delegate, outsource or engage third parties to perform or benefit from all or any portion of its or their rights and/or obligations to any one or more other parties, without accounting, reporting, notification or other obligation or liability to you whatsoever, now or in the future. You also forever waive and relinquish all moral rights or droit moral now or hereafter recognized in connection with your User Content and the rights granted to MTV, the Parent Companies and the Affiliates hereunder.

MTV has the right to license, authorize and/or otherwise enter into agreements and arrangements with any Parent Companies or the Affiliates to do or perform any of the activities, exercise any of the rights and/or undertake any of the responsibilities granted or imposed under this Submission Agreement, in whole or in part. To the extent MTV does so, when you submit User Content each such Parent Company and Affiliate shall be entitled to exercise and benefit from the terms and conditions, rights, licenses and authorizations granted to MTV hereunder and related thereto as if you had entered into this Submission Agreement with such Parent Company or Affiliate directly.

6.   OWNERSHIP.

> The only fair thing in this agreement is that they don't try to get the copyrights in your work, but because they can grant any third party rights in your content, they could effectively take away your ability to make money from your music or video.

MTV retains all right, title and interest in and to the User Content Submission Features, including, without limitation, to all associated intellectual property and proprietary rights existing anywhere in the world and you acquire no ownership, proprietary or other rights, title or interest in or to the User Content Submission Features.

Except for the licenses, authorizations, consents and rights granted hereunder and described in this Submission Agreement, as comprehensive and broad as they may seem or actually be,MTV acquires no title or ownership rights in or to any User Content you submit and nothing in this Submission Agreement conveys to us any ownership rights in your User Content. MTV is acting only as a host, bulletin board or conduit for submitted User Content, with all of the specific rights granted by you hereunder. Although by your submission of any User Content you are requesting and directing us and any of the Parent Companies or the Affiliates with whom we have made arrangements, to take advantage of and exploit all of the rights and privileges granted hereunder (including, without limitation, the right to display and post the User Content on the Platforms), neither we, nor any of the Parent Companies or the Affiliates have any obligation to do any of these things.

> The balance of this form contains legal boilerplate language that, among other details, makes the User guarantee they have all rights in the content they upload and to indemnify MTV against any claims.

. . .

10. GENERAL.

The Terms of Use Agreement, incorporating this Submission Agreement, is the entire agreement between you and us relating to User Content and your use of the User Content Submission Features and supersedes any prior or inconsistent agreements. MTV may terminate this Submission Agreement with you and your right to use the User Content Submission Features at any time without notice to you.

This User Content Submission Agreement was last modified on the date indicated above and is effective immediately.

> Note, there are no signature lines. This is a "Click-through" agreement, meaning very few people read it. In fact, it is doubtful that anyone who actually noticed and read it would submit any music to MTV.

A GOOD DEAL FOR THE ARTIST, SONGWRITER, AND PRODUCER INVOLVING MUSIC FOR A NATIONAL COMMERCIAL CAMPAIGN

This is an example of a great deal for the talent. In this case, a fellow who was commissioned to perform, write and produce a track for a beer commercial. The reasons that make this a pro-talent agreement are set forth in the commentary.

SYNCHRONIZATION & MASTER USE LICENSE

DATE: As of _____ ____, 2017

LICENSOR: _____

LICENSEE: _____ LLC ("Agency"), as agent for [a beer company] ("Licensee")

COMPOSITIONS: "_____ Demo 3A _____" and "_____ Demo 5A _____," including, without limitation, the music, lyrics, arrangements, and title thereof.

MASTER: The master recording of the Composition by _____, including, without limitation, the performances embodied on such master recording

MATERIALS: One x :30 and one x :15 TV commercials tentatively entitled "_____," and any lifts, edits and versions thereof advertising Licensee and its products and services

TERRITORY: North America and its respective territories, commonwealths, and possessions; with respect to the Internet, the Territory shall be Worldwide

It's a good thing that the license is limited to North America, leaving the Licensor completely free to enter into any other deal for the rest of the world.

PERMITTED MEDIA: All media

LICENSE FEE: $10,000.00 USD, the receipt of which is hereby acknowledged.

The fee for the demo was $2,000, so the Licensor received a total of $12,000. Not too shabby for a one year license.

LICENSE FEE FOR OPTION TERM, IF ANY: $10,000.00 USD, which must be exercised prior to the expiration of the Initial Term.

INITIAL TERM: Commencing on the date hereof and ending one (1) year from the first air-date of the Materials

OPTION TERM: Licensee shall have the option to extend the Term for an additional consecutive one year period.

EXCLUSIVITY: During the Term and Option Term, if any, Licensor shall not permit or authorize the use of the Master in advertising or publicity on behalf of malt beverages and hard ciders.

> This is very good. It means that the Licensor can do any other deal he wants for the music with only one exception: he cannot license the music for other beer or "hard cider" commercials.

CREDIT: Licensee will cause Licensor to receive a visable credit as the writer and performer will cause Licensor to receive a visible credit as writer and performer of the music in any webpage including YouTube associated with the spots; and will enable viewers to see such credit if they use Shazam or a similar App in connection with the spots.

OTHER TERMS:

For good and valuable consideration, Licensor hereby grants to Licensee a license to reproduce and use the Composition and the Master, edited or altered as Licensee sees fit, and any portions thereof, in any manner in the Materials and to exhibit, broadcast, publicly perform and otherwise use the Materials, as frequently as Licensee shall determine, in the Permitted Media throughout the Territory during the Term and Option Term, if any. In addition, Licensee and Agency may retain file copies of the Materials for use, during and after the Term and Option Term, if any, in any manner or media anywhere in the world, as frequently as Licensee and/or Agency shall determine, at sales meetings and for intra company, research, file, reference, publicity, (including, without limitation, on Agency's "reel" and website) and award purposes. In the event that any use of the Composition and the Master hereunder is in a medium/venue that does not have a public performance license from Licensor or an organization such as ASCAP or BMI to which Licensor belongs, this agreement shall be deemed to constitute a public performance license for such use for no additional compensation.

> The license contemplates that the Licensor will receive 100% of public performance royalties from his PRO, that is, ASCAP, BMI or SESAC.

Notwithstanding any provision of this agreement, Licensee shall be under no obligation actually to create or use the Materials or to make any use of the Composition or the Master, it being understood that Licensee's sole obligation to Licensor hereunder is to pay the License Fee in accordance with the terms hereof.

Licensor's rights and remedies in the event of a breach or alleged breach of this agreement or any term hereof by Licensee shall be limited to Licensor's right, if any, to recover damages in an action at law and in no event shall Licensor be entitled by reason of any breach or alleged breach to enjoin, restrain, or seek to enjoin or restrain, the use, distribution, or other exploitation of the Materials.

Licensor represents and warrants that it has the sole and unencumbered copyright in the Composition and the Master and the sole and unencumbered right to grant the rights granted to Licensee under this agreement (including, without limitation, the right to use vocal and any other performances embodied on the Master); that there are no third-party samples contained in the Master; and that the exercise of rights granted herein will not violate the rights of any third party or cause Licensee to incur any additional fees. Accordingly, Licensor shall defend, indemnify and hold Licensee, Agency and those working for them or on their behalf harmless from and against any and all claims, losses, damages, costs, and expenses, including, without limitation, reasonable attorneys' fees, arising out of or resulting from a claimed breach of any of Licensor's representations, warranties or agreements hereunder.

Licensor agrees that Licensor will not disclose any trade secrets or confidential information of Licensee (i.e., information that is not publicly available) to any third parties, including, but not limited to, any content of any advertising that Licensee has not yet released and any terms of this agreement.

This agreement constitutes the entire understanding between the parties hereto regarding the subject matter hereof and cannot be altered or waived except by a writing signed by both parties. No waiver by either party of the breach of any term or condition of this agreement shall constitute a waiver of, or consent to, any subsequent breach of the same or any other term or condition of this agreement. This agreement may be executed in separate counterparts each of which when so executed shall be deemed to be an original and all of which, taken together, shall constitute one and the same agreement. Delivery of an executed counterpart of a signature page to this agreement by facsimile or other commonly used electronic means (such as PDF by email) shall be effective as delivery of manually executed counterpart of this agreement. This agreement shall be governed by the laws of the State of New York without regard to the conflict of laws rules or principles which would result in the application of the law of any jurisdiction. Any controversies or disputes arising out of or relating to this Agreement shall be resolved exclusively in either the state or federal courts located in the County of New York, and the parties hereby consent to the jurisdiction of such courts.

IN WITNESS WHEREOF, this agreement has been duly executed by the parties hereto, as of the date first above written.

LICENSOR   LICENSEE

By: _____   By: _____
                                             Authorized Officer

Name _____

FAIR, BUT NOT GREAT SYNC LICENSE FOR MUSIC IN A TV DOCUDRAMA

In this sync license, the Writer granted a non-exclusive right to a production company to use an excerpt of a song he wrote 20 years earlier in a made-for-TV movie on a Pay TV service. He received $12,000, and the company received the right to distribute the movie, including his music, in all media throughout the world in perpetuity. The Writer reserved the right to collect 100% of the public performance royalties including both the Writer and publisher's share. Note, this license did not include a master-use. In this case, the company re-recorded the song rather than using the original master. If they wanted to use the original master, they probably would have had to pay the owner of the master recording another $12,000 under a most favored nations provision.

This is just an "okay" deal because the Writer got a decent, but not great sync fee, and kept his right to performance rights royalties.

MUSIC SYNCHRONIZATION LICENSE

This Music Synchronization (this "Agreement") is entered into as of _____ ____, 2017 by [Pay Television Service] (the "Licensee"), and by [Songwriter] (the "Licensor") and shall confirm the terms according to which Licensee may use a musical composition composed by Licensor in a film titled "_____" (the "Program"):

Musical Composition	Use	Timing
"_____"	Visual Vocal	1:36

1.   TERRITORY. The territory covered by this License is worldwide.

2.   TERM. This License is granted in perpetuity, commencing from the date of first public exhibition, broadcast or transmission of the Program.

3.   GRANT OF RIGHTS. Licensor hereby grants to Licensee the non-exclusive right to use the Composition in the soundtrack of the Program, in trailers and television and radio spots and in the advertisement, promotion, publicity and exploitation thereof, subject to the terms and conditions set forth herein. Licensor gives and grants to Licensee the non-exclusive and irrevocable right and license to record, dub and edit the Composition in synchronization or time-relation with the Program, to copy the Composition in any form, including but not limited to, negatives, prints and/or tape and to publicly distribute, exploit, market, perform, broadcast, transmit and exhibit the Composition as embodied in the Program, perpetually, throughout the territory, in all media by any means or methods now known or hereafter devised excluding Theatrical (including, without limitation, pay television, free television, home video, Internet, mobile devices and non-theatrical distribution) worldwide.

4.   PAYMENT. In consideration of the license and rights granted herein for the Composition used in the soundtrack of the Program, Licensee shall pay to Licensor the aggregate amount of Twelve Thousand Five Hundred Dollars ($12,500.00) if and only if the Composition is included in the Program.

5.   CLEARANCE. Licensee shall be responsible for obtaining appropriate performance licenses and shall make all payments required to be made in connection with Licensee's use thereof.

In this sentence, the Licensor preserves his right to collect public performance royalties.

Licensor agrees to inform Licensee if the permission of any other person in connection with this License is required. Should Licensee be required or desire to obtain the consent of any persons whose performances are embodied in the Composition, Licensor agrees to obtain such permission and deliver same to Licensee. Licensor's failure or inability to provide Licensee with such consents in a timely manner shall give Licensee the option of terminating this License.

6.   HOME VIDEO. The home video rights granted under section 3, above, shall include the right to fix the Composition, as synchronized in the Program, in any manner, medium or form, whether existing now or in the future, including, without limitation, in audiovisual devices (including, without limitation, video cassettes, video discs and other audiovisual devices) ("devices") and to utilize such devices for any and all purposes, uses and performances, whatsoever and to sell, lease, license or otherwise make such devices available to the public as devices intended primarily for non-commercial home use, or otherwise.

7.   RESERVED RIGHTS. Notwithstanding anything contained in this License to the contrary, Licensee hereby acknowledges and agrees that this License does not grant to Licensee the right to include the Composition or any part thereof in any soundtrack phonograph record album (whether disc form, prerecorded tape form or otherwise) or in any other phonograph record, without Licensor's prior written approval thereof.

8.   REPRESENTATIONS AND WARRANTIES. Licensor represents and warrants that Licensor owns or controls One Hundred Percent (100%) of the composition and has the full right, power and authority to enter into and fully perform this License and to grant the rights granted herein; that the consent of no other person, firm or corporation is required to grant such rights; that there are no outstanding liens, encumbrances, nor any claims or litigation, either existing or threatened, which may in any way interfere with, impair or be in derogation of the rights herein granted to Licensee; and that Licensee's use of the Composition will not infringe the rights of any person, firm or corporation.

9. INDEMNIFICATION. Licensor assumes liability for, and shall indemnify, defend, protect, save and hold harmless Licensee and their partners, distributors, assigns and employees and agents of the foregoing (the "Licensee's Indemnified Parties") from and against any claims, actions, losses, penalties, expenses or damages (including, without limitation, legal fees and expenses) of whatsoever kind and nature imposed on, incurred by or asserted against any of the Licensee's Indemnified Parties arising out of any breach or alleged breach by Licensor of any representation, warranty or covenant made, or obligation assumed, by Licensor pursuant to this Agreement. The provisions of this section 9 shall apply, without limitation, to claims brought by Licensee against Licensor.

10. NO OBLIGATION TO USE THE COMPOSITION. Nothing contained herein shall obligate Licensee to actually use the Composition in the soundtrack of the Program or in connection with the exploitation of Licensee's rights in the Program.

11. ASSIGNMENT. Licensee may assign or transfer this License or all of any portion of the rights granted herein to any of Licensee's parent, subsidiary or affiliated companies (collectively an "affiliate") or to any licensee, distribute or transferee of any affiliate or to any person, firm or corporation which acquires the Program or the right to sell, distribute, exhibit or otherwise exploit same or any rights therein. This License shall be binding upon and inure to the benefit of Licensor's and Licensee's respective heirs, successors, licensees, transferees and assigns.

12. ENTIRE LICENSE. This License constitutes the entire agreement between Licensor and License and cannot be modified except by a written instrument and signed by the parties hereto.

13. APPLICABLE LAW AND JURISDICTION. This License shall be governed by and interpreted in accordance with the laws of the State of New York applicable to agreements made and fully to be performed therein, and Licensor consents to the exclusive jurisdiction of the courts of the State of New York and the federal courts located in New York.

14. SEVERABILITY. Nothing contained in this License shall be construed so as to require the commission of any contrary to law, and wherever there is conflict between any provision of this License and any statue, law, ordinance, order or regulation, or collective bargaining agreement or agreement binding on the parties hereto, contrary to which the parties have no legal right to contract, such statue, law provided, that in such event the provision of this License so affected shall be curtailed and limited only to the extent necessary to permit compliance with the minimum legal requirement, and no other provisions of this License shall be affected thereby, and all such other provisions shall continue in full force and effect.

IN WITNESS WHEREOF, the parties have executed this License as of the day and year first above specified.

LICENSOR   LICENSEE

_____   _____

                                     Name: _____

                                         Authorized Officer

CHAPTER **5**

PRODUCER AGREEMENTS

INTRODUCTION: THREE CONTRACTS EVERY MUSIC PRODUCER SHOULD KNOW, HOW ARTISTS SHOULD DEAL WITH PRODUCERS, AND WHAT A PRODUCER SHOULD ASK FOR

This chapter focuses on producer agreements in the context of the indie music business rather than standard producer agreements used by major labels. A producer who works on a major label project will generally have an experienced music attorney who will negotiate these deals on their behalf. The upfront money that a small label or an indie artist can offer, if any at all, often is not enough for a producer to hire a lawyer, so this chapter is meant to help producers, indie artists, and small labels.

Major Label Producer Deals vs. Indie Producer Deals

There are a few key differences in the contracts a producer can expect to find from a major label and in the indie world. If a producer has a track record of making hits, a major label deal will generally include a producer fee upwards of several thousand dollars. The producer would also usually receive a royalty of 3–5% calculated in the same manner as the artist's royalty. For instance, if the artist's royalty is a percentage of the suggested retail price of a record, the producer's royalty will be as well. Like the artist's royalty (which typically ranges from 12–18%), the producer's royalty will be subject to multiple deductions, such as packaging costs and a reduced royalty for foreign sales. The producer's royalty will be deducted from the artist's royalty, in effect making the artist pay for the producer's royalty. Unlike the artist, the producer usually receives his royalty from the first record sold after recoupment of recording costs. This means that once gross income exceeds production costs, the producer is paid for all prior records sales—the artist is not.

When an artist or small label hires a producer, the upfront fees are usually significantly less. In many cases, the artist is also operating his own label, so it does not make sense to base the producer's royalty on the artist's royalty. In that case, the producer's royalty, if any, may be based on net receipts or "profits." See Chapters 2 and 3.

Beats

Particularly in hip hop, R&B, and pop music, artists work with drum, digital or other percussive "beats" as core elements of their recordings. Often, an artist or indie label will search online for the right beat on which to base a song. Although some beats are sampled, others are purchased or licensed from a producer who creates beats with digital drum machines or other studio equipment. Some producers of beats, such as the Neptunes (Pharrell Williams and Chad Hugo), make more elaborate beats than just drum sounds. A Neptunes production also usually employs synthesizer riffs and samples keyboard and other percussive sounds. The Neptunes created some of the biggest hip hop, R&B, and pop hits of the late 1990s and 2000s. So, acquiring a beat from them could be very expensive. However, many new or emerging producers will offer their beats at a low fee. Or, the producer may even waive an upfront fee in exchange for royalties if the artist makes money from the song.

In the studio, a producer is ultimately responsible for the final sound of a recording. However, an artist may buy or license a beat and finish the production himself or with another producer.

Two Copyrights: Sound Recordings and Musical Works

As we discussed in the prior chapter on sync licenses, copyright law protects musical works. In the eyes of the law, a musical work is defined as a song and any accompanying words, as well as orchestral works, librettos, and other musical compositions. But copyright law also protects sound recordings; that is, recordings of musical compositions. A beat is usually both a sound recording and a musical composition because the recording of a beat contains a separately copyrightable musical work.

For many years, producers generally did not create new music. They just recorded and tried to enhance songs created by a songwriter who may have been the artist. However, that has all changed. Now, producers can create new music by providing beats or even complete music floors over which an artist sings or a rapper "spits." In that case, the producer is creating two copyrights: the sound recording and a part of the musical composition. This is why producers sometimes enter into deals with music publishers. See Chapter 6 on music publishing agreements.

Beat Agreements

A producer often sells a beat outright. In that case, the buyer will have the exclusive right to use the beat. Other times, a producer will give a non-exclusive license to use a beat and reserve the right to use the beat for himself or license it to others.

Work for Hire vs. Non-Exclusive License

As discussed in Chapter 4, if the agreement is a sale, it will usually be structured as a "work for hire." In a work for hire agreement, the producer loses all rights in their beat, including the copyright and the right to use the beat again for any purpose. If, on the other hand, the grant of rights is a non-exclusive license, the producer keeps the copyright and retains the right to use it or make other deals. Here is a typical work for hire clause in a producer agreement:

> WORK FOR HIRE: Producer agrees that all of the results and proceeds of his services shall be deemed a "work made for hire" for the Company [or Artist] under the U.S. Copyright Law. Accordingly, the Producer further acknowledges and agrees that Company is and shall be deemed to be the author and/or exclusive owner of the Beat inclusive of the underlying musical composition and sound recording contained in the Beat. Recordings and Musical Compositions contained therein for all purposes and the exclusive owner throughout the world of all the rights of any kind comprised in the copyright(s) thereof and any renewal or extension rights in connection therewith, and of any and all other rights thereto, and that Company shall have the right to exploit any or all of the Beat in any and all media, now known or hereafter devised, throughout the universe, in perpetuity, in all configurations as Company determines. In connection therewith Producer hereby grants to Company the right as attorney-in-fact to execute, acknowledge, deliver and record in the U.S. Copyright Office or elsewhere any and all such documents pertaining to the Beat if he shall fail to execute same within five (5) days after so requested by Company.

It's always in the producer's best interest to retain her copyrights. However, sometimes the work for hire clause will be non-negotiable. In this case, the producer must consider whether the upfront money compensates for the loss of the right to use the beat. Generally, when an artist or indie label hires a producer to create a beat and fully produce one or more tracks, the agreement will be a work for hire, but the producer usually receives an upfront payment and can negotiate a "back-end" royalty.

Fees

The amount of the fee, if any, will depend on a variety of factors including whether the deal is a sale or a license. A sale would generally be more expensive than a non-exclusive license under which the Producer keeps the right to reuse the beat. But, the most important factor in determining the fee is the business reputation of the producer. A producer with a track record of a few successful tracks can demand fees of several thousand dollars or more and a producer with a track record of hits can command much higher amounts. But licensing, or even buying a beat, from a talented but unproven producer can cost a few hundred bucks or less. If the producer receives a royalty in addition to the fee, the fee will be usually structured as an "advance" which will be recoupable prior to payment of the royalty.

Royalty

As noted above, a royalty for a producer hired by an artist or small label may be structured based on net receipts or net profits. A traditional royalty for a producer who works with a big label is 3–5% based on the artist's royalty. Net profits should be defined fairly, for instance, as the gross monies received from the sale or license of the tracks minus the producer's fee and other production costs. See the annotations to last agreement in this chapter.

Mechanicals

Even when an agreement is work for hire, it may be possible for the producer to retain the copyright in his contribution to the underlying musical work (but not the sound recording). In this case, the label or artist will require the producer's permission to use that contribution so that they can exploit the recording. In exchange for that permission, the producer usually receives a "mechanical" royalty, i.e., a royalty tied to the use of the underlying musical composition contained in the record. Mechanical royalties are set by statute. The current mechanical rate is 9.1 cents per song per copy sold (or for songs over five minutes, 1.75 cents per minute or fraction thereof). Since the producer probably did not create 100% of the song—for instance, where someone else (perhaps the artist) wrote the lyrics—the producer's percentage ownership or "split" has to be negotiated. If the producer's negotiated share is 50%, then he would receive 50% of "stat" (i.e., 9.1 cents) for each sale of the record containing the song. This would be in addition to his producer royalty, which is tied to income derived from the record rather than the song. Finally, the label usually asks the producer to accept ¾ of the stat rate. This is called the "Controlled Composition" clause. There is really no good justification for it except it is a standard clause in both producer and artist agreements, and the label can argue that it is an inducement to use the song of the producer or artist in the record.

Three Producer Agreements: Two Simple Agreements for a Beat and a Net Receipts Deal with an Indie Record Label

Re-printed below are three different producer deals that a producer working directly with an artist or an indie label may receive. The first license is a simple work for hire deal for the sale of a beat, the second is a beat agreement in which the producer receives a royalty in connection with the sale or license of the recording as well as an up-front payment, and the third agreement not only provides a royalty for the recording, but also a royalty in connection with the producer's contribution to the underlying musical composition.

SIMPLE WORK FOR HIRE DEAL FOR THE SALE OF A BEAT

This simple work for hire agreement for the acquisition of a beat is favorable to the person or company commissioning the beat. Since the agreement is work for hire, the Producer transfers all of his or her rights to the beat to the commissioning party, and that person or company becomes the "author" of the copyrights in the beat – both the music and the sound recording.

NAME OF ARTIST

ADDRESS

PURCHASE ORDER and AGREEMENT

TO: _____ ("Producer")

Date: _____ ____, 2017

Song and Track: _____

Delivery Date: Previously Delivered

Fee: Five Hundred Dollars ($500.00)

Fee includes all expenses.

RIGHTS TRANSFERRED: WORK FOR HIRE

All services performed in conjunction with the Song and Track including any materials such as rehearsal tracks, outtakes, or other materials provided by Producer ("Materials") shall be deemed to be performed and delivered on a work for hire basis for _____ ("Artist") and Artist shall be deemed to be the author of the Materials and the owner of any copyrights in the same. If such services or Materials are for any reason not deemed to be a work for hire, Producer hereby assigns all rights in the Materials including the copyrights therein to Artist. Without limiting the generality of the foregoing, Artist and any person authorized by Artist shall have the unlimited exclusive right, throughout the universe and in perpetuity, to manufacture or create digital masters of the Song and Track by any method now or hereafter known, derived from the Song or Track and to sell, license, market, transfer or otherwise deal in the same under any trademarks, trade names and labels, or to refrain from such manufacture, sale and dealing. No other compensation shall be due to Producer except the Fee set forth above.

ADDITIONAL TERMS

Time for Payment: Upon execution.

Warranties: Producer warrants and represents that (i) the Materials delivered hereunder shall be original; (ii) Producer has full authority to enter into this agreement; (iii) the Materials will not violate the rights of any third parties; and (iv) that Artist shall be entitled to use the Materials including the Song and Track for any promotional or commercial purpose without permission from or payment to any third party. Producer shall hold Artist harmless and indemnify Artist against any claim, including reasonable attorneys fees, arising in connection with Artist's use of the Materials.

Complete Agreement and Governing Law: The laws of New York applicable to agreements to be made and performed in New York shall govern the terms of this agreement, and the Courts of New York shall have exclusive jurisdiction over any controversy arising hereunder. Once signed by both parties, this shall constitute our entire agreement as of the date first above written.

AGREED:

_____

[Artist]

_____

[Producer]

ROYALTY AND CREDIT FOR PRODUCER

This agreement is more favorable to the Producer as it provides a royalty to the Producer and a credit, although it's still a work for hire and thereby makes the commissioning party (that is, the company or artist) the sole author of the master and the underlying music.

COMPANY

ADDRESS

Names

c/o

Address

As of _____ ____, 2017

This shall constitute the entire agreement between _____ with a residence at _____ (hereafter referred to collectively as "You"), and _____ (hereafter referred to as "Company") with offices at _____, in regard to certain musical recordings to be produced by You (the "Beats").

1.   You shall produce and deliver at least six (6) Beats to Company. The Beats shall include both the sound recordings and the underlying music compositions embodied therein.

This kind of agreement can be used for one beat or a number of beats, as is the case in this particular agreement. It can also be modified to include future beats to be approved by the Company or the Artist, or mutually approved by both parties.

2.   As the sole consideration for Your services hereunder and the rights granted herein, Company shall pay You the following compensation:

(a) One Thousand Dollars ($1,000) upon execution of this agreement and One Thousand Dollars ($1,000) upon delivery and approval of said Beats. Such compensation shall be inclusive of any otherwise required union residuals, re-use fees or other form of compensation.

(b) Company shall also pay You five percent (5%) of any "Profits." Profits shall mean: any monies actually received by Company from exploitation of the Beats throughout the world in any media including sale, license or other use of the Beats minus the payment in Para. 2(a) and any other bona fide actual out-of-pocket recording costs including engineer fees to session musicians, vocalists, other producers, engineers, mixing, mastering, sample and clearance costs. Company shall provide an accounting statement to You and pay You six (6) months after receipt by Company of any Profits. Thereafter Company shall pay You at the end of each additional six (6) month period if it receives any Profits during such period.

(i)   If Company distributes any Beat to the public it shall afford You credit as producer of that Beat if Company receives credit as the Executive Producer, provided that if a Beat is re-mixed or altered, Company shall have the right to credit other persons as additional producers. The size, manner and placement of such credit shall be in Company's discretion.

3.   All Beats to be delivered to Company hereunder shall be deemed to have been created on a "work for hire" basis as that term is defined under the U.S. Copyright Law, and Company shall be deemed to be the exclusive author of the Beats and owner of all rights therein including any copyrights in the Beats. If for any reason this agreement shall not be considered to be work for hire, You hereby assign, grant, sell and convey all rights in the Beats, including the music composition and sound recording copyrights therein, to Company.

4.   Company shall have the exclusive right to perform, distribute, license, assign, sell, and exploit the Beats, or any individual Beat, in any media now known or hereafter developed throughout the world in perpetuity for any promotional or commercial purpose. Without limiting the foregoing, Company shall have the right to edit, re-mix, re-record or make any other derivative use of the Beats whatsoever.

5.   (a) You warrant and represent that the Beats are completely original with You including the music embodied in the Beats. You further warrant and represent that You have all the rights necessary to enter into this agreement and grant the rights herein, that the Beats shall not violate the rights of any third parties, and that Company shall not be required to seek permission from, or pay any compensation whatsoever to, any third party in connection with its exploitation of the Beats. You hereby indemnify Company against any claims arising in connection with Company's exploitation of the Beats, or these warranties and representations, including reasonable attorneys' fees.

(b) Notwithstanding anything to the contrary above, the parties acknowledge that if a Beat includes a sample of any third party music and/or recordings, You shall identify that sample in writing and if Company decides to accept the Beat, Company shall be responsible for clearing that sample. Otherwise Paragraph 5(a) shall apply to all the Beats covered by this agreement.

6.   Company shall have the right to use Your name, approved likeness and bio to promote the Beats in any media throughout the world in perpetuity.

7.   When signed by You and Company, this agreement shall constitute our complete understanding. The laws of Virginia applicable to agreements to be made and performed in

Virginia shall govern the terms of this agreement, and the Courts of Virginia shall have exclusive jurisdiction over any controversy arising hereunder.

> The Company in this case was headquartered in Virginia and therefore wanted Virginia as the jurisdiction if a dispute were to arise between the parties. The party paying the money in any contract typically gets to choose the jurisdiction of courts that would settle a dispute.

Once signed by both parties, this shall constitute our entire agreement as of the date first above written.

[NAME OF COMPANY]

_____ Authorized Signatory

Accepted and Agreed

Name _____

SS# _____

Accepted and Agreed

Name _____

SS# _____

ROYALTY, CREDIT PLUS PUBLISHING ROYALTY FOR PRODUCER

This agreement is for a series of masters to be fully produced for an indie label. It provides a royalty for the sale or license of the recordings, just as the prior agreement did. In addition, it provides for a royalty in connection with regard to the Producer's contribution to the creation of the underlying song. For instance, suppose the Producer created the beat and the artist contributed the lyrics. In this agreement, the label would pay the Producer a royalty for use of the song. The annotations to Paragraph 11 explain the amount that royalty would be.

AGREEMENT made as of _____ ____, 2017, by and between _____ LLC (the "Company") with its principal offices at _____, New York _____ and _____ (the "Producer") with a residence at _____.

The parties hereby agree as follows:

1.   PRIOR RECORDINGS: The parties acknowledge that Producer has produced various audio recordings for Company in connection with various recording artists (the "Prior Recordings"). The Prior Recordings are listed in Schedule A attached hereto. This Agreement will set forth the terms that apply to the Prior Recordings and any other Recordings produced by the Producer at the request of the Company (the "Recordings").

This agreement was designed to cover recordings that the Producer had previously made for the label as well as future recordings.

2.   DUTIES: During the term of this Agreement, Producer agrees to produce and mix the Recordings. Producer shall perform his duties on a non-exclusive basis.

The last sentence means that the Producer may accept work from other labels and artists.

3.   TERM: The term of this Agreement shall commence as of the date hereof and shall continue until either party terminates the Agreement upon thirty (30) days notice.

4.   RECORDING PROCEDURE: Recording sessions for the Recordings shall be conducted by Producer for Company and at such times and places as shall be designated by mutual decision of Company and Producer. All individuals rendering services in connection with the production of the Recordings shall be subject to Company's approval. Each Recording shall embody the performance by an artist of a single musical composition designated by the Company. Each Recording and final mix shall be subject to Company's approval as technically and commercially satisfactory for the manufacture, broadcast and sale of phonorecords. Upon

Company's request, Producer shall re-record any musical composition or other selection until a Recording is technically and commercially satisfactory to Company. The Recordings shall be, at Company's election, maintained at a recording studio or other location designated by Company, in Company's name and subject to its control.

6. COMPENSATION:

(a) As complete and exclusive consideration for the services and rights provided by Producer hereunder, the Company shall pay Producer five percent (5%) of "Net Profits," as defined herein from exploitation of the Recordings. Net Profits shall be defined as follows: "Gross Income" as defined below minus "Expenses" as defined below.

(b) Gross Income shall be any and all income monies received by Company from the exploitation of the Recordings including from sale, license, assignment, lease, or rental of the Recordings or any other use thereof including sale or license of phonorecords in any media now known or hereinafter developed throughout the world for as long as company receives income from such exploitation.

(i) Expenses shall mean any actual recording costs paid by Company (except the royalties payable to Producer hereunder) such as fees payable to session musicians and engineers, costs related to mixing and mastering, and sample and clearance costs, if any.

In essence, the Producer will receive 5% of gross income from the exploitation of his recordings minus production costs.

---

7. GRANT OF RIGHTS

(a) All Recordings recorded hereunder, from the inception of recording thereof, and all Records manufactured there from, together with the performances embodied thereon, shall be the sole property of Company throughout the universe, free from any claims whatsoever by you, the Artist, or any other Person; and Company shall have the exclusive right to copyright such Recordings in its name as the owner and author thereof and to secure any and all renewals and extensions of such copyrights. The product of all persons rendering services in connection with the recording of such Recordings, including Producer shall be deemed "work made for hire" for Company. If such product is determined not to be a "work made for hire," then Producer hereby assigns all rights, including without limitation the copyright in the recordings, to Company.

(b) Without limiting the generality of the foregoing, Company and any person authorized by Company shall have the unlimited exclusive right, throughout the universe, to manufacture records by any method now or hereafter known, be it physical or digital, derived from the Recordings made hereunder, and to sell, market, transfer or otherwise deal in the same under any trademarks, trade names and labels, or to refrain from such manufacture, sale and dealing. Such rights shall exist for the duration of the copyrights in such records.

(i)   Company and Distributor have the exclusive right to distribute the Artist's recordings directly to consumers by means of any and all media, including, without limitation, by means of electronic transmissions.

Note that, although this is a work for hire provision, it applies only to the recording and not to the underlying musical composition. So, if the Producer contributes to creating the song, for instance, by composing the beat, he retains his ownership of that part of the musical composition contained in the recording. In Paragraph 11, Producer grants the label the right to use his contribution to the song in the recording, but retains the right to receive a royalty for that use.

(c)   Company and any Person authorized by Company each shall have the exclusive right throughout the universe, and may grant to others the right, to reproduce, print, publish, or disseminate in any medium the Artist's name, portraits, pictures, likenesses and biographical material concerning you, as news or information, or for the purposes of trade, or for advertising purposes in connection with Records hereunder. During the Term of this Agreement, neither you nor the Artist shall not authorize any Party other than Company to use the Artist's name or likeness in connection with the advertising or sale of Records. As used in this Agreement, "name" shall include, without limitation, any professional names.

8.   ACCOUNTING AND PAYMENT: Company shall account to Producer on a semi-annual basis starting December 31 and continue so long as Net Profits are earned, by furnishing statements and any payments due to Producer after deduction of permissible Expenses. Each such accounting statement shall include a description of any transaction subject to this Agreement including identification of any third party, the amount paid and the nature of the products and/or services for which payment was made. Each such accounting statement shall cover all relevant transactions for the immediately preceding semi-annual period.

9.   AUDIT:

(a)   Producer shall have the right, at any time, to give Company written notice of Producer's intention to examine Company's books and records with respect to each royalty statement. Such examination shall occur no more than once each year and be commenced no sooner than one (1) month and no later than three (3) months after the date of such notice, at Producer's sole cost and expense, by any certified public accountant or attorney designated by Producer, provided that he or she is not then engaged in an outstanding examination of Company's books and records on behalf of a person other than Producer. Such examination shall be made during Company's usual business hours at the place where Company maintains the books and records which relate to Producer, and which are necessary to verify the accuracy of the statement or statements specified in Producer's notice to Company. Company shall have no obligation to produce such books and records more than once.

(b) Unless Producer provides a notice to examine Company's books and records within six (6) months of receipt by Producer of any royalty statement, each such statement rendered to Producer shall be final, conclusive and binding on Producer and shall constitute an account stated. Producer shall be foreclosed from maintaining any action, claim or proceeding against Company in any forum or tribunal with respect to any statement or accounting rendered hereunder unless such action, claim or proceeding is commenced against Company in a court of competent jurisdiction within one (1) year after the date that such statement or accounting is received by Producer.

(i) Producer acknowledges that Company's books and records contain confidential trade information. Neither Producer nor Producer's representatives will communicate to others, or use on behalf of any other person, any facts or information obtained as a result of such examination of Company's books and records, except as may be required by law or judicial decree.

10. NAME AND LIKENESS: Producer hereby grants to Company the right to issue and authorize publicity concerning Producer and to use his name, voice and likeness and approved biographical data in connection with the distribution, exhibition, advertising, and exploitation of the Recordings.

11. CONTROLLED COMPOSITIONS

(a) Producer represents and warrants that each Controlled Composition (as defined below) is original and does not infringe upon or violate the rights of any other person and that Producer has the full and unencumbered right, power and authority to grant to Company all of the rights herein granted to Company. Producer hereby indemnifies Company against any loss, damage or expense (including reasonable attorneys' fees) in respect of any third party claims, demands, liens or encumbrances. "Controlled Composition" shall mean a musical composition embodied in a Recording recorded or released hereunder, which musical composition (i) is written or composed, in whole or in part, by Producer or (ii) is owned or controlled, in whole or in part, directly or indirectly, by Producer.

(i) Producer hereby grants to Company the right to distribute any Recording embodying a Controlled Composition. Company shall pay Producer a mechanical royalty of three quarters (¾) of the current statutory royalty rate in effect at the time of release of the Recording embodying the Controlled Composition at issue, pro-rated by Producer's percentage of ownership in the musical composition.

Under this provision, the Producer grants the label the right to use his contribution to the musical composition. In return, he receives a royalty of ¾ "stat," that is, the statutory rate of 9.1 cents, or 1.75 cents per minute or fraction thereof for songs over five minutes. But this royalty is pro-rated depending on his percentage of ownership. Suppose the Producer contributed the beat and the Artist created the lyrics, they may enter into a deal that each owns 50% of the song. In this case, the Producer's mechanical royalty would be 50% x ¾ x 9.1 cents for songs less than 5 minutes in duration. If the record sold a million copies, his mechanical would be $34,125 (50% x ¾ x 9.1 cents x 1,000,000).

12. <u>LEGAL COUNSEL</u>: Company hereby acknowledges that he has sought and received legal advice from independent counsel or that he has voluntarily waived his right to independent counsel with respect to the terms and provision contained in this Agreement.

13. <u>INDEPENDENT CONTRACTOR</u>: Producer and Company shall have the relationship of independent contractors. Nothing herein shall be construed to place Producer and Company in the relationship of principal and agent, employer and employee, master and servant, partners, or joint venturers, and neither party shall have expressly or by implications, represented themselves as having any authority to make contracts in the name of, or binding on, each other, or to obligate the other in any manner.

14. <u>NOTICES</u>: Notices, reports, accountings or other communication which the Producer or the Company may be required or desire to send to the other, must be delivered EITHER by

- certified mail, return receipt requested to the parties at the addresses first written above or other address to be designated by Producer or Company.
- electronic mail at the following addresses:

   (i)   for Company: _____@___.com
   (ii) for Producer: _____@___.com

15. <u>ASSIGNMENT</u>: Producer may not assign this Agreement. Company may assign its right or any of its rights hereunder to any person, firm, or corporation including a corporation in which the Producer is a principal, provided that (i) Producer shall remain responsible for any payments required to be made under this Agreement, and (ii) the assignee has the necessary cash on hand to make any payments required under this Agreement.

16. <u>ENTIRE UNDERSTANDING</u>: This Agreement constitutes the entire understanding between the parties with reference to this matter, and supersedes all prior agreements, written or oral. This Agreement cannot be modified except by written instrument signed by the parties.

17. <u>GOVERNING LAW</u>: This Agreement is made, and is to be construed under the laws of the State of New York with respect to contracts to be executed and performed in this State, and the courts of New York State shall have exclusive jurisdiction thereto.

18. <u>ENFORCEMENT</u>: If any provision of this Agreement shall be found invalid or unenforceable, then such provision shall not invalidate or in any way affect the enforceability of the remainder of this Agreement.

19. <u>WARRANTIES AND REPRESENTATIONS</u>: Producer hereby agrees that he has the right to enter into this Agreement. He further warrants that no material contributed by him to the Recordings shall violate any rights of any third party, and more specifically that he shall not use any samples of any other copyright work without the express prior written permission of the Company.

20. <u>INDEMNIFICATION</u>: Producer hereby agrees to and does indemnify, save, and hold Company harmless from all damages, liabilities, costs, losses and expenses (including legal costs and reasonable attorney's fees) arising out of or connected with any claim, demand, or action by a third party which is inconsistent with any of the warranties, representations, or covenants made by Producer in this Agreement. Producer agrees to reimburse Company, on demand, for any payment made by Company or Company's designee(s) at any time with respect to any such damage, liability, cost, loss or expense to which the foregoing indemnity applies.

ACCEPTED AND AGREED:

[NAME OF COMPANY]

_____ Authorized Signatory

Accepted and Agreed

Name _____

SS# _____

SCHEDULE A

Reference is made to the Producer Contract made as of _____ ____, 2017, by and between _____ LLC (hereinafter referred to as "Company") with its principal offices at _____, New York _____ and _____ (hereinafter referred to as "Producer") with a residence at _____.

Prior Recordings:

_____ featuring _____

_____ featuring _____

_____ featuring _____

_____ featuring _____

_____ featuring _____

_____ featuring _____

_____ featuring _____

_____ featuring _____

CHAPTER 6

MUSIC PUBLISHING AND SONGWRITER CONTRACTS

INTRODUCTION: EVERYTHING YOU NEED TO KNOW ABOUT MUSIC PUBLISHING AND BASIC PUBLISHING AGREEMENTS: SINGLE SONG, EXCLUSIVE TERM, CO-PUB, AND ADMIN DEALS

This chapter focuses on music publishing. Before discussing the basic forms of agreement, I will answer these basic questions:

- What is music publishing?
- What are the major sources of music publishing income?
- What is a publisher, and why would you need one?

What Is Music Publishing?

Publishing is the commercial exploitation of a musical composition—not the recording. At seminars, I usually hold up a CD to demonstrate the difference between songs or musical works, as the Copyright Act refers to them, and the recording that contains them, i.e. sound recordings. At my last presentation at the New Music Seminar, I brought an album by the great jazz musician, Thelonious Monk. The label on the CD shows that Columbia Records is the record company. It also shows the titles of each song contained in the CD. The recording is owned by Columbia Records. Monk transferred the rights in his performance to Columbia when he signed his record deal, and Columbia Records owns the copyright in the recording. But Columbia did not gain the rights in the songs. For instance, "Ruby, My Dear," written by Monk, is one of the songs included in the album. Columbia owns Monk's recording of the song, but not the song itself. A publisher called Music Sales currently administers the rights in this song on behalf of Monk's estate. The money that flows from the administration of the rights in that song, or any songs, is called publishing income.

What Are the Major Sources of Music Publishing Income?

The major sources of publishing income are public performance royalties, mechanical royalties, and sync fees. Each is explained below. Although minuscule in comparison with the first three, the next largest source of publishing income is sheet music.

Public Performance Royalties

In order for an artist to publicly perform a song they must secure a license and pay a royalty. Songwriters and music publishers use Performing Rights Organizations (PROs) to collect these royalties. In the U.S., there are three major PROs: ASCAP, BMI, and SESAC. A fourth PRO, Global Music Rights (GMR) was recently launched by music industry mogul, Irving Azoff. PROs collect public performance royalties from radio, television, the Internet, and other users of music, such as nightclubs and concert halls. Last year, ASCAP and BMI collected approximately one billion dollars each. As of 2014, SESAC's revenue had grown to $182 million (from $167 million the year prior). It has never been demonstrated that one PRO pays more or less than another, although the PROs will sometimes pay advances based on a songwriter's past success or to lure them away from their current PRO. ASCAP and BMI will serve as a songwriter's PRO automatically. SESAC and GMR are selective and will not sign a writer unless they approve their application. My advice to new and emerging songwriters is to set up appointments with the membership offices of these organizations and try to develop a relationship with a staffer. New songwriters often do not realize that a PRO can be a great resource. These are some of the ways that a PRO can help:

- Evaluate a songwriter's works and provide feedback
- Introduce songwriters to producers and other writers
- Provide workshops in which songwriters can learn about the business and meet executives at publishing and record companies
- Place songwriters who are also artists in showcase concerts

Mechanical Royalties

Mechanical royalties are the monies that songwriters earn from the inclusion of their songs on records. You are owed a mechanical royalty when someone reproduces your work, but also when you record the song on your own album. However, if you are an indie artist and are also your own label, then you won't make any money from these mechanical royalties, because you would essentially be paying yourself. The mechanical royalty rate is set by a tribunal called the Copyright Royalty Board pursuant to the Copyright Act. The current rate is 9.1 cents per song per copy of each record sold (unless the song is longer than five minutes, in which case the rate is 1.75 cents per minute or fraction thereof). This means that if a record containing one song sells a million copies, the "stat" rate would add up to $91,000. With respect to interactive streaming services, such as Spotify, the rate is 10.5% of gross income minus what the service pays to ASCAP, BMI, and SESAC (approximately 6%).

Sync Fees

A sync refers to the synchronization of a musical composition in an audiovisual work such as a movie, TV show, commercial, or video game. The amount of money for a sync placement varies widely depending on the nature of the project and the identity of the song. For instance, the use of a classic pop hit in a major motion picture or TV ad campaign can fetch well over six figures. On the other hand, I recently represented a young producer/songwriter who was paid $12,000 for composing new music for a 30 second beer commercial. The use of an indie writer's song in a basic cable show could garner just a few hundred dollars, or nothing at all except public performance royalties paid to the writer by her PRO.

Sheet Music

Sheet music used to be the primary source of publishing income. Even though sheet music now includes digital as well as physical media, it represents only a small fraction of total publishing income.

Summary

Altogether, these sources added up to approximately six billion dollars in 2014 worldwide. That amount is only slightly higher than the amount earned ten years ago. Accounting for inflation, publishing income has eroded. The major reason is that sales of recorded music have declined dramatically due to a variety of reasons including digital piracy and the transition from CDs and legal downloading to streaming, and consequently mechanical income has sharply declined.

What Is a Publisher?

A publisher is a company that collects the income we discussed above on behalf of the songwriter. Generally, the publisher will take 25% to 50% of the writer's income. Why would a writer give up all that money? Below we will learn what exactly a publisher does and why you need one.

Advances and Royalties

Advances are upfront payments that are usually made to the songwriter to induce her to enter into an exclusive deal in which the writer gives up the right to exploit her songs or license others to do so. For instance, I recently negotiated a publishing deal between a major publisher and a producer who created a beat (which is a musical work as well as a sound recording) for a major record label artist. The publisher offered $150,000 as an upfront advance. Advances are recoupable against royalties. The amount of the royalty varies depending upon the type of agreement. The publisher's share is 50% in a traditional publishing deal and generally 25% in a co-publishing deal (see below). The songwriter does not receive a royalty payment until the publisher "recoups," that is, when the amount of monies earned from the writer's songs exceeds the amount advanced to the songwriter.

Administration

Publishers provide administrative services such as registration of songs with the U.S. Copyright Office and collection societies in the U.S. and throughout the world. They also negotiate deals and get the best fees because they are aware of the going rates for various songs in diverse projects. For instance, if a major ad agency wants to use a song in a national campaign, the publisher is in a better position than the writer to negotiate the most favorable terms because the publisher is aware of what similar songs have received in similar circumstances. The publisher will do its best to collect all of the monies generated by a song from all sources (with the exception of the writer's share of performance monies, which is paid directly to the writer by her PRO).

Exploitation

The publisher is also supposed to exploit a writer's songs and find opportunities to generate additional income. For instance, publishers may encourage producers or artists to re-record the writer's songs. These re-recordings are known as "covers" and can generate a great deal of additional money. For instance, Whitney Houston's cover of "I Will Always Love You" was a much bigger hit than the original record written and recorded by Dolly Parton. The publisher will also try to get songs placed in motion pictures, television shows, video games, and ad campaigns as well as ancillary uses such as greeting cards and toys.

Foreign Income

Publishers have foreign affiliates that collect the money earned by a song in other countries. Major publishers, such as Sony ATV and Warner Chappell, have offices all over the world.

Small publishers can also administer the rights in their songs throughout the world by using "sub publishers." Suppose a European singer re-records a song, and it's a hit in Benelux (Belgium, Holland, and Luxembourg); a writer would need someone on the ground to collect monies from record sales, radio play and streaming in those countries.

Basic Publishing Agreements

The basic types of agreements that songwriters sign with music publishers are:

- Individual or Single Song Agreements;
- Exclusive Term Agreements;
- Co-Publishing Agreements; and
- Administration Agreements.

Single Song Agreement

Under this agreement, a writer transfers the copyright to one song or a limited group of identified compositions to a publisher. In return, the writer receives a portion of the income earned (usually 50%) from uses of that composition or compositions. Because the individual song contract applies only to the song or songs specifically included in the agreement, the writer can go to a number of different publishers with other songs and give each one only those songs that the writer is interested in promoting.

Exclusive Term Agreement

Under this deal, which was, but is no longer, the most common kind of agreement, the songwriter agrees to assign the exclusive right to administer all compositions that he writes during a specified term. For instance, that term could be one or two years with several options that the publisher can use to extend the term of the agreement for additional one-year periods. Sometimes the term is the longer of a period of time or delivery of a certain number of songs. The writer agrees to assign the copyrights in every song that he writes during the term. The publisher keeps the copyright in each song even after the termination of the agreement. However, under the Copyright Act, the writer or his estate has the right to terminate the assignment after 35 years. All publishing income is split on a 50-50 basis, although the agreement may allow the publisher to deduct defined expenses, such as the costs of producing demos. Generally, as discussed above, the publisher pays a songwriter an advance at the beginning of the contract which is recoupable against the writer's royalties. Additional advance payments are usually due if the publisher exercises options to extend the contract.

Co-Publishing

This form of agreement is basically the same as the traditional exclusive publishing agreement except that the writer only assigns 50% of the copyright in each song he writes during the term to the publisher, and the writer generally gets to keep 75% of the publishing income (that is, 100% of the "writer's share" and 50% of the publisher's share). This model became the standard form of deal as singer songwriters such as Bob Dylan, James Taylor, and Simon and Garfunkel became more successful and thereby gained more leverage. An example of a typical co-pub deal is the second agreement included in this article. It is a form used by a major music publishing company. The annotations, which contain suggested changes, demonstrate why an experienced legal adviser is essential when negotiating a publishing deal.

Administration Agreement

Under an administration agreement, the writer retains the copyrights in his songs. The publisher only receives the right to administer a composition or group of compositions for a specified period of time (e.g., 3 years, 5 years, etc.). In return for its services, the publisher usually receives an "administration fee" of 10% to 25% of all income earned during the term of the agreement. This form of agreement is seldom offered to new writers and is generally reserved for writers who have already had great commercial success.

Sync Rep Deals

A variation of a normal publishing agreement is a sync rep deal. It's much more likely that a new or emerging songwriter will encounter this form of agreement than a full-blown publishing deal. Sync rep deals usually do not offer up-front advances and involve companies who specialize in "shopping" songs, including instrumental and lyric versions, for use in movies, TV shows, ad campaigns, and video games. In a sense, these deals are publishing agreements because they involve the exploitation of musical compositions. But unlike true publishing deals, these agreements are intended only for the exploitation of the songs in audiovisual works. They usually do not authorize any other exploitation of the song, such as audio mechanical or licensing sheet music royalties, or the collection of public performance royalties from radio play. Of course there are variations and exceptions. For instance, a sync rep license could include the right to license a song for an audio soundtrack accompanying a movie which includes the song.

It should be noted that there are certain sync reps who will attempt to secure all rights in a song—just like a publisher would. That deal should be avoided, unless the rep is able to exploit songs in all media, as a normal publisher would. In other words, some sync reps "pose" as publishers.

In a standard sync rep deal, the writer grants the rep sync rights in songs that are mutually approved by the writer and the rep. The term is generally limited to one or two years, with automatic renewal terms, subject to cancellation by either party. Again, there are exceptions to this standard structure. Some sync reps will want a longer term or even perpetuity in their right to exploit a song. Generally, however, all sync reps will want the right to enter into perpetual licenses during the term of the agreement. So, for instance, a sync rep will be able to license a song during the term to a movie producer to use that song in the movie in perpetuity.

The most important issue in negotiating or signing a sync rep deal is exclusivity versus non-exclusivity. Sync reps who offer exclusive deals usually give these three reasons to justify exclusivity:

1. *Confusion over who to pay*: The argument is that the writer's PRO may not be able to identify the correct party to pay. In a sync rep deal, the sync rep will usually be listed as the publisher of the song and is paid directly by the PRO. If there is more than one publisher, the PRO may not know who to pay.

   This argument is rebutted by advocates of non-exclusive licenses who argue that, when the song is registered with a PRO, a suffix can be added to the title such as "Blue Skies—#1," "Blue Skies—#2," etc. The cue sheet reporting the use of a song in an audiovisual work, which all the PROs require, can identify the correct title and the right publisher will be paid.

2. *Motivation*: The argument is that publishers will be more motivated if they have exclusive rights in a song.

   The non-exclusive reps will argue that they are just as motivated, and in addition, if exclusive rep loses interest in a writer's songs, the writer loses any chance to make money from them.

3. *Value Reduction*: The argument is that a licensee may cause two sync reps to compete against each other and offer a discount thereby, decreasing the value of a song represented by two different companies.

   The non-exclusive reps will argue this is not the case, as licensees such as ad agencies and music supervisors value their relationships with the reps they work with on a regular basis and would not jeopardize those relationships by going around a trusted rep to get a cheaper price for the same song.

In terms of compensation, sync rep deals vary from company to company. Fifty percent is not unusual. But some companies provide better terms to the songwriter; some only take 20% to 25% and pay the balance to the writer. That percentage is usually based on gross income, including sync fees and public performance monies generated by the transmission of audiovisual works on television or the Internet. An example of a non-exclusive sync rep deal with annotations follows below.

MUSIC LICENSING REPRESENTATION AGREEMENT

This agreement (the "Agreement) is made as of _____ ____, 2017, by and between _____ ("Company") with offices at _____, and _____ ("Music Licensor") with an address at _____. Company and Music Licensor are sometimes referred to individually as "Party" and collectively as the "Parties." This Agreement includes: Summary of Terms below, and Terms & Conditions (the "T&C") and Schedule A attached.

Whereas, Company is a music licensing company that represents musical works for licensing in a wide variety of contexts, including, but not limited to, motion pictures, television programs, documentaries, commercials, video games, websites, and multimedia projects; and

Music Licensor owns and/or represents musical works for licensing purposes and wishes for Company to pursue licenses for certain musical works;

The Parties therefore agree as follows:

SUMMARY OF TERMS

1. NON-EXCLUSIVE GRANT OF RIGHTS: Music Licensor grants Company the non-exclusive right to Represent (as defined in the T&C) and enter into Licenses on behalf of Music Licensor for the use of certain Musical Works (as defined in the T&C) designated by both Parties. Licensor retains the right to license the Musical Works to third parties provided that Music Licensor shall not enter into an "exclusive" license such that any Musical Work could not be licensed by Company for another purpose.

Since this is a non-exclusive agreement, the Writer, referred to as Music Licensor, reserves the right to license his songs directly or authorize others to do so.

---

2. TERM: The duration of this Agreement shall be one (1) year from the date above and shall automatically renew for successive one (1) year terms, provided that either Party shall have the right to cancel the Agreement upon ninety (90) days written notice at any time after the first year of the Agreement.

As we discussed, this is a standard duration for a sync rep deal.

---

3. COMPENSATION: Company shall pay fifty percent (50%) of Gross Revenues (as defined in the T&C) to Licensor payable in accordance with the Terms and Conditions.

This is a standard allocation of monies in sync rep deals, although some companies will pay up to eighty percent (80%) to the Writer. Gross Revenues is defined in the terms and conditions as any monies received from licenses minus recording costs incurred by Company, if any.

---

4. TERRITORY: The grant of rights in paragraph 1 above shall apply throughout the universe.

(a) Music Licensor Information

Mailing Address: _____

Phone Number: _____

Email: _____

AGREED AND ACCEPTED BY:

COMPANY: MUSIC LICENSOR:

_____   _____

Authorized Signature

TERMS & CONDITIONS

1. DEFINITIONS

(a) "Musical Work(s)" is defined as (i) the sound recordings and the underlying musical compositions contained in such recordings and (ii) those recordings that the Parties mutually agree shall be covered by this Agreement. Those Musical Works are listed in Schedule A. Company has no rights in any other songs or recordings than the Musical Works. The definition of Musical Work shall also include all musical, artistic, literary material (including liner notes, song titles and other metadata), and all other intellectual property connected with the any Musical Works, including associated names and logos.

Note that the Musical Work is defined to include both the recording and the underlying song. If the Company makes a deal in which the song is re-recorded by any third party, such as a movie producer, the income from the license of the song will be shared on a 50/50 basis between the Writer and the Company, even though the producer is only paying for the song and not the original recording.

(b) "Represent" is defined as copying, distributing, marketing and promoting the use of the Musical Works and services to the general public and potential licensees, and to include the Musical Works on any website and controlled by Company, and to offer for license to others and license to third parties the Musical Works listed in Schedule A.

(c) "Licenses" is defined as contracts issued by Company permitting third parties to use Musical Works in any audiovisual work including, but not limited to, films, television, video games and audiovisual ad campaigns as well as any other synchronization in any and all media now know or hereinafter developed. Such rights shall also include the right authorize lyric reprints, and to make a musical arrangement to the extent necessary without changing the basic melody, fundamental character or the lyrics of the composition. Company shall be entitled to enter into any license with any third party except for pornography and shall be entitled to negotiate any terms that are reasonable in the sole judgment of Company, provided that no License shall be "exclusive" such that the Musical Work could not be licensed for another purpose. For the purpose of this Agreement, Licensor hereby authorizes to enter into any such License on behalf of Licensor, and for this purpose Licensor hereby grants power of attorney to enter into such License and collect monies from the licensee on behalf of the Parties hereto.

> Although the Company's rights are non-exclusive, the Writer has no right to approve any deal. That means that the Company can enter into any license it wishes, so long as that license is non-exclusive. A writer with leverage (meaning that they are successful or the Company badly wants to enter a deal with them) may be able to negotiate an approval right.

(d) "Gross Revenues" is defined as any monies that Company actually receives from Licenses for the Musical Works minus actual approved out of pocket expenses such as recordings costs if Music Licensor wishes company to produce any Musical Works.

2. REGISTRATION

(a) Music Licensor shall be responsible for, and required to, register the musical compositions embodied in the Musical Works with the Music Licensor's Performing Rights Organization (that is, ASCAP, BMI or SESAC in the United States). Music Licensor shall list the Company as the publisher of the Musical Works,

> It is important that a song is registered at a PRO so that the Writer and the Company receive performing rights royalties.

(b) In the event that Company enters into a License for the Musical Works, Company will add a registration with the appropriate PRO for the Musical Works with a tag. For instance, if the name of the Musical Work is "The River," Company will reregister the Musical Work at the same PRO as "The River-Company." With respect to such re-registration, Company shall be the publisher. Licensor hereby authorizes Company to re-register the Musical Work for the purposes set forth in this paragraph, and hereby grants Company power of attorney to implement such re-registration on its behalf. For placements that Company secures, Company shall receive 100% of the publisher's share of performance rights royalties and synch license fees which will result in the 50-50 division of Gross Revenues set forth in the Summary of Terms.

> This provision solves one of the arguments made by the proponents of exclusive licenses. That argument is that the "publisher's share" of performance royalties could be paid to the wrong party. In this agreement, since the Company is receiving 50% Gross Revenue, the Company would be entitled to 100% of the "publisher's share" of performing rights income. This subparagraph makes clear that the Company will be receiving that money directly from the PRO. All the PROs are now able to track particular performances of a song in any audiovisual work that is transmitted on television or the Internet. For instance, if the Company makes a deal with the producers of *Veep* on

HBO (for use of the song in a particular episode), the PRO will be able to track that particular song through the use of watermarking or other technical means. So, if a different company licenses the same song on behalf of the Writer to a different TV show, or even a different episode of *Veep*, the PRO will not pay the Company. Instead, the PRO will pay the other company the publisher's share of the performance fee.

c. Company reserves the right to register the Musical Works at SoundExchange for purposes of collecting royalties for the public performance of a Musical Work in included in a soundtrack album in connection with a film or television show for which Company licensed such Musical Work. Any royalties payable by SoundExchange shall be subject to 50–50 division of Gross Revenues set forth in the Summary of Terms.

This provision is tied to the Company's right to license a Musical Work for a soundtrack album in connection with a film or TV show, in which the Company placed a Musical Work. For instance, if Pandora or SiriusXM performed the Musical Work, SoundExchange, the organization responsible for collecting royalties for the digital public performance of sound recordings, would collect royalties in connection with the performance of the music recording contained in the Musical Work.

3.   TERMINATION OF AGREEMENT

After the initial one (1) year term, either party may choose to terminate this Agreement without cause with ninety (90) days written notice; the result of which will be the termination of this Agreement at the end of the ninety (90) day notice period. In addition, Licensor or Company may remove any Musical Work from the Company service after the first year upon written notice, provided that if Licensor provides such notice Company shall have ninety (90) days to remove the Musical Work and any license secured during that time shall be valid.

4.   REPRESENTATIONS AND WARRANTIES

(a) Music Licensor hereby represents and warrants that Music Licensor is the sole and exclusive owner of any and all rights in and to Musical Works as defined herein, including the copyrights, and/or an authorized representative or agent of the owner(s) (with written authority to act on behalf of the exclusive owner) of any and all such rights for the purposes of Company use of the Musical Works as set forth in this Agreement. Licensor represents and warrants that Music Licensor is free to enter into and abide by the terms of this Agreement and that Music Licensor owns and/or controls all necessary rights required to legally provide/license/offer the Musical Works submitted to Company in accordance with the terms of this Agreement. Music Licensor represents and warrants that no Musical Work will contain unauthorized samples, covers, or any part of any third party's music or literary work.

(b) Licensor agrees and acknowledges that Licensor is responsible for clearing any third party material including songs or samples written, controlled or recorded by third parties, and to pay any required royalty payments. Company shall use a tag line in promotional materials that will read as follows: "Original songs pre-cleared for film, television, new media and advertising.

(c) Music Licensor is responsible for notifying Company in writing in the event Music Licensor no longer represents 100% of the rights of Musical Works.

(d) Music Licensor further agrees to and shall indemnify and hold Company (and its owners, officers, directors, employees, agents, representatives and/or affiliates) harmless against any and all losses, damages, costs, claims, actions and proceedings, including without limitation attorneys fees and costs, resulting from the breach of the warranties and representations above.

(e) This Agreement is personal to Licensor. Licensor may not assign and/or otherwise transfer Licensor's rights and duties under this Agreement without prior consent of Company. Company may assign this Agreement to any third party in which Company is a principal owner.

5.   ACCOUNTING AND PAYMENTS

(a) Company shall make the required payments here to the Music Licensor within 45 days after the end of each calendar quarter (March 31, June 30, September 30, and December 31). All fees will be payable in U.S. dollars. All payments shall be accompanied by a statement showing the source of the payment to Company.

(b) In the event Music Licensor or Company elects to terminate this agreement, all monies owed to Music Licensor will be paid upon termination.

(c) All payments and notices will be made by delivering payment to the Music Licensor's address as specified above. All returned mail will be held until a current address is received by Company.

6.   CONTENT DELIVERY, MARKETING & PROMOTION

(a) Music Licensor agrees to deliver the Musical Works and all associated metadata in accordance with Company's instructions.

(b) Music Licensor will make reasonable efforts to promote its association with Company and the availability of its Music Works in the Company Music Licensing websites.

(c) Licensor may deliver additional Musical Works which shall be subject to all the terms of this Agreement by submission of the Musical Work and required metadata in accordance with Company's instructions.

(d) Company, solely at its own discretion, reserves the right to not to license, promote or include in its music library any Musical Work that it considers inappropriate for its service.

7. GENERAL PROVISIONS

(a) If either Party breaches any term or condition of this Agreement, the breaching party will have thirty (30) days to cure such breach after the first day of written notice from the non-breaching party. If after thirty (30) days, the breach has not been cured or a resolution has not been made, the non-breaching party may terminate the Agreement.

(b) This Agreement is governed by the laws of the State of New York applicable to contract made and to be performed there and the courts of the State of New shall have exclusive jurisdiction over any disputes arising from this Agreement.

(c) This Agreement and all rights and obligations hereunder will be binding upon the successors, licensees and assigns of each party.

(d) Should any part of this Agreement be determined to be invalid or unenforceable by a court of competent jurisdiction, the remainder of this Agreement shall remain in full force and effect.

(e) The parties agree that this Agreement is the complete and exclusive understanding between the parties. This Agreement may not be modified or altered except in writing signed by both parties.

SCHEDULE A

MUSICAL WORKS

Song Title	Performed by	Album (if any)/Label (if any)	Writer(s)

CO-PUBLISHING AGREEMENT

> This is an agreement used by a major publishing company that I received for a producer/writer client who wrote the beats for two songs for an artist who had just been signed by a major label. The songs were to be included in that artist's first album release. The client told me he got a "four song deal for $150,000." That sounded great until I reviewed the agreement. It was more like "sign here, we will send you $100,000, maybe you'll get the other $50,000 later, and by the way, you're our writer for the rest of your life."

_____ Music Inc.

p/k/a _____ (ASCAP)

> Most publishers are affiliated with all three U.S. PROs (ASCAP, BMI and SESAC). But, they will insert in the agreement the name of the PRO with which the writer is affiliated. In this case, the producer/writer was affiliated with ASCAP. Writers can only be affiliated with one PRO at a time, although they can change PROs after the term of their agreements with their then current PRO ends.

Dated: As of _____ ____, 2017

The following, when signed by you and by us, will constitute the terms and conditions of the exclusive co-publishing agreement between you and us (the "Agreement") with respect to _____ ("Writer," "You" or "Your"):

1.   TERM:

1.1. The "Term" of this Agreement shall consist of an initial period of one (1) "Contract Period" (as defined below) commencing as of the above date (i.e., the "First Contract Period"). In addition, we shall have three (3) successive options each to renew the Term for a period of one (1) Contract Period (i.e., the "Second Contract Period," the "Third Contract Period," and the "Fourth Contract Period"). It is understood and agreed that our options are consecutive and successive, so that our failure to exercise any particular option will cause any remaining option(s) to lapse as well.

> Notice that the "Term" and "Contract Period" have no definite duration. This is because, as we discuss bellow, they will each continue indefinitely until the Writer satisfies the "Delivery Commitment."

1.2. Contract Period/Delivery Commitment:

    1.2.1. Subject to the terms of paragraph 1.3. below, each "Contract Period" shall continue for the later of twelve (12) months, or, until thirty (30) days following our receipt of notice (all references to notice in this Agreement are to notice in the manner prescribed in paragraph 9 below) from you of the completion of your "Delivery Commitment" (as defined below) for such Contract Period.

The most important word in this provision is "later." Although each Contract Period could end in 12 months, that period will not actually end then, unless the writer has satisfied the "Delivery Commitment."

1.2.2. Your "Delivery Commitment" for each Contract Period shall consist of four (4) 100% newly-written compositions (or the fractional equivalent thereof) which shall be initially commercially released on an LP length recording (embodying no less than ten (10) different musical compositions) in CD format and embodied on the "standard" CD version of such LP as initially commercially released (e.g., and not embodied solely on a so-called "bonus track," "deluxe," "digital-only," "expanded," "limited edition," or "re-released" version of such LP or any other such "non-standard" version of such LP or, if LPs are no longer primarily released in CD format, the then-current, industry-wide dominant commercial release format in a permanent configuration) in the United States during such Contract Period by a "Major Record Company" (i.e., WEA, Sony Music Entertainment, EMI, Universal, or another company then regularly distributed by one of such companies) with a signed mechanical license from the applicable Major Record Company confirming payment of mechanical copyright royalties in the United States at rates not less than 100% of the then-current United States minimum statutory mechanical copyright royalty rate with respect to each such 100% newly-written composition (or the fractional equivalent thereof) but in no event less than $.364 in the aggregate for such four (4) 100% newly-written compositions (or the fractional equivalent thereof) each such 100% newly-written composition a "Recorded and Released Composition" or "RRC."

This is perhaps the most important provision in this agreement. It ties the duration of the agreement to delivery of songs, but not just any songs. They must be songs included in a physical album released by a major record company. Bonus or digital only releases don't count.

Also, the four songs must be 100% written by the Writer "or fractional equivalent thereof." What does this mean? Suppose the Writer, who in this case was a producer who creates beats, had 33% writing credit in ten songs, which were included in physical albums and each released by a major label. The total could add up to 3.3 (10 x .33%). The Delivery Commitment would not be met, and the contract would continue.

An even greater burden on the Writer is imposed by these words:

". . . with a signed mechanical license from the applicable Major Record Company confirming payment of mechanical copyright royalties in the United States at rates not less than 100% of the then-current United States minimum statutory mechanical copyright royalty rate."

This is a nearly impossible hurdle for a producer who makes beats for artists. Major record companies almost always make producers accept a lower mechanical rate than 100% of stat. This clause would pretty much guarantee that the Writer could never satisfy his Delivery Requirement. The result is that the Writer would have to deliver an unlimited number of songs for the rest of his career (subject to the Writer's right to terminate the grant in 35 years, a provision in the 1976 Copyright Act intended to benefit creators who sign bad deals at the beginning of their careers when they have little bargaining power).

The above quoted words also mean that the Publisher may never have to pay additional advances otherwise due if the Publisher exercised additional option periods. In other words, this "four song" deal is nearly an indefinite song deal, and this is the reason that no Writer should sign a music publishing deal except with the help of competent legal counsel to negotiate provisions in a music publishing agreement that are seriously detrimental to the Writer.

1.3. In each instance, our option shall be exercisable by written notice to you at any time during the Term up to thirty (30) days after your delivery to us of notice from you of the completion of delivery of your Delivery Commitment for the then-current Contract Period, provided that in no event shall we be required to exercise our option prior to the end of the twelfth month of the then-current Contract Period. For the avoidance of doubt, only written notice from you to us as prescribed in paragraph 9 below will trigger the thirty (30) day period during which we can exercise our option (i.e., submission of your delivery obligation to your creative product manager or to any other employee of Warner Music Group shall not constitute constructive notice as a substitution for written notice as described herein). Notwithstanding the foregoing, in the event we fail to timely exercise any particular option as provided above, you shall send us notice confirming same and expressly referring to this paragraph 1.3. (the "Option Cure Notice") and we shall have fifteen (15) days following our receipt of your Option Cure Notice to exercise the applicable option in which case the Term shall continue without interruption. If, however, we fail to exercise such option within such fifteen (15) day period, then the Term will end at the end of such fifteen (15) day period. For the purpose of calculating the thirty (30) day and fifteen (15) days periods set forth above, it is understood and agreed that any day on which our offices in Los Angeles are closed for business shall not be included in the calculation thereof.

2.   TERRITORY: The World.

That fact that the territory is the world is not a problem because this is a major publisher with offices all over the world. However, if this was a small publisher, the Writer may want to investigate the competence of that publisher's agents or "sub-publishers" in other countries.

3.   SCOPE OF AGREEMENT:

3.1. Subject Compositions:

3.1.1. Writer, including, without limitation, any and all of your music publishing entities and we will each own an undivided fifty percent (50%) share of your and Writer's interest in (i) all compositions presently owned or controlled by you and/or Writer, including, without limitation, all compositions included on the attached Schedule "A" (collectively, the "Existing Compositions"), and (ii) all compositions written, co-written (to the extent written), owned or controlled by you and/or Writer during the Term (or written prior to the Term and reacquired by you during the Term) (collectively, the "New Compositions"). The Existing Compositions and the New Compositions are sometimes collectively referred to below as the "Subject Compositions" or "SCs." We will have exclusive life-of-copyright administration of the SCs throughout the Territory. A composition first recorded and/or released during the Term or within three (3) months following the expiration of the Term shall be deemed to have been written and composed during the Term unless you can conclusively prove that such composition was written after the Term.

The Writer should try to delete the words "all compositions presently owned or controlled by you and/or Writer, including, without limitation," in (i) above. There is no reason the Publisher should own the Writer's previously created songs unless the Writer wants the Publisher to exploit those works, or the Publisher is willing to increase the advance payment. Also, the Writer may have entered into licenses for prior songs with a licensee, sync rep, or other third party.

3.1.2. You shall submit each SC to your creative product manager (such submissions include a CD, MP3, or then current format of audio recording, together with complete writer/ publisher/ split/ rate/ sample and lyric information with respect to each such SC delivered) utilizing the attached Schedule "C." In the case of co-written compositions, such co-ownership and administration shall only extend to your fractional interest which shall be calculated by multiplying one hundred percent (100%) by a fraction, the numerator of which is the number one (1) and the denominator of which is the total number of contributing writers unless we have received notice prior to the initial U.S. release of the specific composition indicating a different ownership share (accompanied by a fully executed writer acknowledgment of such shares utilizing the form on Schedule "C"). For clarification, nothing contained herein shall relieve you of your Delivery obligation.

3.2. Administrative Requirements and Restrictions: Although it is intended that we and our foreign subsidiaries, affiliates and licensees have the fullest possible rights to administer and exploit the SCs, to utilize your name(s) and approved likeness(es) (subject to paragraph 3.2.5. below) in connection therewith and to execute PA forms (and other routine copyright documents, copies of which we shall provide to you upon our receipt of notice from you requesting same) in your name and on your behalf as your attorney-in-fact (which appointment is coupled with an interest and is therefore irrevocable), neither we nor our foreign subsidiaries shall do any of the following (nor shall we authorize any affiliate or licensee to do any of the following) without your prior written consent in each instance (which consent shall not be unreasonably withheld by you it being understood and agreed that any request by you to revise the financial or other terms of any request with respect to the use of any SC as a condition of securing such consent or approval with respect to such use of such SC shall ipso facto be deemed unreasonable):

3.2.1. (a) Change or authorize any change in the English-language title and/or lyric of any SC, alter the harmonic structure of any SC, alter the melody of any SC (except insubstantial changes necessary solely to accommodate the syllabic requirements of foreign languages) or register any local translation of an SC with a performing rights society unless a recording embodying such translation has been released;

(b) Except to the extent that the rules and regulations of local mechanical and/or performing rights societies prescribe the share of royalties to be allocated to local adapters/translators/arrangers (which share shall be deducted "off the top" in determining "Gross Receipts," as defined below), all fees and/or royalties to any such persons shall be borne by us;

3.2.2. Issue a mechanical license for the use of any SC on a "top-line" record at less than the prevailing statutory or society rate, except in connection with those types of uses for which reduced-rate licenses are customarily granted in the country in question (provided, that our inadvertent, non-repetitive failure to obtain your prior written consent to such license at less than the full rate shall not be deemed to be a breach of this Agreement) and provided, further, that we will issue mechanical licenses as required by the terms of your current "controlled compositions" and related clauses (as annexed hereto as Schedule "B"), as well as with the corresponding clauses of any future agreement in respect of your recording and/or producing services, so long as such clauses comply with the provisions of paragraph 7.2.1.1., below;

3.2.3. Authorize the use of the title or lyric of any SC or any portion thereof as the title of a play, film or TV program, or authorize the dramatization of any SC or exploit any so-called "grand rights";

3.2.4. Authorize the inclusion of any SC in: any film rated "NC-17" or "X" (or the equivalent) provided that we have been made aware of such rating (except as may be required pursuant to any applicable blanket or similar license under foreign performing rights and/or mechanical rights society regulations now or hereafter in effect or otherwise); any commercial for feminine hygiene products, firearms or political candidates and/or issues or religious causes and/or issues; or any merchandising use, "tie-in," or endorsement;

A Writer with clout may be able to negotiate that any sync licenses would be subject to her approval.

3.2.5. Utilize any name, photograph or likeness of, or biographical material concerning, you [provided, that any such material (as well as any album cover artwork)] utilized by a record company with your written consent, or under circumstances deemed to constitute consent pursuant to the applicable agreement with such company, shall be deemed approved for use hereunder, free of charge as between you and us but subject to any necessary third-party clearance). Notwithstanding the foregoing, our use of Writer's name(s) in connection with our administration and/or exploitation of SCs, or in connection with advertising and publicity for our publishing companies, to designate our writers and catalog, or (with your consent) in respect of a profile of you on our so-called "web site" (such advertising, publicity and web site use being at no cost to you) shall not require your consent or prior approval.

3.2.6. Notwithstanding anything to the contrary contained in this paragraph 3.2., we shall not be required to obtain your prior written consent for any usages contained herein which are subject to any and all blanket or similar licenses now or hereafter in effect.

It's very important to be clear that the Writer will be paid for blanket licenses that include his songs. The contract should state that the Writer will be paid on a proportionate basis depending on the number of songs included in the license or the number of "plays," to be negotiated on a case by case basis. Here's the reason why: the major publishers are currently trying to go around ASCAP and BMI and negotiate "direct" licenses for public performance rights with digital music providers such as Pandora, Spotify and YouTube. If they succeed in changing the consent decrees, which now require ASCAP and BMI to include all the songs in their repertoires, the Writer may not see a dime of performance revenues if the publisher takes the position that they don't have to pay the Writer for public performance of songs included in a blanket license. As digital streaming services continue to grow in popularity, they could soon become a major source of income for writers, but not if the publishers are allowed to enter into direct licenses and the publishing contracts are not clear that the write must be paid.

3.3. Co-Administration Provisions:

3.3.1. Co-Administration of SCs: (a) Notwithstanding the provisions of paragraph 3.1.1. above, you and Writer (or your and Writer's music publishing designees) shall have the right by notice to us to undertake co-administration rights solely with respect to your applicable share (inclusive of Writer's songwriter royalties) of the SCs [i.e., you shall have the right to directly license solely your applicable co-publisher share (as set forth in paragraph 3.1.1. above) and 100% of Writer's songwriter share of the SCs and we shall have the right to license solely our applicable co-publisher share (as set forth in paragraph 3.1.1. above) of the SCs] as of the accounting period immediately following the accounting period during which occurs the later of: (1) the fifteen (15) year anniversary of the expiration of the Term; (2) your receipt of an accounting statement reflecting the recoupment of all advances hereunder; and (3) our receipt of notice from you requesting such co-administration. It is understood and agreed that your co-administration rights shall be subject to the terms and conditions of all licenses and other agreements entered into by us prior to the effective date of such co-administration, copies of which shall be delivered to you within a reasonable time following the effective date of such notice.

This clause belongs in the category of "giving ice in winter." That's because the Writer only gets to administer his share of publishing in his songs 18 years after the termination of the contract at earliest. This is also another example of a clause that could be seriously improved by a lawyer working on behalf of a writer with clout.

(b) In the event of such co-administration, it shall be your sole responsibility to provide written notice to all applicable third parties (including, but not limited to, record companies, mechanical rights societies, licensing agents, and your performing rights society) (provided that, upon your request, we shall provide you with the information required for you to contact such third parties) instructing them to make direct payment to you or your music publishing designee (or a third party on your behalf) of your share of Net Income, as well as Writer's songwriter royalties in respect of Gross Receipts which are earned by the SCs subsequent to the effective date of such co-administration (and you shall provide us with copies of all such notices), and we shall have no obligation to collect any part thereof. Notwithstanding the foregoing, if, after the effective date of your co-administration, third parties debit our account for an overpayment of income in respect of the SCs (and we had theretofore accounted to you for such income), the amount of the debit, less our share of such income, shall be considered an overpayment to you and, at our election, shall be immediately paid back to us by you upon demand or deducted from any payments due or thereafter becoming due to you.

3.3.2. Post-Co-Administration Collection: We shall have the right for twenty-four (24) months following the commencement of your co-administration rights with respect to the SCs to collect all income earned by the SCs prior to the commencement of your co-administration rights but not collected prior thereto ("Post-Co-Administration Collection Period") and such income shall constitute Gross Receipts hereunder and shall be processed and paid pursuant to the terms of the Agreement. Notwithstanding the foregoing, following the termination of the Post-Co-Administration Collection Period for the SCs, we shall have no further obligation to collect and/or pay to you any monies attributable to the SCs, provided, however, if, after the termination of the Post-Co-Administration Collection Period for the SCs any third party debits our account for an overpayment of income in respect of the SCs (and we had theretofore accounted to you for such income), the amount of the debit, less our share of such income, shall be considered an overpayment to you and, at our election, shall be promptly paid back to us by you upon written demand or deducted from any payments due or thereafter becoming due to you.

4.   COLLECTION AND DIVISION OF INCOME:

4.1. We will be entitled to collect (and shall employ best efforts consistent with our reasonable business judgment to collect) all writer/publisher income (except the so-called "writer's share" of public performances collected by societies and any other amount normally paid directly to songwriters by a disbursing agent, which, except as otherwise provided in this Agreement, shall be collected by you for your own account) generated by each SC, regardless of when earned (including without limitation pre-Term earnings on Existing Compositions).

4.2. Royalties/Net Income Share:

4.2.1. Except with respect to print income, we shall credit your account hereunder with the following percentages of "Net Income" (as defined in below), which shall be inclusive of Writer's songwriter royalties:

(A) Mechanical Income: Seventy-five percent (75%)

(B) Public Performance Income: Fifty percent (50%) of the Net Income derived solely from the so-called "publisher's share" of public performance income, provided; however, if we license any public performance use directly, we shall be entitled to collect all writer/ publisher income in connection therewith and we shall pay you seventy-five percent (75%) of the Net Income derived from such license, it being understood and agreed that the so-called "writer's share" (i.e. the first fifty percent (50%) of the aggregate seventy-five percent (75%) of Net Income) of which shall be paid to you with our next regular accounting and without regard to the recoupment status of your account.

(C) Synchronization Income: Seventy percent (70%)

Even a writer without great past success may be able to negotiate this percentage to 75%, matching her share of performance royalties.

(D) Other Income: Seventy percent (70%), provided, however, such percentage shall be forty percent (40%) in respect of any source of income which pays the so-called "writer's share" in respect of such exploitation directly to Writer (and for which such so-called "writer's share" was not collected by us).

4.2.2. With respect to print income, we shall pay you fifty percent (50%) of Net Income in addition to Writer's songwriter print royalties as set forth on Schedule "A".

4.2.3. As used herein, "Gross Receipts" shall be deemed to be the following:

(A) Except with respect to printed editions, amounts received by us in the United States (or credited to our account in reduction of an advance previously received by us in the United States) specifically and identifiably in respect of the use or exploitation of SCs, including but not limited to, from licensees and performing (publisher, not writer's share) and mechanical rights societies, it being understood and agreed that our share of amounts collected by our foreign music publishing subpublishers (which shall be calculated by them "at the source," i.e., as received by them from performing and mechanical rights societies and other licensees, and shall not be reduced by intermediate distribution between various units of our music publishing group) shall be deemed to be ninety percent (90%) of such amounts (other than the publisher's share of public performance income and mechanical income from "local cover recordings," as defined below), eighty percent (80%) of the publisher's share of public performance income, and eighty percent

(80%) of mechanical income from "local cover recordings" (i.e., recordings of SCs not performed and/or produced by you in whole or in part, which are initially recorded and commercially released outside of the United States).

(B) With respect to printed editions manufactured and sold by us or by our exclusive licensees or affiliates in the United States and/or Canada, "Gross Receipts" shall be deemed to be the following percentages of the marked or suggested retail list price ("List") on copies sold and not returned for which payment is received or credited to us in reduction of an advance previously received ("Net Paid Sales"), prorated where less than one hundred percent (100%) of a composition is an SC and also prorated where any edition does not consist solely of SCs (such proration to be based upon the number of copyrighted, royalty-bearing compositions included therein):

(1) twenty percent (20%) in the case of piano/vocal sheet music;

(2) twelve and one half percent (12.5%) in the case of Piano/Vocal folios [with an extra five percent (5%) in the case of a so-called "personality" folio featuring SCs written or co-written by you, together with your name and likeness as a recording artist] or a "matching" folio [i.e., compositions from a specific album on which you are a featured recording artist, together with a replica of the album cover artwork therefrom which is not an "educational edition" as described in paragraph 4.2.3.(B) (3) below]. Such royalty shall be reduced prorata in any case in which a "personality" or "matching" folio features you together with another recording artist. For example: the royalty in respect of an "A, B & C" personality folio would be ⅓ of five percent (5%), or 1.667%, while the royalty in respect of an "A, B, C & D" matching folio would be ¼ of five percent (5%), or 1.25%;

(3) ten percent (10%) in the case of so-called "educational" editions (including, but not limited to, choral, band, guitar, guitar tab, easy piano, orchestral arrangements and other pedagogical editions) and "fake books."

(C) In the case of printed editions manufactured and sold by us or by our exclusive licensees or affiliates outside of the United States and Canada, "Gross Receipts" shall be deemed to be twelve and one half percent (12.5%) of List on Net Paid Sales (subject to the prorations set forth above).

(D) In the case of printed editions sold through an in-house mail order and/or direct to consumer programs, "Gross Receipts" shall be deemed to be fifty percent (50%) of each of the above royalties.

(E) In the case of printed editions sold by third party print licensees and in respect of income from the rental of orchestral material, "Gross Receipts" shall be deemed to be fifty percent (50%) of all sums received by us in respect of such uses.

4.2.4. "Net Income" is hereby defined as Gross Receipts less:

(A) Solely in respect of print income, your songwriter print royalties as prescribed in Schedule "A";

(B) Actual copyright registration fees and the actual and reasonable third party costs of preparing lead sheets;

(C) Actual and reasonable out-of-pocket audit, litigation, and collection expenses (provided, that you have approved or consented to the commencement of such audit or litigation action and such expenses to be prorated in the event that such expenses are incurred in an action involving other compositions we control); and

(D) "Demo costs" (approved by both parties in writing).

5. ADVANCES: We shall make the following nonrefundable payments (subject to any with-holding which may be required by the rules and regulations of any taxing authority having jurisdiction), which shall be recoupable from Writer's songwriter print royalties pursuant to Schedule "A" and your share of Net Income hereunder:

5.1. In respect of the First Contract Period:

5.1.1. $100,000 promptly following the full execution of this Agreement and our receipt of all supporting documents and information described herein (including, without limitation, written confirmation from your performing rights society of the full registration of your publishing entity);

5.1.2. $50,000 promptly following our receipt of notice from you confirming completion of fifty percent (50%) of the Delivery Commitment.

Note that the advance is split into two parts. In this case, the Producer wrote 50% of two songs that were to be included in an album to be distributed by a major label. As we point out in the second comment in connection with 1.2.2., there is no guarantee that the Producer/Writer will ever achieve this goal.

5.2. In respect of optional Contract Periods:

5.2.1. In the event that we exercise an option, an amount [payable fifty percent (50%) upon commencement of the applicable option period with the balance payable upon our receipt of notice from you confirming completion of fifty percent (50%) of your Delivery Commitment for the applicable option period] equal to sixty-six and two-thirds percent (66.67%) of your Net Income share of U.S. mechanical royalties (including income derived from so-called "dpds" or "digital downloads") as reported on the first two royalty statements for the immediately preceding Contract Period, but not less than nor more than the following:

Contract Period	Minimum	Maximum
Second	$175,000	$350,000
Third	$200,000	$400,000
Fourth	$225,000	$450,000

These numbers can be negotiated upwards even by writers without a proven track record of success.

5.2.2. The amounts for the optional Contract Periods in paragraph 5.2.1. above shall be reduced by any then-current unrecouped balance in your account (as reflected on your accounting statement for the accounting period immediately preceding the accounting period during which the applicable optional Contract Period commences), provided that in no event shall the minimum amount in respect of such optional Contract Period be so reduced by more than fifty percent (50%). For the avoidance of doubt, the foregoing amounts set forth in the immediately preceding sentence shall be further reduced by any "Extra-Contractual Advances" (as defined below).

5.3. In the event that you request (and we pay) an advance ("Extracontractual Advance") at a time when such advance is not due hereunder, such Extracontractual Advance shall constitute a pre-payment (in whole or in part, as applicable) of the next advance(s) becoming due and payable hereunder, unless we otherwise agree in writing at the time the Extracontractual Advance is made.

6.   ACCOUNTING AND PAYMENT:

6.1. We will account to you (and make payment where appropriate) within sixty (60) days following the end of each semi-annual calendar period. However, if the amount due for a specific statement is less than $50, payment (but not the statement) may be deferred until the aggregate amount due to you exceeds $50. The exchange rates used by third parties in accounting to us shall be used by us in accountings hereunder.

6.2. We will only be required to account and pay with respect to amounts actually received by us in the U.S. (or credited to our account in reduction of a previous advance received by us in the U.S.); provided, that amounts collected by our foreign music publishing subsidiaries which are specifically and identifiably in respect of the use or exploitation of the Subject Compositions shall (subject to the "blocked currency" provisions set forth below) be deemed to have been reported by them to us and received by us in the U.S. no later than the end of the semi-annual accounting period next following the semi-annual period during which such amounts are actually collected by such subsidiaries.

6.3. Audit and Suit:

6.3.1. You [by way of a mutually approved certified public accountant on your behalf, it being understood and agreed that our approval shall not be unreasonably withheld and that we shall not disapprove of an auditor (if at all) more than once per audit] shall have the right to audit our books and records (solely on-site at our offices in Los Angeles, CA) once as to each statement for a period of three (3) years after such statement is received (or deemed received as provided below). Legal action with respect to a specific accounting statement or the accounting period to which such statement relates shall be barred if not commenced in a court of competent jurisdiction within three and one half (3.5) years after such statement is received (or deemed received as provided below).

6.3.2. For the purposes of calculating such time periods, you shall be deemed to have received a statement when due unless we receive notice of no receipt from you within sixty (60) days thereafter. However, your failure to give such notice shall not affect your right to receive such statement (and, if applicable, your Net Income payment) after such sixty (60) day period.

6.4. In "blocked currency" situations, we shall not be required to pay you until the blockage shall have been removed, but if requested to do so, we shall provide you with notice of such blockage and deposit blocked currency royalties in the local currency in a depository of our choice.

6.5. All payments hereunder shall be subject to all applicable taxation statutes, regulations and treaties.

7.   WARRANTIES AND REPRESENTATIONS:

7.1. By your signature below, in each instance in which SCs are delivered to us, you warrant and represent with respect to each such SC: (1) that you own such SC and have the right to grant the rights set forth herein and own the copyright interests being conveyed hereunder, (2) the SC is original, in whole or in part, (3) that the SC does not infringe any third party's rights or violate any applicable criminal statute, including but not limited to such third party's copyright, trademark, service mark, or right of privacy or publicity, (4) that the SC is not defamatory, and (5) that you and your respective music publishing entities are and will remain affiliated with ASCAP, BMI, or another recognized performing rights society [and in the event of your failure to so affiliate and for the purpose of preventing loss of income due to such failure, we shall be entitled to claim one hundred percent (100%) of the publisher's share with the performing rights society and account to you for income derived therefrom per paragraph 4 above until such time as you formally affiliate and notify us of such affiliation]. In each instance in which we provide you with a document which is necessary to vest our rights and/or interests in the SCs, you shall execute and return such document to us within ten (10) business days following your receipt of the same. In the event that you fail to do so, in addition to any other rights and/or remedies available to us hereunder, we shall be entitled to execute such document in your name and on your behalf as your attorney-in-fact (which appointment is coupled with an interest and is therefore irrevocable).

7.2. Additional Warranties and Representations:

7.2.1. Except as set forth in the annexed Schedule "B" [your current controlled compositions clause(s)], neither you nor your respective music publishing designees, nor anyone acting on your and/or your respective music publishing designees' behalf or deriving rights from or through you or your respective music publishing designees: (A) has received or will receive an advance, loan or other payment from a performing rights society, record company or other third party which is or may be recoupable from (or otherwise subject to offset against) monies which would otherwise be collectible by us hereunder, (B) is presently subject to any so-called "controlled compositions" clause under a recording agreement or (C) is presently subject to any provision of a recording agreement which would allow a record company to charge any amount against mechanical royalties.

7.2.1.1. Notwithstanding the foregoing, we shall comply with the licensing requirements of the "controlled compositions" clause of any recording agreement into which you (or an entity furnishing your services) have entered into or may enter subsequent to the date of this Agreement, and your and/or such entity's acceptance of such clause shall not constitute a breach of this Agreement, provided such other agreement contains the following:

(A) for "top line" LPs the applicable mechanical rate in the United States with respect to the physical distribution of records embodying SCs is not less than seventy-five percent (75%) [but with respect to the digital distribution of records embodying SCs not less than one hundred percent (100%) of the then-current rate established by the Copyright Royalty Board] of the minimum statutory mechanical license rate in effect on the date of delivery of the first record embodying a specific SC, and the rate in Canada with respect to the physical distribution of records embodying SCs is not less than seventy-five percent (75%) [but with respect to the digital distribution of records embodying SCs not less than one hundred percent (100%)] of the full rate in effect on the date of delivery of masters to your record company in the U.S.;

(B) the per record maximums are not less than ten (10) times such rate in the case of full length records (LPs, cassettes, CDs) (with your reasonable efforts to secure in such recording agreement payment on fifty percent (50%) of LP length "free goods"), three (3) times such rate in the case of 12" singles, and two (2) times such rate in the case of 7" singles or cassette singles;

(C) no advances or other charges under the recording agreement are recoupable from, or capable of being offset against, mechanical royalties in respect of SCs (with the exception of budget overruns and union late payment penalties); and

(D) accounting provisions providing for the rendition of semi-annual accountings and payments with respect to the SC.

7.2.1.2. If (and to the extent that) one or more of the standards set forth above is not met, and/or in the event of any recoupment and/or offset pursuant to subsection 7.2.1.1.(C), above, we shall nonetheless calculate our share of income as though such standards had been met and no such recoupment or offset had occurred.

7.2.1.3. In the event that you or any entity acting on your behalf or deriving rights from you directly distributes recordings embodying SCs without the involvement of any record company or any similar such entity who undertakes the obligation to obtain mechanical licenses and make mechanical royalty payments (each a "Self-Releasing Entity"), such Self-Releasing Entity shall pay mechanical royalties to us on the same terms as set forth in paragraph 7.2.1.1. above.

7.2.2. Notwithstanding the foregoing, in the event that any record company to whom you (or an entity furnishing your services) are or may hereafter be under contract charges any advance(s) or other amount(s) against mechanical royalties earned by the SCs from recordings made under such recording agreement or reduces the amount of mechanical royalties otherwise due to you because the mechanical royalties payable with respect to "outside material" embodied in your recordings causes aggregate mechanical royalties to exceed the per-record maximum rate(s) prescribed in the controlled compositions clause of your recording agreement or fails to pay mechanical royalties in respect of all records for which record royalties are payable unless due to Record Company's breach or error, then, in addition to any other rights and remedies available to us, we shall be entitled to (A) send a letter of direction in your name advising your record company of the terms of this paragraph 7 and instructing such record company [upon recoupment from record royalties of any portion(s) of the advance(s) or other amount(s) so charged] to re-credit us directly to the same extent (not to exceed the total amount originally recouped from or charged against mechanical royalties) and (B) reimburse ourselves from any and all monies (including your writer/ publisher royalties) earned or due hereunder, for any amount charged against mechanical royalties, except to the extent later recovered through the re-crediting process.

See the second comment in connection with 1.2.2 above. Record companies nearly always make artists who write their own songs accept a reduced mechanical rate—usually ¾ of stat, and they nearly always reduce the mechanical payable to artists who write if the aggregate mechanical payable, including monies paid to outside writers, exceeds a "cap" of, for instance, 10 x ¾ stat. The Writer should not be punished for signing a deal with a record company that has a "Controlled Composition" clause because record companies will generally refuse to delete the Controlled Composition clause except for superstars.

7.2.3. In the event of a breach of this paragraph 7.2., we shall (in addition to any other remedies available to us) be entitled to reimburse ourselves from monies otherwise becoming due to you or your music publishing designee hereunder to the extent that monies are not collectible by us by reason thereof.

8.   <u>INDEMNITIES/CLAIMS; CURE OF BREACHES; WAIVER; ASSIGNMENT:</u>

8.1. Indemnities/Claims:

8.1.1. Each party will indemnify the other against any loss or damage (including actual court costs and reasonable third party attorneys' fees) resulting from a third party claim due to a breach of this Agreement by that party which results in a final, adverse judgment against the other party or which is settled with the other party's prior written consent (not to be unreasonably withheld or delayed). In addition, your indemnity shall extend to the "deductible" under our errors-and-omissions policy without regard to judgment or settlement.

8.1.2. Each party shall give the other prompt notice of any third party claim which such party receives in respect of any SC and each party shall make a good faith effort to consult with the other prior to responding to such claim.

8.1.3. Each party is entitled to be notified of any action against the other brought with respect to any SC, and to participate in the defense thereof. However, if you wish to participate in the defense by counsel other than our errors and omissions counsel, such participation shall be at your sole cost and expense. Furthermore, in respect of any action alleging that any SC infringes a third party's rights or violates any applicable criminal statute, including but not limited to such third party's copyright, trademark, servicemark, or right of privacy or publicity, we shall at all times have the right to tender the defense thereof to you (i.e., require you to assume the obligation of defense).

8.1.4. If a claim is made against us and/or with respect to any SC, we may withhold a reasonable amount (i.e., an amount reasonably related to the scope of the claim and potential liability including anticipated reasonable third-party attorneys' fees and litigation costs) from monies due or to become due to you, but if requested to do so by notice in the manner prescribed in paragraph 9, below, we will notify you of the amount on legal hold and we will release it if (and to the extent that) suit is not brought with respect to that sum within one (1) year thereafter, and provided that you have reasonably responded in writing to any written inquiry we have made in respect of such claim, and we won't withhold if you provide us with a satisfactory commercial surety bond.

8.1.5. To the extent necessary in our sole reasonable business judgment, we may prosecute, settle, and compromise all claims, suits, and actions respecting SCs. In the event of recovery by us of any monies as a result of a judgment or settlement from any claim, suit, action, or proceeding instituted or initiated by us, such monies shall be deemed Gross Receipts hereunder. Should the cost of any such claim, suit, action, or proceeding (which has been previously approved by you) exceed the amount recovered by us, any cost over and above such recovery shall solely be borne by you. If we have not instituted any suit, action, or proceeding within sixty (60) days after your notice requesting same, you shall have the right (and it shall be your sole remedy), exercisable any time thereafter, to institute such claim, suit, action, or proceeding in your own name, in which case one hundred percent (100%) of the recovery (net of your documented out-of-pocket attorney fees and costs) shall be retained by you, less the amount of the then current unrecouped balance (if applicable) of your royalty account, which shall promptly be paid to us.

8.2. Cure of Breaches: Neither party will be deemed in breach unless the other party gives notice and the notified party fails to cure within thirty (30) days after receiving notice [fifteen (15) days in the case of payment of monies]; provided, that if the alleged breach is of such a nature that it cannot be completely cured within thirty (30) days [or fifteen (15) days, as applicable], the notified party will not be deemed to be in breach if the notified party commences the curing of the alleged breach within such thirty (30) day [or fifteen (15) day] period and proceeds to complete the curing thereof with due diligence within a reasonable time thereafter. However, either party shall have the right to seek injunctive relief to prevent a threatened breach of this Agreement by the other party. All payments required to be made by us hereunder shall be subject to any rights and/or remedies which may otherwise be available to us in the event of a breach of this Agreement on your part not cured in the manner prescribed above.

8.3. Waiver: The waiver of the applicability of any provision of this Agreement or of any default hereunder in a specific instance shall not affect the waiving party's rights thereafter to enforce such provision or to exercise any right or remedy in the event of any other default, whether or not similar.

8.4. Assignment: We may assign our rights under this Agreement in whole or in part to any subsidiary, affiliated or controlling corporation, to any third party owning or acquiring a substantial portion of our stock or assets, or to any partnership or other venture in which we participate, and such rights may be similarly assigned by any assignee. We may also assign our rights to any of our licensees if advisable in our sole discretion to implement the license granted. You shall not have the right to assign this Agreement or any of your rights hereunder without our prior written consent. Any purported assignment by you in violation of this paragraph shall be void from the making thereof.

9. NOTICES/STATEMENTS/CONSENTS:

9.1. Except as expressly provided herein, all notices shall be in writing and shall be sent by certified mail (return receipt requested), registered mail, Federal Express or any other nationally recognized overnight courier that provides for proof of delivery to you and to us at the following addresses, or to such other addresses as the parties may designate from time to time by notice in like manner:

            To You: c/o _____

                        _____

                        _____

Phone: _____

Fax: _____

Email: _____

To Us: Attn: Head of Legal & Business Affairs

_____

_____

Fax: _____

9.2. Statements (and payments, as applicable) shall be sent by ordinary mail to:

[PLEASE PROVIDE]

9.3. Requests for creative approvals/consents pursuant to paragraph 3.2. above shall be sent by e-mail to you:

c/o [PLEASE PROVIDE]

Phone: _____

Fax: _____

Email: _____

9.3.1. Where the consent or approval of a party is required, it shall not be unreasonably withheld (unless expressly provided otherwise herein) and shall be deemed given unless the party whose consent or approval has been requested delivers notice of nonconsent or disapproval to the other party within fifteen (15) days after receipt of notice requesting such consent or disapproval.

9.3.2. Notwithstanding the foregoing, with respect to the use of any SC pursuant to paragraph 3.2. above, consent or approval shall be deemed to have been given unless we are notified of disapproval from you or your manager or attorney within ten (10) business days [three (3) calendar days in respect of uses pursuant to paragraph 3.2.4.] following your receipt of faxed or emailed notice requesting such consent or approval.

10. FIRST NEGOTIATION RIGHT/MATCHING RIGHT:

10.1. You shall not sell, transfer, assign or otherwise dispose of or encumber any of your interests in the SCs without first according to us a "First Negotiation Right" (as defined below) and a "Matching Right" (as defined below) in each instance.

10.2. "First Negotiation Right"—prior to negotiating with any third-party, directly or indirectly, relating to the rights concerned you shall give us notice (such notice which shall not be given until you seek, in good faith, to actively pursue third-party offers in connection with the rights concerned) and negotiate with us exclusively for a period of no less than thirty (30) days (unless we send you a notice waiving such period).

10.3. "Matching Right": No party other than us will be granted the rights to purchase or, as applicable, exploit the assets or rights concerned unless (a) you first send notice to us specifying all of the material terms of the offer and the identities of all parties and furnish to us a copy of the offer, and (b) you offer to enter into an agreement with us containing the same terms described in your notice. If we do not accept your offer within thirty (30) days after our receipt, you may then enter into that proposed agreement with the parties referenced in your notice, provided that agreement is consummated within ninety (90) days after the end of that thirty (30) day period upon the terms (or better terms) set forth in your notice. If that agreement is not consummated within the latter ninety (90) day period, no party except us will be granted those rights to purchase or exploit the assets or rights concerned unless you first offer to enter into an agreement with us as provided above. If we do accept your offer, both parties shall proceed promptly and in good faith to complete our due diligence review and financial audit and industry-standard documentation. We will not be required, as a condition of accepting any such offer, to agree to any terms which cannot be fulfilled by us as readily by any other person (for example, but without limitation, the ability to secure a full mechanical rate from a record company affiliated with that other party), nor be obligated to match any offers that specifies any financing contingency or fails to evidence the ability of the offeror to finance.

11. LAW AND FORUM:

11.1. This Agreement has been entered into in and is to be interpreted in accordance with the laws of the State of California. All actions or proceedings seeking the interpretation and/or enforcement of this Agreement shall be brought only in the State or Federal Courts located in Los Angeles County, all parties hereby submitting themselves to the jurisdiction of such courts for such purpose.

11.2. Service of Process:

11.2.1. Service of process in any action between the parties may be made by registered or certified mail (return receipt requested) addressed to the parties' then-current addresses for notice as prescribed in paragraph 9, above.

11.2.2. Service shall become effective thirty (30) days following the date of receipt by the party served [unless delivery is refused, in which event service shall become effective thirty (30) days following the date of such refusal].

Very truly yours,

_____

By: _____

_____

Chairman and CEO, _____

AGREED AND ACCEPTED:

_____

p/k/a _____ (ASCAP)

Except for the Schedule below, we are not printing several schedules and exhibits containing legal formalities, which are referred to and originally attached to the agreement above. Unlike those attachments this Schedule contains substantive provisions.

Schedule "A" to Agreement dated as of _____ ____, 2017

Re: _____ ["Writer"]

WRITER PRINT ROYALTIES

Calculated on Net Paid Sales of printed editions by us or by our subsidiaries, affiliates or exclusive licensees:

(A) U.S. and Canada

Piano/vocal sheet: 7 cents

Piano/Vocal Folios (other than "fake books" or "educational editions," described below): Twelve and one-half percent (12½%) of wholesale (prorated in the case of "mixed" folios to reflect number of royalty-bearing compositions). "Personality" folios [featuring Writer(s)' name and likeness as a featured recording artist] or "matching" folios [featuring album cover artwork and songs from specific album featuring Writers]: an additional five percent (5%) of wholesale. Such royalty shall be reduced prorata in any case in which a "personality" or "matching" folio features Writers together with another recording artist. For example: the royalty in respect of an "A, B & C" personality folio would be ⅓ of five percent (5%), or 1.667%, while the royalty in respect of an "A, B, C & D" matching folio would be ¼ of five percent (5%), or 1.25%.

"Fake books" and "educational editions": (including, but not limited to, choral, band, guitar tab, easy piano, orchestral arrangements and other pedagogical editions) and other printed editions not otherwise expressly provided for in this agreement: 10% of wholesale (prorated to reflect number of royalty-bearing compositions).

(B) Outside the U.S. and Canada: Fifty percent (50%) of Gross Receipts.

(C) Other Income: Fifty percent (50%) of Gross Receipts.

(D) In-House Mail Order/Direct to Consumer Sales: Fifty percent (50%) of the above royalties (as applicable).

All royalties above to be prorated based on that portion of a composition which is an SC.

CHAPTER **7**

MUSIC AND THE MOVIES: COMPOSER AGREEMENTS (WRITTEN WITH ROBERT SEIGAL, ESQ.)

INTRODUCTION: WHAT A COMPOSER FOR A MOVIE SHOULD GET IN WRITING, AND LICENSING PRERECORDED MUSIC FOR A FILM

This chapter focuses on basic agreements for music and the movies. The aim is to help musicians who have been offered the opportunity to write new music for a film or license their pre-existing works. We will discuss three different forms of agreement. The first two are "composer agreements" for the creation of a "score," i.e., music used throughout a film. The third agreement is a license from a composer to a filmmaker for the use of a single song in a movie.

If you are a filmmaker seeking previously recorded and commercially released music, you may be interested in reading my book, *The Future of the Music Business*. That book includes a comprehensive guide on how to license (or "clear") music for movies. Producers should be aware of at least one fact: licensing popular, pre-recorded music can be very expensive. For instance, a client recently received a quote of $50,000 for a Tom Petty song for a feature film, even though the movie was a low budget Dutch language production with extremely limited commercial potential. This quote was just for the underlying musical composition. The client would have had to pay another $50,000 to use Petty's recording. If you are a filmmaker, hiring a composer to create music for your movie can save you a great deal of money.

Composer Agreements

The key terms of a contract between a film producer and a composer are:

- Whether the composer will be responsible for recording as well as writing the music;
- The fee payable to the composer;

- The time schedule for the delivery of the music;
- The composer's credit;
- How a composer would be compensated if there is a soundtrack album; and
- The permitted use and ownership of the music itself.

Fees

In a conventional composer agreement, the composer is responsible for producing or supervising the production of the music as well as composing it. The composer is paid a fee for those services, and the filmmaker sometimes pays for costs associated with rendering those services, such as studio time, compensation to engineers, mixers, arrangers, and the rental of recording equipment. Alternatively, these costs may be built into the composer's fee (see the discussion of the Package Deal below).

The composer's fee is generally paid in installments. Part of the fee may be payable upon the signing of the agreement or the commencement of "spotting"—i.e., when the production team and the composer screen the movie to determine where and what type of music should be used in the movie's score. Another portion of the fee may be payable upon the commencement of the recording of the score. A third installment of the fee may be payable upon completion of all services, including delivery of the master recording in a format specified in the contract, and the producer's acceptance of the master recording (see below).

The Package Deal

With low budget movies, a producer and a composer often enter into a "package deal." Package deals work well when a composer is using few instruments and relies on synthesizers and her own equipment and recording facilities. The producer pays the composer a fee designed to compensate the composer as well as cover costs associated with the recording of the score. The composer assumes responsibility to pay for musicians, arrangers, studio time, and instrument rentals, and retains any monies remaining after she pays these costs. But, if the composer incurs expenses in excess of the package fee deal, the composer assumes the costs of such overages.

However, there are usually certain costs excluded from the "package deal" which the producer assumes. If the producer hires another composer to re-write the score or re-record, the producer must pay the new composer and any licensing fees for any music not written by the original composer. The composer should try to limit the right of the producer to demand changes after delivery and to negotiate a "kill fee" in case the producer is dissatisfied with the score (see "Producer's Acceptance" below and Paragraph 2(b) of the second contract analyzed in this chapter).

Work for Hire vs. Exclusive License

A key provision in any composer agreement is the section that addresses the ownership rights in the music. In a typical composer agreement, the producer and the composer agree in a signed writing that the music which the composer creates and records is deemed a "work for hire" and that the producer owns all rights including the underlying music and recording of that music. This provision also states that, if for any reason the music the composer creates and records is not deemed a "work for hire" under Federal Copyright Law, the parties agree that the composer has transferred all rights in the underlying music and recordings to the producer.

A work for hire contract gives the producer total control of the music and the recordings. The producer can use or modify the music in any manner, and include the music in the trailers, marketing materials, advertisements and any other form of promotion for the movie.

However, the producer can also act as a music publisher and label by licensing the music and the recordings to any third party whether or not such third parties have any connection to the movie. For instance, the producer could license the music and/or the recordings to a person or entity that may want to use it in a commercial or ad campaign. Although the composer has no say in how the music is used and does not share in the income from licensing of the music to third parties, the composer may be entitled to compensation from public performances. This is the one income stream in which a writer subject to a work for hire agreement usually gets paid.

As discussed in prior chapters, the publisher's share and the songwriter's share are generally divided on a 50/50 basis. Although the filmmaker receives the publisher's share for the music license, the composer retains the songwriter's share regardless of who owns the rights to the music. In the U.S., a composer does not receive public performance income from the distribution of DVDs, permanent downloads, or when a movie is played in a theater. However, public performance royalties can be collected from a movie broadcast on TV or from the Internet (e.g. Netflix). The composer should be very careful that proper cue sheets are prepared and presented to his or her performance rights organization ("PRO") to ensure that he or she will be credited by the PRO. As discussed in Chapter 4, a cue sheet is a log of all the music used in a production. Cue sheets are the primary means by which performing rights organizations track the use of music in films and TV. Without filing the cue sheet, the composer will not be compensated by a PRO.

Work for hire agreements are standard and usually non-negotiable when a major studio hires a composer. But, major studios generally pay significant fees. A composer who is approached by an independent producer with a more financially modest offer may be able to retain the rights to her music or at least share additional income streams besides just the writer's share of public performance royalties. If a producer cannot afford to pay a composer her customary fee, the composer may agree to a reduced fee provided that she is permitted to share the rights to the underlying music (the publishing rights) as opposed to just the rights to the recordings. For example, if the composer's music from the movie is licensed, the composer could negotiate to receive the full songwriter's fee (50%) and perhaps one-half of the publisher's share (25%). In this scenario, the producer would retain the remaining one-half of the publisher's share (25%).

Since producers are generally not music publishers and may not have an interest in engaging a music publisher to exploit the music rights on their behalf, a producer may offer a reduced fee to a composer and permit the composer to retain the publishing rights. In this scenario, the composer usually grants an exclusive license for the use of the music in the movie as well as in any trailers, advertisements or other promotional materials related to the movie, but retains the copyright to his music and recordings, and the right to use them in other projects. In this case, the producer may also negotiate to secure the right to create and distribute a soundtrack album in connection with the movie. The composer agreement can go into extensive detail in calculating how a composer will be compensated for the use of her music and recorded performances on the soundtrack album, or the parties can agree to negotiate such terms in good faith at a later time if the possibility of a soundtrack album is more certain, such as when a distributor agrees to commercially release the movie.

If the producer agrees that the composer will retain the rights to her music and recordings, the producer will usually require the composer to agree that she cannot use or allow others to use the music in any other movie, television program or audiovisual project for a certain period of time without the producer's written consent. This period may be several years, and could start from the initial commercial release of the movie or from the signing of the composer agreement. After the duration of the agreed upon period, the composer can use the music however she pleases.

The composer's agreement may also have a provision limiting the amount of the movie's music that may be used in an album. This is to prevent an album containing the composer's music from becoming potentially competitive with the movie's soundtrack album, thereby undercutting the marketability and value of the actual soundtrack album. If a composer creates her own album and uses any portion of the movie's music, she is usually required to credit the movie as the source of the music.

Producer's Acceptance

Prior to accepting the final score, the producer usually retains the right to request certain changes, omissions, or additions to the movie's music. In addition, the producer generally has the right not to use the composer's score in the final version of the movie, provided that the composer has been fully compensated for creating and/or recording the score. This is known as a "play or pay" clause, and it is used in a wide variety of forms of entertainment business agreements (such as an agreement for an actor's services).

Play or pay provisions are usually non-negotiable because they are inherently fair by pre-supposing that the producer has paid one hundred percent of composer's fee; it would be overreaching to demand that the producer use the composer's score even if the producer does not think it works for the movie. However, to increase the likelihood that a composer and producer are on the same page regarding the movie's music, the two can agree that the composer will provide scoring and recording services for a portion of the score, at which point the producer can decide whether or not to continue to work with the composer for the remainder of the score. If the producer chooses to terminate the relationship, the composer would receive an agreed upon "kill fee," and the producer generally retains the right to use the composer's music and recordings rendered during the trial period.

Credit

Composers should negotiate their credit carefully because a good credit can be vital to getting higher fees for future work. A composer may request a "single card" credit in the main credit sequence of the movie, meaning that his name and credit is the only name to appear on screen at a given time. The producer will usually only promise to provide a credit if they actually use the music in the movie.

Single Song Agreements

Acquiring music for movies can take all kinds of forms. The last agreement that we analyze in this chapter is for a single song that was previously written but unreleased. The filmmaker wanted the composer, who was also a record producer, to record the song so that he could put the recording in a music video that would be shown with the end credits. Because the producer and composer both knew that the producer wanted to use the composer's pre-existing song, the composer had a great deal of leverage. As a consequence, the composer was able to negotiate a license rather than a work for hire.

You could imagine a situation where the filmmaker wanted the composer to create and record an entirely original song. In that case, the contract would look more like a work for hire agreement.

PRO-FILM PRODUCER AGREEMENT

This contract is a standard pro-film producer form of agreement. It makes all the music a Composer creates and records a work for hire for the filmmaker. It also gives the filmmaker the right to demand that the Composer make an unlimited number of changes and revisions in the music without obligating the film producer to pay any additional compensation to the Composer.

[PRODUCTION COMPANY NAME]
[PRODUCTION COMPANY ADDRESS]

Dated as of _____ ____, 2017

[NAME OF COMPOSER]
[COMPOSER ADDRESS]

Re: "[TITLE OF FILM]"/Composer Agreement

Dear _____:

This letter, when executed by you and [PRODUCTION COMPANY NAME] (referred to as "Company" or "us"), will set forth the material terms of the agreement between you and us relating to your creation and delivery to us of musical score for the motion picture tentatively titled "[TITLE OF PICTURE]" (the "Picture").

All of Company's obligations herein are expressly conditioned upon Company's receipt of fully executed copies of this Agreement and the Certificate of Authorship attached hereto and incorporated herein.

1. SERVICES: You will compose, conduct, perform, record, arrange, produce, and mix the score (hereinafter, the "Compositions" or the "Score") for the Picture in accordance with the schedule set forth below. Company hereby engages the services of Composer to write, compose, arrange, adapt, interpolate, orchestrate and conduct the recording of the Score for the Picture and to supervise the music editing, dubbing and so-called "sweetening" of the recording of the entire Score and to deliver a fully recorded and edited digital audio file or DAT or such form as Company requires for all original and duplicate master recordings embodying the Score (the "Master" or the "Masters") all for and as directed by Company. The Master shall be suitable for synchronization with the Picture and with audio-visual discs, cassettes and other audio-visual devices embodying the Picture or substantially all of the Picture ("AV devices") and, upon Company's request, for manufacture of audio products embodying the Score, upon and subject to the terms and conditions herein set forth. Without limiting the generality of the foregoing, but subject to the specific terms of this Agreement, Composer shall perform all services or duties customarily performed in the motion picture industry by a composer, scorer, conductor, arranger and adapter with respect to the Picture. Company shall

have the right to require Composer to make such reasonable changes, modifications or additions to the Score, and to any and all musical compositions, production numbers, or special material composed by Composer hereunder as may be reasonably required by Company.

In this agreement, the Composer is not only responsible for writing the score; she must also deliver the recording of the music.

2. TERM OF ENGAGEMENT: The term of Composer's engagement ("Term") hereof shall commence upon the date set forth above and shall continue until complete and satisfactory delivery of the Score. Composer shall deliver the Master in accordance with a schedule to be provided by Company and, subject to the terms herein, perform any re-writes, if any, requested by Company until a Score commercially and technically satisfactory to Company shall have been delivered.

This provision is very favorable to the filmmaker. It would allow him to order the Composer to make an unlimited number of changes. An alternative is to limit the filmmaker to demand the Composer make one round of changes with a payment schedule for additional changes. See the next contract and the comments for Paragraph 3 for another alternative for the Composer.

3. COMPENSATION: In full and complete consideration for Composer's full and faithful performance of all services hereunder and for all rights granted to Company hereunder (including, without limitation, all right, title and interest in and to the results and proceeds of Composer's services rendered hereunder), provided Composer is not in material breach hereof and subject to Company's rights of suspension and/or termination in the event of force majeure, disability or default, Composer shall be entitled to be paid an "all-in" fee of _____ Thousand Dollars ($___,000), payable in the following manner: (i) _____ Thousand Dollars ($___,000) upon signature of this Agreement by Composer and commencement of Composer's services; and (ii) _____ Thousand Dollars ($___,000) promptly following the satisfactory delivery of the Score as set forth herein. (Notwithstanding the foregoing, no synchronization fees, royalties or other consideration (excluding only mechanical royalties and any public performance fees, if applicable) shall be payable to Composer for the use of the Score, Master or the Compositions (collectively the "Work"), or any part thereof in the Picture or in connection with any advertising, publicizing or exploitation thereof, regardless of the method, media or types of devices utilized for the exhibition or exploitation thereof.

As confirmed in the next paragraph, this agreement is "all-in" meaning (i) the Composer is responsible for any expenses such as studio time and musicians' fees; and (ii) the Composer will make no more money than the fees in Paragraph 4 except for the "writer's share" of public performance royalties and use of some excerpts of the score in an album.

4.   RECORDING COSTS: You will be responsible for all recording costs incurred in connection with the Score and your services hereunder. You agree that you will be solely responsible for, and warrant that you pay, all such recording costs, even in the event such costs exceed the compensation payable to you pursuant to paragraph 4 above.

> The Composer must be careful not to accept a fee that is not adequate to compensate her for her time plus paying for recording costs.

5.   OWNERSHIP: Subject to the terms and conditions hereof, you hereby acknowledge and confirm that we shall own all right, title and interest in and to the Compositions of the Score (including, without limitation, the worldwide copyrights therein including any extensions and/or renewals thereof) and your performances thereon, throughout the universe and in perpetuity, and that we shall have the right to secure registration of copyright in the Score and the Masters (i.e., the individual master recordings comprising said Score) and the individual compositions comprising the Score (the "Compositions") and your performances thereon in our name, pursuant to the United States copyright laws, as "work made for hire." We shall have the exclusive right, insofar as you are concerned, to use and to authorize others to use the Score and any and all portions thereof throughout the world or any part thereof in any manner we see fit, and to refrain from any or all of the foregoing. If for any reason the results and proceeds of your services hereunder are not deemed to be a work made for hire, you shall and hereby do assign such results and proceeds and all rights therein and thereto to us, for use in any and all media (whether now known or hereafter devised), throughout the world, irrevocably and in perpetuity. The payments made by Company or its assignees under this Agreement are deemed to include sufficient remuneration for all so-called rental and lending rights pursuant to any directive, enabling or implementing legislation, laws and regulations enacted by any nation throughout the world, including the member nations of the European Union. You hereby waive all rights of "Droit Moral" or "Moral Rights of Authors" or any similar rights or principles of law which you may now or later have in the Work.

> This is the "work for hire" clause that we discussed in the Introduction. If the Composer cannot get a license deal in which he gets to keep his copyright in the music, he can at least try to get more money for giving up his rights in the music.

6.   CREDIT: Provided you fulfill your material obligations hereunder and further provided that the total background musical score embodied in the Picture as released in the United States consists of the Score, we will accord you the following credit: "Original Music by [NAME OF COMPOSER]." The foregoing credit shall appear in the main credit roll in the Movie. All other aspects of such credit, including size and placement, shall be determined by Licensee.

Credit is often a highly negotiated provision. But in this agreement, the obligation to provide any credit at all only applies if the "total background music" in the movie consists of the score. If another composer is brought in to contribute even incidental passages of music, the filmmaker is not obligated to credit the Composer. Composers should seek a credit provision more like the one in Paragraph 12 of the next agreement.

7. SOUNDTRACK ALBUM:

(a) Should Company enter into an agreement with a record distributor ("Distributor") for the exploitation of the soundtrack album ("Soundtrack Album"), if any, and should the Soundtrack Album or any audio product embody any of the Score as performed by and/or conducted by Composer and/or the Compositions, then Company shall negotiate in good faith with Composer for a royalty with respect to such audio products manufactured and sold hereunder. Any "Artist's royalty" (as such term is customarily known in the music industry) payable to Composer for use of Composer's recorded performance of any composition on the soundtrack album for the Picture shall be computed, reduced and determined in a no less favorable manner as Company's basic royalty under its agreement with any recording company.

As indicated in the Introduction, instead of the Composer agreement going into extensive detail in calculating how the Composer shall be compensated for the use of her music and recorded performances on the soundtrack album, the parties agree to negotiate such terms in good faith at a later time if and when the possibility of a soundtrack album is more certain, such as when a distributor agrees to commercially release the movie.

(b) The parties acknowledge and agree that Composer shall have the right to include selections from the Score on any record album featuring Composer's solo work (with Company's prior written approval which shall not be unreasonably withheld by Company) provided that the following credit be placed by any of such composition's title: "Music from the motion picture feature [TITLE OF PICTURE]."

Although this is generally a pro-producer form, this provision is a big concession to the Composer because, under a work for hire agreement, the composer generally has no rights in the music after delivering it to the producer.

8. PUBLISHING: You acknowledge that we will be the sole owner of all right, title, and interest to the Compositions, including (a) the worldwide copyrights therein and any renewals or extensions thereof, and (b) the sole, exclusive, perpetual worldwide rights of administration, exploitation, and promotion associated therewith. Nothing in this agreement shall limit Composer's right to receive Composer's performing rights income derived from the exploitation of the Score, whether in whole or in part. Composer shall be entitled to receive the "writer's" share in and to the Compositions.

As discussed in the Introduction, this is the one form of income, aside from the inclusion of some of the music in a Composer's own album, that the Composer is entitled to under a work for hire agreement.

9. USE OF NAME, LIKENESS, ETC.: Company may use, and permit others to use, Composer's name, likeness, voice and biographical material in and in connection with the Picture, the Work, any project or product derived from the Picture, if any, and the sale, distribution, promotion and advertising thereof. Company and its assignees shall have the sole and exclusive right to issue publicity concerning the Picture and concerning Composer's services with respect thereto except for Composer's own publicity provided that there shall be no derogatory statements or references concerning the Picture or any party or entity associated with the Picture.

10. MUSIC CUE SHEETS: The music cue sheets for the Picture shall be filed with the proper performance rights societies by Company accurately reflecting Composer's ownership of all Compositions. The cue sheets shall be prepared in consultation with Composer, and Company shall promptly provide Composer with a copy upon its availability. Company will be responsible for submitting cue sheets to distributors (including non-US) and to broadcasters.

The Composer should make sure the producer complies with this provision and files a proper cue sheet before the release of the movie on television or on Internet Video On Demand (VOD).

11. NO OBLIGATION TO EXPLOIT: Company or its assigns shall not be obligated or required to print, publish, promote or otherwise exploit the Work or the Picture, or any part of them, in any manner or to exercise any of the rights granted to Company or its assigns hereunder.

12. NOTICES: All notices which either party is required or may desire to serve hereunder shall be in writing and shall be served to the addresses specified herein. A courtesy copy of such notices shall be sent to: _____, Esq., _____; Tel: (_____) _____-_____; E-Mail: _____.

13. FEDERAL COMMUNICATIONS ACT: Reference is made to Section 507 of the Federal Communications Act which makes it a criminal offense for any person in connection with the production or preparation of a picture or program intended for broadcasting to accept or pay, or agree to accept or pay, money, service or other valuable consideration for the inclusion of any matter or thing as a part of such picture or program, without disclosing the same to Company thereof prior to the telecast of such picture or program. Composer warrants and agrees that Composer has not and will not accept or pay any money, service, or other

valuable consideration for the inclusion of any plug, reference, product identification, or other matter in any material prepared or performed by Composer hereunder.

14. INDEPENDENT CONTRACTOR: Composer warrants that he or she is an independent contractor and is not an employee of Company. As an independent contractor, Composer is responsible and liable for any income tax, unemployment insurance, FICA (Social Security), or any other payment normally associated with an employee relationship.

15. ASSIGNMENT: Company shall have the right to assign this Agreement at any time to any person or entity. Neither this Agreement nor any rights hereunder are assignable by Composer at any time to any person or entity. This Agreement inures to the benefit of Company's successors, assigns, licensees, grantees, and associated, affiliated and subsidiary companies.

16. ADDITIONAL COVENANTS OF COMPOSER: Composer agrees that Composer shall:

(a) Not disclose to any party information relating to the subject matter of this Agreement or to the activities of Company with respect to the Picture or otherwise except: (i) to Composer's financial and legal advisors; and (ii) regarding any incidental and non-derogatory references by Composer to third parties concerning Composer's Score in connection with the Picture.

(b) Not incur any liability or expense on Company's account without Company's prior written approval (except as otherwise stated herein), and if such approval is given, Composer will provide Company with any information necessary to satisfy such obligation, including copies of any necessary agreements.

17. GOVERNING LAW; DISPUTE RESOLUTION: This Agreement will in all respects be governed by and interpreted, construed and enforced in accordance with the laws of the State of New York. Any dispute or controversy arising under this Agreement (including, without limitation, the validity and enforce ability of this Agreement) shall be subject to arbitration in the State of New York in accordance with the Rules of the American Arbitration Association as decided by One (1) arbiter mutually approved by the parties and whose decision shall be binding, final and non-appealable and may be entered in a court of competent jurisdiction. The prevailing party shall be entitled to reasonable outside attorneys' fees and costs. For the purpose of enforcing such arbitrator's decision, any action arising out of or relating to this Agreement and its enforcement will have jurisdiction and venue in a state or federal court situated within the State of New York, and the parties consent and submit themselves to the personal jurisdiction of said courts for all such purposes.

18. REMEDIES: The parties acknowledge and agree that Composer's remedy for any breach of a term of this Agreement by Company shall be limited to monetary damages at law. Composer shall not have the right to rescind this Agreement or to any equitable or

injunctive relief or otherwise in which there would be an interference or prevention of Company's right to finance, produce, market, distribute or otherwise exploit any and all rights in and to the Picture.

19. DVD/BLU-RAY AND SOUNDTRACK ALBUM: Provided that Composer has rendered services as stated herein and Composer is not in breach of any material term stated herein, Company shall provide Composer with one (1) DVD or Blu-Ray copy and (1) soundtrack album CD (if and when available) of the Picture in its completed form which shall be used by Composer solely for private, non-commercial or resume reel use.

20. ENTIRE AGREEMENT; MODIFICATIONS: This instrument constitutes the entire agreement of the parties hereto relating to the subject matter specified herein. This Agreement can be modified or terminated only by a written instrument executed by both Composer and Company or Company's successors and assigns. The parties acknowledge and agree that signatures may be by hand, facsimile, electronic or optically scanned (e.g., pdf) and any of these methods shall be deemed as binding on the parties.

21. MISCELLANEOUS: You warrant and represent that neither the Score, the Masters or the Compositions shall infringe the rights of any third party, and that you are not under any disability, restriction or prohibition, whether contractual or otherwise, with respect to the performance of your services hereunder. Without limiting the foregoing, you specifically warrant and represent that (a) you have the full right, power, and authority to enter into this agreement, (b) you have obtained all requisite rights, clearances and permission to enter into this agreement from all applicable third parties, including, without limitation, [record company], [publishing company], and each of their respective affiliates, and (c) we shall not be required to make any payments of any nature for, or in connection with, the rendition of your services or the acquisition, exercise or exploitation of rights by us pursuant to this agreement, except as specifically provided herein (it being understood, for the avoidance of doubt, that you shall be solely responsible for any artist and other third party royalties or other sums payable arising out of our exploitation of the Masters, Compositions and other rights granted hereunder). You further warrant and represent that you have consulted with counsel with respect to the execution of this agreement. You agree to and do hereby indemnify, save and hold us harmless of and from any and all liability, loss, damage, cost or expense (including reasonable attorneys' fees) arising out of or connected with any breach or alleged breach of this letter agreement or any claim which is inconsistent with any of the warranties or representations made by you in this letter agreement.

If the foregoing terms are acceptable, kindly sign on the signature line set forth below and fax this letter to our attention for countersignature. This letter with the Certificate of

Authorship, attached hereto, shall constitute the entire agreement between the parties and can only be modified in writing.

Very truly yours,

[PRODUCTION COMPANY NAME]

_____

An Authorized Signatory

ACCEPTED AND AGREED IN
ALL RESPECTS:

_____

COMPOSER S.S. No.: _____

This bit of boilerplate drives home that the Composer is indeed transferring the copyright in both the recording and music to the producer. The Composer also waives "moral rights," which means that the producer can make any changes to the score that she wishes whether the Composer approves or not.

EXHIBIT "A"

CERTIFICATE OF AUTHORSHIP

For One Dollar ($1.00) and other good and valuable consideration, the receipt and sufficiency of which is hereby acknowledged, the undersigned hereby certifies that the undersigned will write or has written an original musical score (the "Score"), and will produce and record or has produced and recorded master recordings embodying the Score, each intended for initial use in the theatrical motion picture currently entitled "[TITLE OF PICTURE]" (the "Picture"), at the request of [PRODUCTION COMPANY NAME] ("Company") pursuant to a contract of employment between Company and the undersigned dated as of _____, 2017 (the "Agreement") (the Score, the Masters and all other results and proceeds of the undersigned's services hereunder and under the Agreement are hereinafter referred to as the "Work"). The undersigned hereby acknowledges that the Work has been specially ordered or commissioned by Company for use as part of a contribution to a collective work or as part of the Picture or other audio-visual work, that the Work constitutes and shall constitute a work-made-for-hire as defined in the United States Copyright Act of 1976, as amended, that Company is and shall be the author of said work-made-for-hire and the owner of all rights in and to the Work, including, without limitation, the copyright therein and thereto throughout the universe for the initial term and any and all extensions and renewals thereof, and that Company has and shall have the right to make such changes therein and such uses thereof as it may deem necessary or desirable including but not limited, to the right to include the Work in the Picture in all media now and hereafter devised and on phonorecords and trailers, advertisements, promotions and co-promotions with respect thereto. To the extent that the Work is not deemed a work-made-for-hire, and to the extent that Company is not deemed to be the author thereof in any territory of the universe, the undersigned hereby irrevocably assigns the Work to Company (including the entire copyright therein and any extensions and/or renewals thereof), and grants to Company all rights therein, including, without limitation, any so-called "Rental and Lending Rights" and "Neighbouring Rights" pursuant to any European Economic Community directives and/or enabling or implementing legislation, laws or regulations (collectively, "EEC Rights"), throughout the universe in perpetuity, but in no event shall the period of the assignment of rights being granted to Company hereunder be less than the period of copyright and any renewals and extensions thereof.

Company's rights hereunder shall include, without limitation, the rights to authorize, prohibit and/or control the renting, lending, fixation, reproduction, performance and/or other exploitation of the Work in any and all media and by any and all means now known or hereafter devised, as such rights may be conferred upon the undersigned under any applicable laws, regulations or directives, including, without limitation, all so-called EEC Rights. The undersigned hereby acknowledges that the compensation paid hereunder and under the Agreement includes adequate and equitable remuneration for the EEC Rights and constitutes a complete buy-out of all EEC Rights. In connection with the foregoing, the undersigned hereby irrevocably grants to Company, throughout the universe, in perpetuity, the right to collect and retain for Company's own account any and all amounts payable to the undersigned with respect to EEC Rights and hereby irrevocably direct any collecting societies or other persons or entities receiving such amounts to pay such amounts to Company.

The undersigned hereby waives all rights of droit moral or "moral right of authors" or any similar rights or principles of law which the undersigned may now or later have in the Work. The undersigned warrants and represents that the undersigned has the right to execute this Certificate, that the Work is and shall be new and original with the undersigned and not an imitation or copy of any other material and that the Work is and shall be capable of copyright protection throughout the universe, does not and shall not, (i) violate the trademark, service mark, or copyright of any third party; and (ii) to the best of undersigned's knowledge, violate or infringe upon any common law or statutory right of any party including, without limitation, contractual rights, and rights of privacy, or constitute unfair competition and is not and shall not be the subject of any litigation or of any claim that might give rise to litigation, including, without limitation, any claim by any copyright proprietor of any so-called "sampled" material contained in the Work. The undersigned further warrants and represents that the undersigned has attained the legal age of majority in the United States, and is at least eighteen (18) years of age. The undersigned further warrants and represents that, to the best of undersigned's knowledge, the undersigned will not utilize any persons who have not attained the legal age of majority and will not utilize the services of any undocumented alien in rendering services hereunder. The undersigned shall indemnify and hold Company, the corporations comprising Company, and its and their employees, officers, agents, assignees and licensees, harmless from and against any losses, costs, liabilities, claims, damages or expenses (including, without limitation, court costs and attorneys' fees, whether or not in connection with litigation) arising out of any claim or action by a third party which arises from a breach of any warranty or representation made by the undersigned in this Certificate or in the Agreement. The undersigned agrees to execute any documents consistent herewith and do any other acts consistent with this Agreement which may reasonably be required by Company or its assignees or licensees to further evidence or effectuate Company's rights as set forth in this Certificate or in the Agreement. Upon the undersigned's failure to do so after ten (10) business days of Company's written request, the undersigned hereby appoints Company as the undersigned's attorney-in-fact for such purposes (it being acknowledged by the undersigned that such appointment is irrevocable and shall be deemed a power coupled with an interest), with full power of substitution and delegation. Company shall promptly provide the undersigned with any documents exercised pursuant to the foregoing power of attorney.

The undersigned further acknowledges that in the event of any breach by Company of this Certificate, the undersigned will be limited to the undersigned's remedy at law for damages (if any) and will not have the right to terminate or rescind this Certificate or to enjoin the distribution, exploitation or advertising of the Picture or any materials in connection therewith, that nothing herein shall obligate Company to use the undersigned's services or the Work in the Picture or to produce, distribute or advertise the Picture, and that this Certificate shall be governed by the laws of the State of New York.

Company's rights with respect to the Work may be freely assigned and licensed and its rights shall be binding upon the undersigned and inure to the benefit of any such assignee or licensee.

The undersigned affirms and acknowledges that the undersigned has been advised and counseled with respect to the negotiation and execution of this document by an attorney of the undersigned's own choice or acknowledges waiver of such advice and counsel.

IN WITNESS WHEREOF, the undersigned has signed this Certificate as of _____, 2017.

    Signature
    Printed Name: [NAME OF COMPOSER]
    Social Security No.

AGREED AND ACCEPTED:

[PRODUCTION COMPANY NAME]

By: _____
    An Authorized Signatory

_____ ____, 2017

COMPOSER-FRIENDLY AGREEMENT

The second agreement is much more composer-friendly. It is not a work for hire agreement. Instead, the Composer merely grants the filmmaker the right to use the music in his movie and retains all other rights, except that the Composer agrees not to license the music for another full length film for a period of time. In addition, the second contract limits the time that the filmmaker can make the Composer make changes to two days after the Composer delivers the final mix. It also provides for a "kill fee" if the filmmaker decides that the music delivered by the Composer is unacceptable.

[PRODUCTION COMPANY NAME]
[PRODUCTION COMPANY ADDRESS]

Dated as of _____ ____, 2017

[NAME OF COMPOSER]
[COMPOSER ADDRESS]

RE: Original Music for the motion picture feature, currently entitled [TITLE OF PICTURE]

Dear Colleagues,

This letter shall confirm the agreement (the "Agreement") by and between [PRODUCTION COMPANY NAME] located at [ADDRESS] ("Company") at _____, and [COMPOSER], at _____ ("Composer") in connection with the motion picture feature presently entitled [TITLE OF PICTURE] (which together with all trailers, promotion, publicity, advertising and DVD supplemental material therefrom, is collectively referred to as the "Picture"). All of Company's obligations herein are expressly conditioned upon Company's receipt of fully executed copies of this Agreement.

1.   Company hereby engages Composer to compose, arrange and produce original musical compositions (the "Compositions"), as further described in the attached Schedule A, for the score of the Picture, and to record and produce master recordings embodying the Compositions (the "Masters") used in the Picture. The music composed hereunder and all other results and proceeds of Composer's services are referred to herein as the "Work."

Similar to the first agreement, this deal requires the Composer to produce as well as write the score.

2. Composer will render your services hereunder during the Term, as defined below, on a first priority basis. You will deliver to us the final mix of the Score no later than _____, 2017.

This provision is favorable to the Composer as it does not require him to turn down other jobs while he is working on this movie.

3.   Composer shall deliver the Work to Company pursuant to the following schedule (the "Delivery Schedule"):

(a) Composer shall begin the production of the Work on approximately _____, 2017; (or upon signing of the agreement and first payment, whichever comes first).

(b) Composer shall essentially complete the work by _____, 2017. Company shall be entitled to hear the Work prior to the final mix, which shall be subject to final approval by an individual designated by Company (or Company's designee) for such final approval. Composer agrees to be available for up to two (2) days of consultation, and shall make such revisions during that time in the Work as Company may reasonably require, provided that if after such revisions are made, and Company does not accept the Work as acceptable, then Company shall pay Composer a "kill fee" of 25% of the total compensation otherwise payable under Paragraph 5 below in addition to the initial fee and Composer shall retain all rights in the Work and Company shall have no right to use the Work for any purpose.

> This is far better than the first agreement, where the Composer agrees to keep changing the music at the producer's request without limitation to the number of times the producer can demand changes.

(c) Upon Company's approval of final mixes of the fully produced Work, company shall make delivery ("Delivery") of the Work to _____ ("Company's Designee") via disc(s), DAT(s) or computer files (at Company's discretion). Simultaneously with Delivery of the Work or prior to Delivery, Composer shall submit a properly completed music cue sheet for the Picture, provided Composer shall not be responsible for procuring or providing information needed to complete the cue sheets related to third party licensed music. Company shall be responsible for filing final cue sheets to Composer's performance rights organization prior to the initial release of the Picture.

> See the Introduction for explanation of a cue sheet and its importance.

(d) Composer shall deliver all Materials to Company's Designee, pursuant to the Delivery Schedule defined herein, to the following address and contact: _____

4.   Composer shall be responsible for the production of the Work, the payment for all expenses related to the production of the Work, including, but not limited to, the hiring of musicians, the booking of recording sessions, the programmer and engineer. Composer shall not be responsible for a music editor. Company shall have approval over all stages of production of the Work and all constituent elements thereof including the final composition and orchestration. In addition, Composer shall consult with Company throughout the production of the Work.

> As with the first agreement, this Composer deal is "all-in," that is, the Composer is responsible for expenses.

5.   The term of this Agreement (the "Term") shall commence upon delivery of first payment and the signing of this agreement. The Term shall end upon delivery to Company of final Work (i.e., final mixes of the Masters), delivery of all documentation necessary for the full exercise of all rights granted hereunder and completion of all services required by Company hereunder but shall not extend past _____, 2017. Time and full compliance of all delivery requirements are of the essence of this Agreement. During the Term, Composer shall not, without prior written consent of Company and/or Company's Designee, render or agree to render any services of any kind for any other person or entity which would or might conflict with, interfere with or prevent the complete rendition of the services required to be rendered by Composer hereunder. Notwithstanding the foregoing, the Work shall be delivered in accordance with Company's production schedule.

6.   In consideration of the rights granted by Composer hereunder, Composer's services and the use by Company of the results and proceeds thereof, Company shall pay to Composer an aggregate amount of _____ Thousand Dollars ($_____,000.00) (the "Fee"), which shall be inclusive of any and all expenses incurred by Composer in the production and delivery of the Work to Company, payable as follows: (i) $_____,000.00 after (a) commencement of Composers' services hereunder and (B) receipt of an executed copy of the Agreement; (ii) the final $_____,000 upon delivery to Company of the Materials. But Composer has agreed to defer the money due in _____, 2015 until a mutually agreeable time not to exceed six months (_____, 2015). All payments made by Company and/or Company's Designee to Composer hereunder shall be inclusive of any sales tax or use taxes required to be paid by Composer to any governmental authority.

7.   (a) It is expressly agreed that Composer is performing services hereunder as an Independent Contractor. Composer retains the copyright to the supplied Work but irrevocably grants Company, all synchronization, performance rights and licenses, the rights to secure copyrights throughout the world, the absolute and unrestricted right and permission to reproduce, adapt, edit, copyright, televise, exhibit, distribute, license, disseminate, display and otherwise exploit in any or all markets and media (collectively "use") the Compositions and Masters that Composer supplies to the production in the context of this film. This grant of rights is made without limitation upon time, circumstance, location, market or medium or use of this material in and related to the motion picture feature tentatively entitled "[TITLE OF PICTURE]."

Unlike the first agreement, here, the Composer retains his copyright in the music—both the underlying music and the recordings. This is a huge difference, as it allows the Composer to re-use the music and make additional money from exploiting it.

(b) Notwithstanding the foregoing, Company acknowledges that Composer is a member of ASCAP and the worldwide non-dramatic public performance royalties in the Work shall be licensed through ASCAP. Company hereby acknowledges Composer's one hundred percent (100%) of the writer's share of the worldwide non-dramatic public performance royalties in the Work; and one hundred percent (100%) of the publisher's share of the worldwide non-dramatic public performance royalties in the Work with Composer's music publishing designee, _____ (ASCAP).

Unlike the first agreement, here, the Composer will collect 100% of the public performance royalties.

(c) Composer shall own and separately administrate one hundred percent (100%) of the publishing and one hundred percent (100%) of the so-called writer's share of the publishing rights in and to the Compositions. Composer shall own any and all rights in and to the Masters prepared in connection with the Picture subject to the terms stated herein.

(d) Company and its assigns, licensees, successors and designees shall have the unrestricted right of access to use the Compositions composed by Composer and the masters recorded by Composer in all media, now known or hereafter devised, throughout the universe, in perpetuity in connection with the Picture.

(e) Without limiting the generality of the foregoing, Composer hereby acknowledges that Company shall have the right to synchronize, perform, and use the Work in the soundtrack of the Picture, and uses ancillary to the Picture, including, without limitation, in trailers, promotions and co-promotions, and advertisements for any or all of the foregoing, and in connection therewith, the parties acknowledge and agree that Company shall have the perpetual right, throughout the universe, to exploit the Work in or related to the Picture in all media including, but not limited to, theatrical release, subscription, satellite, pay/cable and free TV, audio-visual devices (including but not limited to video-cassettes and discs), trailers, advertisements and publicity therefore, any computer-assisted media including but not limited to CD-ROM, CD-I and similar disc systems, interactive cable and in all other uses associated with any new technology and media, whether now known or hereafter devised. Subject to the terms stated in this Agreement, any and all rights to the Work are owned by Composer.

(f) Company shall be free, at its sole discretion, to make any further use, recording, exploitation, publishing, and distribution of the Work and every arrangement, version, orchestration and adaptation thereof, and of recordings thereof as Company may desire in the Picture and any promotion or advertising for the Picture, free and clear of any and all claims by, or asserted, and all claims by, or asserted on behalf of, Composer or any third parties (including, without limitation, any and all composers, musicians and other persons who provide services, performances or materials in connection with the performance of the Work).

(g) Composer agrees to look solely to such society and/or Composer's music publishing designee for such royalties and waive any claim against Company for its publisher's share of such royalties received by Company. Notwithstanding the foregoing, if Company shall receive monies due to Composer, Composer's performing rights society or its publishing designee, then Company shall remit such monies promptly to Composer, Composer's performing rights society or its publishing designee.

(h) Composer shall have the right but not the obligation to exploit the Work in any other form or manner within Composer's sole discretion, throughout the universe and in perpetuity for any purpose except (i) in another feature length motion picture including documentary or "feature" motion picture for a period of three (3) years from the commercial release of the Picture, except with the prior written consent of Company; and (ii) use the Work in an album subject to subparagraph (i) below.

This pro-Composer provision allows the Composer to exploit the compositions and the masters for any other purpose except in another movie or full length album. So, for instance, the Composer can license the compositions and masters for ad campaigns or video games and collect 100% of the revenues.

(i)   The parties acknowledge and agree that Composer shall have the right to include selections from the Work on any record album featuring Composer's solo work (with Company's prior written approval which shall not be unreasonably withheld by Company) provided that the following credit be placed by any of such composition's title: "Music from [Title of Picture]"

(j)   Company, its successors and assigns shall have the right to make, distribute, or sell or authorize others to do the same, any phonorecords, including, without limitation, discs, tapes and devices of any speed or size of type, whether now known or hereafter devised, for the recording of the music material in any soundtrack album(s) for the Picture (the "Soundtrack Album"). The parties shall enter into negotiations in good faith terms for Composer's participation in such Soundtrack Album subject to record company's approval.

8.   Company agrees not to exploit or use the Work other than as embodied in the soundtrack of Picture or in advertisements and promotional materials for the Picture. In connection with any other use or exploitation of the Work not set forth herein, Company shall consult with Composer in connection therewith; which such consent shall not be unreasonably withheld. In the case of a soundtrack album, Company shall consult with Composer whereby an agreement shall be negotiated in good faith.

9.   The parties acknowledge and agree that Company is not and shall not be a signatory to any union, guild or collective bargaining organization concerning any musicians or performers who have rendered or shall render services in connection with the Work.

10. Composer hereby warrants, represents and covenants to Company as follows:

(a) Composer hereby represents and warrants to Company that Composer has the right to enter into this Agreement and perform all of its obligations pursuant to this Agreement.

(b) Composer shall be the sole author of all material contained in the Work; and that the Work shall be completely original with Composer and shall not infringe upon or violate any copyright, common law right or any other right, of any person, firm or corporation;

(c) That neither the Work nor any element of, or material contained in, the Work will infringe upon or violate the right of privacy of, or right of publicity of, or constitute a libel or slander against, or defame, or violate any copyright, trademark or service mark, common law or other right, of any person, firm or corporation or violate any other applicable law;

(d) Composer has acquired all rights necessary to its grant of rights to Company hereunder, including without limitation, all copyrights, music synchronization and music performance rights licenses;

(e) That no part of the rights herein granted to Company have been transferred to any third party and that said rights are free of any liens, claims and encumbrances whatsoever in favor of any other party, and that said rights and the full right to exercise the same, have not been in any way limited, diminished, or impaired; and that there are no claims, litigation or other proceedings pending, outstanding or threatened adversely affecting or that would or might in any way prejudice Company's rights hereunder.

11. (a) Composer assumes liability for, and hereby agrees to indemnify, defend, protect, save and hold harmless Company, its partners, divisions, subsidiary and affiliates, divisions and companies, distributors, assigns, licensees and the respective shareholders, directors, officers, employees and agents of the foregoing (the "Company's Indemnified Parties") from and against any and all claims, actions, suits, costs, liabilities, judgments, obligations, losses, penalties, expenses or damages (including, without limitation, reasonable legal fees and expenses) of whatsoever kind and nature imposed on, incurred by or asserted against any of Company's Indemnified Parties, arising out of any breach of any representation or warranty made by Composer herein or out of any other breach by Composer of this Agreement.

(b) Company assumes liability for, and shall indemnify, defend, protect, save and hold harmless Composer from and against any and all claims, actions, suits, costs, liabilities, judgments, obligations, losses, penalties, expenses or damages (including, without limitation, legal fees and expenses) of whatsoever kind and nature imposed on, incurred by or asserted against Composer arising out of any breach or alleged breach by Company of any representation, warranty or covenant made, or obligation assumed, by Company pursuant to this Agreement.

(c) In order to seek or receive indemnification hereunder:

(i) the party seeking indemnification must have promptly notified the other of any claim or litigation to which the indemnification relates; and

ii) the party seeking indemnification must have afforded the other the opportunity to participate in any compromise, settlement, litigation or other resolution or disposition of such claim or litigation.

12. Provided that Composer fully performs all of her material obligations hereunder and is not in material breach of any of Composer's representations, warranties, obligations or agreements hereunder and the Work is synchronized to the Picture's visuals, Company shall accord Composer a credit substantially in the following form: "Original Music by [NAME OF COMPOSER]".

> These credit provisions are much more favorable to the Composer than the first agreement, and composers should seek to include these terms into any agreement they sign. A good credit can be essential in advancing a Composer's career and securing higher fees in future projects.

(a) Such credit shall be on a separate card, in the main credit roll in the Picture.

(b) Credit in the same form as set forth herein shall be provided in any paid advertising and posters for the Picture, wherever the full billing block for the Picture appears.

> The "billing block" is the list of names on the bottom portion of the official movie poster. In the layout of film posters and other film advertising, the billing block is usually set in a highly condensed typeface. A successful Composer can negotiate for a larger size name.

(c) Except as set forth above, any and all other characteristics of Composer's credit shall be at Company's sole discretion. No casual or inadvertent failure to comply with the provisions of this Paragraph 11 nor any failure by third parties to comply with the credit provision shall constitute a breach of this agreement by Company. In the event of any failure by Company to comply with the foregoing credit provisions, and upon written notice from Composer thereof, Company shall take reasonable steps to prospectively cure any such failure which is economically practicable to cure (i.e., no recall of copies).

> An established Composer can negotiate for a credit in advertising any time the director or principal actors receive credit.

13. Composer and Company are independent contractors with respect to each other, and nothing herein shall create any association, partnership, joint venture or agency relationship between them. Composer shall be fully responsible for all persons employed by it, in connection with its performance hereunder, whether as independent contractors or as employees, and shall be fully responsible for them, for all compensation and/or withholding

taxes, worker's compensation insurance or other required payments in connection with such persons, except as otherwise specifically and explicitly provided herein.

14. Company may use, and permit others to use, Composer's name, approved likeness, voice and approved biographical material (which shall not be unreasonably withheld or delayed by Composer) in and in connection with the Picture, the Work, any project or product derived from the Picture, if any, and the sale, distribution, promotion and advertising thereof. Except as otherwise stated under this Agreement, Company and its assignees shall have the sole and exclusive right to issue publicity concerning the Picture and concerning Composer's services with respect thereto except for Composer's own publicity provided that there shall be no derogatory statements or references concerning the Picture or any party or entity associated with the Picture

15. (a) All notices and other communications from either party to the other hereunder shall be in writing and shall be deemed received when delivered in person or five (5) days after deposited in the United States Mails, postage prepaid, certified or registered mail addressed to the other party at the address specified at the beginning of the Agreement, or at such other address as such other party may supply by written notice.

(b) Composer shall execute any and all further documents that Company may deem necessary and proper to carry out the purposes of this Agreement.

(c) This Agreement contains the full and complete understanding among the parties hereto, supersedes all prior agreements and understandings, whether written or oral pertaining thereto and cannot be modified except by a written instrument signed by each party hereto.

(d) This Agreement is to be governed by and construed in accordance with the laws of the State of New York, applicable to contracts entered into and to be fully performed therein. Any litigation, action or proceeding ensuing out of or relating to this agreement shall be instituted in a court of competent jurisdiction (whether state or federal) in New York.

(e) Composer shall not assign any of its rights or obligations hereunder without the prior written consent of Company, and any purported assignment without such prior written consent, shall be null and void and of no force and effect. Company shall have the right to assign this Agreement at any time to any person or entity, provided that person or entity which assumes Company's obligations in a writing signed by such assignee's duly authorized signatory.

(f) The parties acknowledge and agree that Composer's remedy for any breach of a term of this Agreement by Company shall be limited to monetary damages at law. Composer shall not have the right to rescind this Agreement or to any equitable or injunctive relief or otherwise in which there would be an interference or prevention of Company's right to finance, produce, market, distribute or otherwise exploit any and all rights in and to the Picture.

(g)   Provided that Composer has rendered services as stated herein and Composer is not in breach of any material term stated herein, Company agrees to provide a DVD of the Picture in its completed form in a professional format (preferably mini-DV or Video DVD) for use solely as a sample of Composer's professional work, not for any commercial use or distribution.

(h)   All representations and warranties contained herein or made in writing by Composer in connection herewith shall survive the execution, delivery, suspension and termination of this Agreement and any provision herein.

(i)   No waiver by either party hereto, or any failure by any party hereto to keep or perform any covenant or condition of this Agreement, shall be deemed to be a waiver or breach of any preceding or succeeding covenant or condition.

(j)   If any part of this Agreement shall be held to be void, invalid or unenforceable, it shall not affect the validity of the balance of this Agreement.

(k)   The parties acknowledge and agree that this Agreement may be signed in counterparts (with the counterparts deemed to be one fully executed document) either manually, by facsimile or optical image scanner (e.g., pdf) and such signatures shall be deemed as binding upon the parties.

Kindly indicate your agreement to and acceptance of the foregoing by signing the enclosed copy of this Agreement where indicated below.

Company: [PRODUCTION COMPANY NAME]

By: _____

Print Name: _____

Its: _____

Composer: _____

By: _____

Print Name: _____

Its: _____

AGREEMENT FOR A SINGLE SONG FOR A FILM

This agreement is for the recording of a single song that the Composer previously wrote but never recorded. Similar to the second agreement, the Composer grants a non-exclusive license to the filmmaker and retains all other rights in the song.

This agreement (the "Agreement") is entered into as of _____ ___, 2017 (the "Effective Date") by _____ LLC (the "Licensee") with principal offices at _____, and _____ _____ (the "Composer/Producer") with an address at _____.

Licensee and Composer/Producer shall each be referred to as a "Party" or collectively be referred to as the "Parties".

For good and valuable consideration, the receipt and adequacy of which is hereby acknowledged, the Parties agree as follows:

1. <u>PRODUCTION</u>: The Composer/Producer shall produce a recording of a pre-existing musical composition titled "_____" (the "Song") written by Composer/Producer. That recording shall be hereafter referred to as the "Recording" and shall be inclusive of the Song. The Recording will feature the vocal performance of Ms. _____ ("Artist") who is featured in the movie titled "_____" (the "Movie"). The recording shall take place on a date and time and at a location approved by Licensee.

Since the Composer/Producer is retaining rights in the Recording, she needs to have a separate agreement with the Artist so the Composer/Producer and the Artist know their respective rights and obligations with regard to the use of the Recording outside of the movie.

2. <u>NON-EXCLUSIVE LICENSE</u>:

(a) Composer/Producer hereby grants to Licensee a non-exclusive license to use the Recording, including the Song, in the Movie in any manner determined exclusively by Licensee, and to distribute the Movie in all media now known or hereby developed, throughout the world (the "Territory") for the duration of the Term (as defined below), as well as in advertising, publicity, and promotion of the Movie.

Since this is a non-exclusive license, the Composer/Producer retains the right to use the Recording, including the Song, outside of the movie and retain all the income. In this case, the Composer/Producer even retained the right to license the Song and Recording for use in another movie.

(b) Licensee shall be permitted to edit or modify the Recording or perform post-production mastering alterations to the Recording without the prior written consent of Composer/Producer. Nothing in this Agreement requires the Licensee to use the Recording in the Movie and the Licensee may use the Recording in whole or in part in Licensee's sole discretion. All rights in and to the Movie shall be owned solely by Licensee, and Composer/Producer shall have no rights therein.

3.   VIDEO: Composer/Producer hereby grants to Licensee the non-exclusive right to use the Recording, inclusive of the Song, in a video to promote the Movie (the "Video"), and to distribute the Video in all media now known or hereby developed, throughout the world (the "Territory") for the duration of the Term (as defined below).

> In this case, the licensee movie producer wanted to make a video including the Recording to promote the movie.

4.   PUBLICITY: Licensee shall have the right to publish, advertise, announce and use the Composer/Producer's name, approved likeness and bio in connection with Licensee's exploitation of the Movie or the Video.

5.   CONSIDERATION: As complete and exclusive consideration for the services rendered and the rights granted to Licensee hereunder, Licensee is obligated to pay Composer/Producer the sum of _____ ($_____) (the "Composer/Producer Fee"). The Composer/Producer Fee includes her travel to and accommodations in New York City. Composer/Producer hereby acknowledges that Licensee has paid the Composer/Producer Fee in full.

> In this case the Composer/Producer had traveled from L.A. to New York and recorded the Song for the licensee filmmaker and the licensee had already paid her fee by the time I was asked to do the paperwork.

6.   TERM: All licenses and rights granted in this Agreement shall commence on the Effective Date and extend for the duration of the copyrights in the Recording, the Song and the Video.

7.   LIMITATIONS: Composer/Producer reserves all of its right title and interest in the Recording and the Song not expressly granted herein.

8.   CREDIT:

Licensee shall accord Composer/Producer screen credit in the Movie, substantially as set forth below, with respect to the Recording and the Song:

"[Name of Song]"
Words and Music by _____
Performed by [Artist]
Copyright (P) © 2017
Produced and arranged by _____

The foregoing credit shall appear in the main credit roll in the Movie. All other aspects of such credit, including size and placement, shall be determined by Licensee.

9.   CUE SHEET: Licensee agrees to prepare an accurate music cue sheet for the Movie and the Video and file the cue sheet with ASCAP, with a copy provided to Composer/Producer, within 30 days after completion of the Movie.

In this case, ASCAP was the Producer/Composer's PRO.

10. NOTICES: Notices in regard to this Agreement shall be delivered by certified mail at to each Party at the addresses listed above or to a new address provided by either Party.

11. REPRESENTATION AND WARRANTY: Composer/Producer represents and warrants that Composer/Producer is the sole author of the Song, that the Song is completely original and contains no samples or other third party created content; that there are no liens or encumbrances on the Song and that Composer/Producer has the full right, power and authority to enter into this Agreement and to grant the rights agreed to be granted hereunder.

12. INDEMNITY: Composer/Producer shall at all times indemnify and hold harmless Licensee from and against any and all third party claims, damages, liabilities, costs and expenses, including legal expenses and reasonable counsel fees, arising out of breach by Composer/Producer of any warranty, representation or agreement made by them herein.

13. MISCELLANEOUS: Notwithstanding any provision of this Agreement to the contrary, nothing herein shall be construed to create a partnership or joint venture between the Parties, to authorize either Party to act as agent for the other, to permit either Party to undertake any agreement for the other, or to use the name or identifying mark of the other, all except as it is specifically provided herein. Neither Party shall be construed for any purpose to be an employee subject to the control or direction of the other. This Agreement is binding and shall inure to the benefit of the Parties' respective successors and assigns. Licensee may not assign any rights or obligations under this Agreement without the express written consent of Composer/Producer, which shall not be unreasonably withheld or delayed. This Agreement contains the entire understanding of the Parties relating to the

subject matter hereof and supersedes any prior understanding or agreements. This Agreement may not be modified or amended except in writing signed by each of the Parties. This Agreement shall be governed by and construed in accordance with the laws of the State of New York, without giving effect to its principles of conflicts of laws. This Agreement can be signed in counterparts.

IN WITNESS WHEREOF, the Parties hereto have executed this Agreement as of the day and year first written above.

Composer/Producer

_____ LLC

_____

_____

Authorized Signatory

Name: _____

Title: _____

CHAPTER 8

LIVE PERFORMANCE AND BOOKING AGREEMENTS (A LAWYER'S GUIDE TO STRUCTURING PAID MUSIC GIGS)

INTRODUCTION: PASSING THE HAT—THE TIP JAR, DEALING WITH VENUES, AND USING PROMOTERS

This chapter focuses on the business of live music performances. We will focus on what indie musicians face when starting out as well as artists who are more advanced in their careers. We will discuss how it really works in the trenches and how to navigate over that rough terrain for the best outcomes.

When an indie musician is just starting her career, playing for no money can be good exposure. However, eventually, you will want to make money from your music so you can quit your day gig. Live performance is one of the main income streams that can support indie musicians in addition to record sales, merch, sync placements, and public performance royalties.

Part I of this Introduction provides tips for artists just starting out, as well as emerging live bands or singer-songwriters. This also includes advice from Nashville based singer/songwriter, Jennifer Sullivan, and interviews with an indie rock promoter and promoter-publicist, Fiona Bloom.

Part II discusses artists who are successful enough to work with booking agents and includes a booking agency's standard-form contract with a venue, which is designed to be good for the artist and the agent. Included are comments showing the changes that the venue would likely request.

Part III deals with the way that the Internet has converged with live performance to generate new revenue streams for both artists and venues. It includes an interview with Spike Wilner, a jazz pianist and co-owner of Smalls, a jazz club in Greenwich Village, about a new "Revenue Share" program which offers artists the opportunity to make money by allowing off-site fans to listen to live performances on demand.

Part I: New and Emerging Artists

Passing the Hat—Tip Jar

There are many venues, such as small clubs and restaurants, that will allow musicians to book a set and entertain diners or drinkers for free and then "pass the hat" after their session. For tips from Nashville based singer/songwriter, Jennifer Sullivan, on maximizing contributions to the "tip jar," see her comments below. Performing in public places, such as on the street or in subways, for gratuities ("busking"), is another way to make money from live performance. In fact, New York City has a special program that allows musicians to busk legally. Performers can audition for "Music Under New York (MUNY)," an official program that sets up schedules of performances and locations for MUNY members.

Jennifer Sullivan's Thoughts on the Tip Jar

"I make an average of $50/hour in tips at these kinds of gigs (I don't busk, so this only applies to live club performances). The longer the gig and the more frequently you perform, the better! I typically perform about four hours per gig and five gigs a week. Here's a few ways I maximize my tips:

- You can't expect people to come up and give you a tip. Don't be afraid to ask for it! For example, I like to say, 'Thank you guys so much for being such a great audience! I'm going to come around and shake hands, see if you guys have any requests, and pass around this tip jug. This is how I make a living on Broadway, so if you like what you're hearing, please show your support and leave a tip. And if you don't like what you're hearing, put some love in the jug anyway so I can take some lessons!' It usually makes people laugh.
- Having an obvious tip jar is key! Make your own with a gourd, a huge champagne glass, or just a regular old bucket. Decorate it and write TIPS on it. Make sure your tip jar is impossible to miss, right in front of the stage, maybe on a stool. THERE IS NOTHING WRONG WITH WORKING FOR TIPS. I even ask for tips at my paid gigs— why not? It helps you make a lot more money, and as indie musicians, we need as much as we can get! But don't be desperate. Be charming, funny, and confident.
- Be funny and sincere. If people are being rude or awkward, don't take it personally. Make them give you a high five and maybe you will brighten their day. People remember things like that. Then, just move on to your next fan.
- When starting out, it's important to use unpaid gigs as opportunities to make fans. Have an email list, business cards, and demos of your music at the ready. If you have CDs, always take them with you when you pass the hat. People are more likely

to buy things they can touch and see. I sell my CDs for $5, and I notice that people end up buying a couple extra to share with their friends. I definitely make extra income at gigs by selling CDs, and people have something to take away with them.

- Last but not least, the MORE songs you know, the better the chance you will make good tips. Be humble—if you're starting out and want people to hear your songs, that's great; but if you want to be a professional musician, you MUST be a good entertainer. And that means playing cover songs and requests. Know your audience and play to THEM in order to make the most tips. I ask for $20 per request. Know what songs work well with your original repertoire, and know your venue. Cover songs and sing-alongs are a great way to make fans AND tips!"

Dealing with Venues Directly

Beyond passing the hat, there are thousands upon thousands of small clubs in every city (and most towns) that charge admission to listen to live music. Some small jazz and singer/songwriter oriented clubs will pay non-established musicians a fistful of cash to show up for an evening (think $50 to $100 for a single musician and $100 to $250 for two or three, plus often a bar tab, and perhaps a free or discount meal). Other clubs offer a split at the door (*i.e.*, money from fans who pay to see particular artists). Often, they offer 40% to 60% in favor of the artist, and the venue keeps 100% of the revenue from the bar. Some clubs require 100% of ticket sales from the first certain number of people who come to see the band. Other clubs will deduct expenses for things such as sound and amps, in-house production staff, and even refreshments in the green room. If it sounds like this presents opportunities for clubs to be less transparent in paying artists, you would be correct. And, if dealing with clubs directly sounds like a tough way to make a living, you would be right. Some clubs are worse than most, and others are total nightmares for artists. For instance, certain clubs will take a band's credit card at the beginning of the night. Unless a certain number of people pay at an inflated ticket price determined by the venue, the club will charge the band's card to make up the difference. For the details of good, bad, and very bad club deals, read "Should You Pay to Play? The Worst to Best Club Deals in the World," by Ari Herstand (http://www.digitalmusicnews.com/2014/04/16/should-you-pay-to-play). The article is based on a wealth of experience. For Jennifer Sullivan's colorful comments on bad deals and playing for no money, see below.

Jennifer's Comments on Clubs that Require the Artist to Sell a Minimum Number of Tickets

"I hate this style of promoting, it's such bullshit. Unless you are a highly established act, these kinds of performances make no money. Unfortunately, a legitimate agency doesn't usually sign you unless you have a proven track record of high profile live performances already under your belt. So usually, this is how it works: Let's suppose you want to play at the local pub. They may have a third party booker that books their Friday and Saturday nights, so you contact them. The booker agrees to book you, and your deal is they get the first ten covers ($10/cover = $100), which they split 50/50 with the pub. You make 100% after that. If you're a new artist just starting out, that means you'll probably bring 8 people to pay $10, and you'll make zero money. You might get one free drink at the bar, if you're lucky. And, you'll do this so many times and keep failing and realize that this kind of deal is a waste of time."

Jennifer's Comments on Whether an Artist Should Ever Play for Free

"KNOW YOUR WORTH!!! If you are truly talented, driven, confident, humble, professional, and friendly, you can get paid gigs. Especially if you provide your own little sound system, many dinner places and private events will hire you for $300+ to play for a few hours.

Know your CRAFT! You need to be able to play 4 hours' worth of original and cover music to be a full time, independent (unsigned) working musician. Until that big break comes along and you get signed and get to play your music for stadiums of adoring fans, this is how you get started—working your butt off at gigs. It ain't easy! But don't short yourself on what you can do. If you play an unpaid gig, agree to at least a bar tab and MAKE SURE that the venue has a built-in audience. If they expect you to bring all the people AND not pay you, there's a problem. One way to get around annoying third party promoters is to find the direct contact to the club and offer them a better deal. Instead of them splitting 50/50 with a booker and the venue only making $50, offer them a 70/30 deal, where at least if you bring $100, instead of seeing $0 you get $30!"

Promoters

One way a musician can enhance their chances of actually making some money, or increasing the amount of money they are likely to make, is by working with a promoter. This is because promoters often can make better deals for artists because of their knowledge and experience, and because promoters come with a certain amount of credibility. Venues are more likely to book artists represented by promoters because they trust the promoter's musical tastes from prior dealings and know that the promoters would not waste their time with artists who cannot draw a crowd. Most importantly, good promoters use all of their skills and experience to bring the largest possible crowd to their artist's shows.

However, some promoters should be avoided. According to Ari Herstand, there is a "new wave of 'promoters' who actually don't promote at all except upload one post on Facebook and rely on the artists to sell all their tickets." Ari also warns about "pay to play" promoters. These promoters require bands to pre-purchase tickets and then split the money with the venues without guaranteeing any money for the artist. Since the promoter has already made money, there is little incentive for him to do much to promote the show.

Below are two interviews with legit promoters who work with new and emerging artists. Before reading these interviews, a word about booking agents: like a promoter, they book shows for their musician clients. However, booking agents usually only work with artists who have established followings, whereas promoters can help you now.

We start out with an interview with a staffer at an indie promotion company who preferred to remain anonymous in order to provide full disclosure. The second interview is with seasoned promoter and publicist, Fiona Bloom.

INTERVIEW WITH AN INDIE ROCK PROMOTER

SG: Tell us briefly about yourself and what you do.

I work for a small concert promotion company based in New York City. The company was started in order to supply a growing need for promoters who would work in the local scene and solely with the agenda of nurturing rising talent.

Although we work primarily with local talent, we also pride ourselves on having worked with talent both nationally and internationally, including bands from Japan and Sweden.

SG: In general, what does a promoter do? And how is it different than a booking agency?

A promoter brings a show to the attention of the public and gets people to come through a variety of means including social media, hand-outs, posters, and flyers and gets media attention and press for the event. A booking agent's main function is to book venues for an artist.

SG: As a promoter, what unique things do you do for the artists you work with?

My promotion company serves as a platform for local bands to gain greater exposure and helps those bands play bigger and better shows as long as they are talented and hardworking. The company primarily exposes bands to the music industry, media, new fans, and other great acts in the New York region. In addition, we work with prestigious mid-size venues in Manhattan, such as Gramercy Theatre and Irving Plaza, as well as more intimate venues in Manhattan and Brooklyn.

I am the primary booker and promoter for my company. My role ranges from discovering new talent to serving as the liaison between the venue and the artist. If I decide to organize a show, I am responsible for setting dates with the venue, negotiating financial terms, and making sure the talent shows up on time—whether it's one band or six. I am also responsible for promoting the show on my company's website, social media platforms, and at the venue.

I make sure that all bands are made aware of their responsibilities before the show, including draw requirements (how many tickets they must sell before receiving a portion of the proceeds) and backline provisions (fees that the venue charges for equipment such as a microphone, sound amplification, instruments and security). In addition, I am also responsible for the show running smoothly, which includes handling any problems that may arise during load-in, show time, and load-out. I also "settle up" with the venue—meaning I pay for any expenses incurred, which are always agreed upon prior to the show. And, I pay remaining monies to my company, as well as to the artists after the show.

SG: What kind of artists do you work with?

My company strictly books and promotes rock and metal bands. We feel that over the years, a void has grown in the rock and metal genres—at least in New York. So, we strive to support the talented bands pursuing a career in this genre. Our goal is to bring rock and metal back to New York City.

My company also mainly works with "baby bands," which usually means they are not yet signed to a label. However, the range of experience these bands possess can vary from the recently-formed to the very experienced.

We offer the more experienced bands great opportunities, such as getting them opening-act positions for nationally well-known bands.

SG: Does your company have contracts with the artists? If not, do you confirm terms by email, or is everything done on a handshake basis?

We do not have formal contracts between the company and our artists. That being said, all of our communications with the artists are confirmed in writing; there are no oral agreements. Issues are avoided by simply making the bands aware of everything in writing ahead of time.

For example, if I were hosting a show, I would secure the talent for that show after securing the venue. This ensures that I will be able to convey, in writing, the requirements to the artists. I let the artists know, in writing, what the venue charges for room rental (if applicable), sound, lighting, and security. I transmit all of the expenses up front. That way, I can give the artists a pre-sale arrangement—a ticket amount that the artist should sell prior to the show to ensure expenses are accounted for and to ensure the artist gets paid. The number of tickets that must be sold pre-sale will naturally vary depending on the price per ticket and the venue. And, for some local venues, the expenses are low enough that pre-sale is not necessary. But in any event, everything will be in writing.

The most important concept to understand is that we maintain close relationships with the bands we work with. My company is not a "one-and-done" promotion company; we often have a continuing relationship with our artists. There are many artists we work with over and over again because they are hardworking, talented, and we have a mutually beneficial relationship with them. A certain level of trust is built so that a formal contract becomes unnecessary. While the same cannot be said for a band we are working with for the first time, we are still able to avoid misunderstandings by having everything in writing.

I think it's important to point out that we never require bands to work with us exclusively. In fact, we encourage bands to work with multiple local promotion companies. This will give the bands greater exposure. The only requirement we have regarding exclusivity is that we ask the band to have at least three weeks of down time in between shows. For example, if Band X plays a show in NYC with another promoter on Week 1, we will not book Band X to play one of our shows in NYC until Week 4.

SG: What about venues? How do contracts work with them?

We usually do not have formal contracts with the venues, but, similar to when we work with artists, there are almost always emails confirming all terms. When working with smaller venues, all expenses are laid out when we secure the venue for the show date. This usually occurs two to three months before the show for a smaller venue, and four to five months in advance of a larger show. All communications with the venue are in writing, and we determine how much it will cost to rent the venue and how much it will cost for venue staff (i.e., lighting, security, door person). During these communications, we also negotiate whether or not there is a bar guarantee for the venue, meaning the minimum amount of money the bar has to make for the night. This is important because we often host shows on weekend nights, which can often result in a high bar guarantee ($1,500 to $3,500 for the evening). If we are not prepared for this, it is very easy to fall into a situation where the bar guarantee is not met by audience consumption, and we end up having to pay the remainder out of pocket.

This leads me to discuss the reason local bands feel it is useful to have a promotion company running the show. Promoters are the cost-bearers. Anything and everything that could go wrong with a show and result in costs incurred gets placed directly on the shoulders of the promoters. Therefore, if bands decide to organize a show without a promoter, the bands can often incur these expenses and make very little money, if any, by failing to ask the venue the right questions. For example, there are many local bands who have fallen prey to excessive bar guarantees because they just didn't think to discuss with the venue whether or not a bar guarantee exists, and who bears the cost of paying off the remainder if the minimum is not met. The promoter is the advocate for the artist by knowing the right questions to ask and negotiating a fair deal.

SG: Can you tell us about the money; what the venue gets, what the artist gets, and what the promoters take?

We typically make 40% of sales at the door, after expenses. The artist gets the other 60%. If the show is a flop, we ensure the bands get paid or at least don't wind up owing money to the club, and we bite the cost and pay the club the unrecouped expenses.

Our larger shows work in a similar manner. The company will only get paid after the venue's expenses are paid. Typically, we retain a 40% profit for these shows as well, and the artists receive 60%.

What the artist will actually make varies depending on the show. At a small, local show (think "dive bar"), expenses for the venue range from $250 to $350. Let's assume the expenses are $250, at $10 per ticket; thus, a band has to sell more than 25 tickets to break even. If they don't, neither the band nor the promoter gets paid. A band in the headlining slot(s) will generally sell around 35 tickets, and that may generate $400. But, due to expenses, there is no guarantee they will actually make money, and this is always conveyed to the bands before they agree to play a show.

At a larger show at a mid-size venue, the payouts are better because ticket prices are higher and more tickets are sold. Pre-sale requirements for this type of show range from $75 to $200 depending on the band's slot in the show. At this type of show, the opening and closing bands will usually make $300 to $400 for the night, direct support bands will make $400 to $600 for the night, and the headliner will make $800 to $1,000 for the night.

When there is a promoter on the show, the venue does not pay the artist. The promoter(s) receive the payment for the show, then must distribute the payment to the artists, and then finally gets to pay itself.

SG: Tell us about sponsorships. Can artists make more money if they get a sponsor?

Everyone makes more money with sponsors, but they are very hard to secure, and my company has not been able to work with them in a long time.

I do know that securing a sponsor for the show results in a huge increase in pay to the bands. The amount of the sponsorship will depend on (1) the size of the venue, (2) whether the venue has an existing arrangement with the sponsor's brand, and (3) whether there is a requirement for a certain amount of product to sell at a show, along with varying other factors. Nevertheless, a sponsorship can really make or break a show. For example, most music festivals are only able to exist because of arrangements with one or more sponsors.

SG: If you do get sponsorships, do you do contracts or just an email correspondence confirming terms?

As I said, the company hasn't worked with sponsors in a long time, so I don't have personal knowledge whether there were any contracts.

INTERVIEW WITH PROMOTER AND PUBLICIST, FIONA BLOOM

SG: Tell us briefly about you and what you do.

I own a branding/PR agency called The Bloom Effect. We offer a plethora of services including social media, traditional and digital publicity, international consulting, event promo, product launches, and shopping artists to record companies and publishers. Our specialty is looking after international acts in the U.S., and also giving them platforms for their debuts and performances.

SG: In general, what does a promoter do?

A promoter should wear many hats. We work to secure talent, which initially involves researching and being "up" on all the hottest bands, as well as knowing the competition and what's happening in the music scene during the timeframe we're looking to bring in an act. We also publicize and promote talent via the usual methods of general publicity—print, digital, radio, local TV, and social media—as well as create some visuals for the show or tour.

Promoters should also do text campaigns, email blasts, and newsletters to their network or following to promote the show. In addition to this, my company offers ticket giveaways to radio stations and blogs, and allows for guest lists for VIPs and industry personnel where applicable. Furthermore, we work with other organizations to ensure more ticket sales and the overall promotion of the venue and of the show.

A good promoter should have access to all venues and contacts in the various markets where they work. They should also have great relationships with artist managers, agents, and other live promotion companies. Great communication skills and the ability to follow-up and maintain relationships are also key. Personally, I work with all kinds of artists and in all genres of music. In fact, I always like to say there are two genres: good and bad, and I work with the good!

Promoting has made my life more colorful, and there's variety to everything I do; I never treat any two projects the same. There is a set template of doing things, but the formula and ingredients change.

SG: When you act as a promoter, what unique things do you do for the artists you work with?

Let's just say that I answered that in the previous question because most promoters don't go all out like I do.

SG: What kind of artists do you work with?

I try to work with great artists. The artists I work with must be very original, and they have to be pretty amazing live! Everything from DJ's to R&B, hip hop, soul, rock, reggae, folk, and jazz—I've done it all. I love all genres and styles.

SG: Does your company have contracts with the artists? If not, do you do email correspondence confirming terms, or is everything done on a handshake basis?

It depends on the work. If I'm producing several shows with an artist then yes, we have contracts with the artists. If it's a one-off, then we generally have an invoice for my services or an email confirming all of the terms for my services.

SG: Same question regarding venues.

With the venue, I have an offer sheet with all of the terms laid out with back-line, tech riders, comps, guarantee versus door, bonus after X amount of revenue reached, the merchandising agreement, and anything else discussed.

SG: Can you tell us about the money? Do you put up money to rent venues?

I try not to put up my own money. If there are costs involved, I work with vendors or sponsors who will pay for them, or an investor who takes it off the back-end.

SG: Do you pay for any expenses such as travel or equipment rental?

Sometimes we pay for hotels, MC's to host the show, and some equipment—although I like to get the equipment donated by the band.

SG: Do you work on a flat fee basis or a percentage?

Depending on the specific deal and its outcome, I work on either flat fee or a percentage. However, I prefer the former.

SG: How much money does the artist make? If it's a percentage, what is the percentage? And of what is it a percentage? For instance, is it a percentage of ticket sales? How much does the venue make?

The Artist either makes their guarantee, which is worked out beforehand based on the size and capacity of venue. Or, the artist can make a percentage of door, ranging from 60% to 75%. On rare occasions, the artist can make up to 80% of door. This percentage is compiled from ticket sales minus any venue expenses such as sound and/or security and back-line costs. It all depends on what kind of deal and the sorts of terms you have.

The venue generally doesn't survive off of door sales, which are generally considered "extra" for them. Rather, the venue makes their money from the liquor, bar, and food costs for the night. Promoters and artists do not share in these costs.

SG: Do you ever get sponsorships for shows? If so, how do you find them, what do they want from the artist or the show, and what are they willing to pay?

Yes, I love having sponsors. They help to pay expenses and promote the show by creating fliers and posters, and the like.

I find sponsors by contacting like-minded brands. By "like-minded," I mean brands that attract the same demographic as the artist I am working with, have a "hipness factor" with said demographic, and have worked in the area where the show will be held. By doing so, we can capitalize on the good will, history, and interests of the brand.

I scout brands through industry contacts, conferences, and referrals, or by researching them online (namely, their Twitter, Facebook, or LinkedIn profiles). Usually, the brands want the artist to promote their shows hard. This means shouting out the brand's name a few times and wearing their clothes if it is a clothing, shoes, or liquor brand. Brands and sponsors can pay up to $5,000 or more a show depending on the market, the show's date, and the size of the audience.

SG: If you get sponsorships, do you form contracts or just email to confirm terms?

Any work I do with sponsors will definitely be contractual. These are professional businesses we're dealing with who are a lot more conservative than the music industry. Thus, the agreements are always formal.

SG: How can potential clients get in touch with you?

I'm always open to receiving new clients, and it's very easy to get in touch. Find me on http://www.thebloomeffect.com. I can also be contacted directly at fiona@thebloomeffect.com. I'm open to phone, and potential clients can get in touch with me at 646-764-0004. Finally, I'm all over social media: @fionabloom.

Part II: Artists Working with Booking Agents

As noted above, booking agents work almost exclusively for artists with established followings. To do this, they usually negotiate with in-house "talent brokers" at the venues. Generally, booking agents negotiate a guaranteed amount of money for their artists, and the artist will occasionally earn more if they sell more than a certain number of tickets. Below is a booker's standard agreement with venues. The comments explain how the agreement is favorable to the artist and the changes that a venue will usually request.

PERFORMANCE ENGAGEMENT AGREEMENT

Date: _____ ____, 2017

THIS CONTRACT for the personal services of the entertainer(s) on the engagement described below is made between the undersigned Promoter of Entertainment (herein called "Promoter") and the Artists' Representative (herein called "Agent"), designated below.

Promoter: _____, Hong Kong

Agent :   _____, NY, NY USA

The Artist is engaged in accordance with the terms and conditions on the face hereof. The Artist, by its undersigned leader, represents that the Artist has agreed to be bound by said terms and conditions. Each member of the Artist may enforce this agreement.

1.   ARTISTS, PLACE AND DATES OF ENGAGEMENT:

[Name of Artist]

Place: TBD

Date: December 19, 2017, 4:30 pm and 8:00 pm (two shows)

* Hours of Engagement: 100 minutes.

2.   COMPENSATION AND PAYMENT TERMS: The total compensation for services of the Artist and flight travel expenses for the above is USD $35,000 (this is the net amount, free of taxes).

The initial deposit of USD $17,500 is due upon signing the contract (non-refundable), no later than October 10th, 2017 to purchase air tickets to and from Hong Kong.

And the Balance of $17,500 is due on December 1, 2017.

The Promoter will insist that the second payment will be contingent upon the Artist actually showing up and playing the gigs. So, they will insist on changing December 1st to December 19th and specify that the second payment will be paid upon completion of the second show.

Payment must be made in cash or certified funds. If payment is not made as provided herein, Promoter is responsible for all costs and expenses, including, but not limited to, attorneys' fees and legal expenses incurred by the Artist in collecting the amount owed, whether or not suit is commenced. Said costs, expenses and attorneys' fees shall also include without limitation any such costs, expenses and fees in any proceeding under any present or future bankruptcy act or state receivership.

The Promoter would probably request an additional provision along the following lines:

"If, for any reason, Artist cannot or does not perform due to no fault of Promoter, Artist shall refund the initial payment to Promoter no later than December 20, 2017."

DIRECT DEPOSIT BANK WIRE Instruction.

Please wire transfer the Deposits to the following account.

Account Name: _____

Bank Name: _____

Account Number: _____

3.   ADDITIONAL TERMS AND CONDITIONS: Promoter Agrees to Pay and Artists Rep. Agrees to ACCEPT the Guarantees set forth in this contract, plus, Artists Rep. also agrees to pay AIRFARES for all its members and crews of the ARTISTS.

The Promoter will want to clarify the exact additional amount that they will have to pay for the Artist's band, and they will want to know exactly what "crew" are coming and the reason for them coming at all.

Promoter agrees to provide First Class HOTEL accommodations, plus INTERNAL Ground. Hotel requirement details will be provided later.

Promoter shall provide and pay for First Class Sound and Lights, First Class Back-line, and Any and All Rider Equipment.

Artists shall arrive in Hong Kong, no later than December 18th 2017. (Detailed Travel itinerary will be available on a later date).

The contract should make clear that this is for two nights. That clarification would benefit both parties as it would avoid misunderstanding and a possible dispute.

4.   CANCELLATION: Except as provided herein, this agreement may not be canceled for any reason or at any time by Promoter. Payment is due according to the payment schedule set forth above even if the event for which the Artist was retained is canceled for any reason. Promoter understands that this is a personal services contract and the Artist will not be offering its services to anyone else for the hours on the date of the engagement set forth above in reliance on this agreement to perform for the Promoter.

5.   It is agreed and understood that the Promoter shall be responsible for the safety and security of the Artist and the Artist's representatives, crew, guests, their baggage and equipment for the duration of the engagement.

> The venue will insist that the Promoter is not responsible for the actions or omissions of 3rd parties. So, if a cabdriver gets the Artist into an accident, the Promoter cannot be held responsible.

6. All artwork and/or use of the Artist's name/likeness is to be approved by the Artist.

> The Promoter may want to insert a clause that, if they provide artwork for the Artist to approve and she does not notify them of her approval or disapproval within a certain number of days, approval may be assumed.

7. It is agreed and understood that this contract is only binding for a live performance. The ARTIST reserves the right for their merchandise and any other rights outside the field of live entertainment including without limitation any so-called audio records (in whatsoever formats) and/or audio visual devices (in whatsoever formats) embodying the Artist's performance whether in whole and/or in part.

8. It is agreed and understood that the Promoter shall provide and pay for all catering requirements for the band and crew. Artist/Artist's Tour Manager will advise Promoter of these requirements.

9. The Promoter agrees to provide, pay and be responsible for all visas, work permits, driving permits and other documentation, including payment of visa consulate fees that are necessary for the Artist to undertake the engagements herein. Any payments due are to be paid directly to the Artist or as advised by the Artist's Tour Manager. Once all the documents are prepared by the Promoter. It is Artists' responsibility to apply and obtain the visa stamps at the consulate in their own country of domicile.

10. RELATIONSHIP: The Artist is retained by Promoter only for the purposes and to the extent set forth in this agreement, and Artist's relationship to the Promoter during the period of their engagement shall be that of independent contractors and not that of Employees of Promoter for any purpose whatsoever.

11. JURISDICTION: In accordance with the laws of the State of New York, the parties will submit every claim dispute, controversy or difference involving the entertainment services arising out of or connected with this contract and the engagement covered hereby for a determination and said determination shall be conclusive, final and binding upon the parties. In connection with the foregoing, the parties do hereby consent to the jurisdiction of the courts of the County of Manhattan, State of New York, USA.

12. <u>RECORDING</u>: No performance or engagement shall be recorded, reproduced or transmitted from the place of performance in any manner or by any means whatsoever, in the absence of a specific written agreement with the Artist relating to and permitting such recording, reproduction or transmission.

13. <u>FORCE MAJEURE</u>: If a performance is prevented, rendered impossible or infeasible, by sickness, inability to perform, any act or regulation of any public authority or bureau, civil tumult, strike, epidemic, interruption in or delay of transportation services, weather, war conditions or emergencies, or any cause beyond the control of Artist, it is understood and agreed that there shall be no claim for damages by either party to this Agreement and Artist's obligation as to such performance shall be deemed waived. Provided, however, if such inability is caused or contributed to by Promoter, Promoter's obligation to make payment as provided in paragraph 6 above shall not be waived and Promoter shall be liable for the amount due and owing Artist.

14. <u>INDEMNITY</u>: Promoter agrees to indemnify, defend and hold Artist harmless from and against any and all claims, costs or liability for damage, injury to any person or property during Artist's engagement, including time of set up and take down.

WHEREAS, the AGENT, in signing this contract himself, or having same signed by a representative, acknowledges full authority and responsibility to do so and thereby assumes liability for the amount stated herein. and NO deposits will be returned.

WHEREAS, the Promoter shall conduct all its official communication to the Artist through the AGENT.

AS WITNESSED HEREOF THE PARTIES HERETO HAVE HEREUNTO SET THEIR HANDS THE DAY AND YEAR FIRST ABOVE WRITTEN.

PROMOTER: _____

_____
Authorized signatory

AGENT _____

_____
Authorized signatory

Part III: The Internet's Impact on Live Performance

Here we will discuss the way the Internet has converged with live performance to generate new revenue streams for both artists and venues. As an example, this chapter includes the "Revenue Share" agreement offered by Smalls, a jazz club. This contract offers artists who play at the club the opportunity to make money by allowing off-site fans to listen to their live performances both simultaneously and on demand.

Below is my interview with Spike Wilner, co-owner of Smalls. The interview took place in 2014 and originally appeared in the fourth edition of my book, *The Future of the Music Business* (Hal Leonard 2015). After the interview took place, Spike launched the Revenue Share program.

INTERVIEW WITH SPIKE WILNER, JAZZ PIANIST AND CO-OWNER OF SMALLS JAZZ CLUB IN NYC

Spike Wilner uses the Internet to expose the artists who play at Smalls, located in New York's Greenwich Village, to a worldwide audience by simulcasting live shows every night (click on "live video" at www.smallsjazzclub.com). In addition, over seven years ago he started creating an archive of recordings of the live music performed at the club. This interview covers Spike's experience with expanding Smalls' audience by using the Internet, and his vision of the future.

SG: Give us a brief description of what happens at SMALLS: the music, the artists featured there, and what folks can expect if they visit the club.

Smalls Jazz Club is generally open from 4:00 PM to 4:00 AM, with some exceptions. Normally we have 3 bands per night. We do two, two-set shows followed by an "after-hours" set and finally a jam session at the very end. Jam sessions are an important part of Smalls, and traditionally, there's a jam every night of the week quite late (sometimes not even starting until 2:00 AM). We also have afternoon jam sessions on Friday and Saturday. On Wednesday afternoons we host a tap dance jam session and the tap community comes out for that. On Wednesdays and Thursdays we do a 9:30 PM "main show," which usually features a famous musician or band. The same goes for the weekend, but the show starts at 10:30 PM. Our "after-hours" shows start either around midnight or 1 AM and all seasoned veteran players host. Sundays we are open all day with a vocal workshop at 1 PM, a showcase show at 4 PM, a duet show at 7:30 PM and then at 10PM we have the legendary Johnny O'Neal in a permanent residence with his trio.

Smalls has a "no reservation" policy; first come first serve. Our cover is $20 until after-hours and then it's $10. We have a one-drink minimum for those seated or at the bar but standers in the back don't have to buy a drink. It gets crowded and the vibe changes as it gets later. The after-hours is the coolest vibe and not for everyone. But the music is always great at Smalls, from the beginning of the day to the end.

SG: You have been experimenting for some time now with harnessing the power of the Internet to create a broader audience for artists who play at Smalls. You are now streaming every show at Smalls. Tell us more about your live simulcast including how you implement it, how many people are tuning in, and the feedback you have received from fans and the artists themselves.

I recall a story that John Hammond, the great record producer, was driving to Chicago when he picked up a radio broadcast live from a Jazz club in Kansas City. The music blew his mind so he turned his car around and drove straight to Kansas City to sign whoever that artist was. It turned out to be Count Basie, and the rest is history.

What fascinates me about that story is the idea of a club putting a radio wire to transmit to the world. I wanted to do this as well, so I decided to use the Internet. We started live streaming about seven years ago with a very simple system. As the years progressed, the technology for live streaming has grown in leaps and bounds. Now, it's possible for anyone to inexpensively create their own "television studio." We began to generate an enormous audience worldwide, with jazz fans checking in from all parts of the globe. I was in Italy last year and it shocked me how famous Smalls has become internationally. I attribute this to the Internet and the nightly live broadcasts. The other thing is, I firmly believe that the music being played nightly at Smalls will be of historic importance to future generations. Therefore, my mission has been to record every single show and have it organized by a date, who the leader was, and who was in the band. What started with setting up a recording device seven years ago has created an incredible collection of about 8,000 recordings so far. And now, this library includes HD videos as well.

SG: Recently, you had a crowd funding campaign. What were your goals, did you succeed, and what challenges did you face?

Our goal with the crowd funding campaign was to raise money for a new piano and new equipment for our live streaming (i.e., computers and cameras). We were successful and hit our goal. We bought a new Steinway for the club and installed a new and up-to-date streaming system and in-house recording studio.

As far as the crowd funding experience, while it helped us, it is a terrible way to fund a business. For one thing, you tap the good will of everyone that likes or supports you. Secondly, you can't do it again; it's a one-time shot. The other thing that nobody talks about is that if you do get your money there's this huge tax liability at the end of the year. If you don't properly prepare for that and spend all the money then you're going to get hit.

Furthermore, Indiegogo took a big chunk in fees. I don't like crowd funding and hope it's just a passing fad.

SG: I understand that you would like to use the Internet to monetize your archive of recordings of the shows performed at the club in the last seven years and share revenues with the artists.

My idea is to build a website platform where we can disseminate our huge library of recordings and videos. This has proved more complex and expensive than I had planned. I would like to do a full revenue share with all of the artists that are in our archive. We want to charge a small subscription rate for fans to access our ever-growing library. The revenue from the subscriptions would be pooled and distributed to artists based on how much their work gets listened to. The more popular an artist is, the more they make—law of the jungle economics. This is a big system and I realized I had to take on partners to make SmallsLIVE LLC real. I've since partnered with two guys. One is a programmer and has his own successful website development company. The other partner is an investor who is financing the building of this site. Once the site is up and launched, we will be able to use it to accommodate an entire range of related media projects including our live stream and video library, as well as educational videos, downloads, and merchandise.

SG: You now have over 4,000 subscribers on your YouTube channel. How has your experience been with them? What other social networks do you use?

At first, we were excited about YouTube. It seemed amazing that you could have a CDN [Content Delivery Network] host your live stream for free. But, it's not really free in the sense that you don't have real control over the content that you stream. YouTube screens your video and scans for illicit use of copyrighted material. It turned out that when we played our iPod on breaks, we get flagged even though we are paying for the right to publicly perform that music to the appropriate music collection societies. But, if you get flagged, YouTube will not allow you to stream any music including our live performances. It's a headache. On the other hand, it's very affordable to rent time on a good CDN such as Bit Gravity. Then you have full control of your stream and the content that you're creating.

We have a large fan base on Facebook and also Twitter. We also have a rapidly growing email list and regularly do a newsletter and post to our social media. Facebook is great because it's very affordable and reaches a lot of people who you know are already interested in what you're doing.

THE SMALLSLIVE ARTISTS' INTERNET REVENUE SHARE AGREEMENT

**THE SMALLSLIVE
ARTISTS' REVENUE SHARE AGREEMENT**

This Agreement (the "Agreement") is between SmallsLIVE LLC ("SmallsLIVE") and you in regard to the SmallsLIVE Archive and the Artist Revenue Share Project.

TERMS OF USE:

By accepting this Agreement, you also agree to SmallsLIVE's Terms of Use as they appear in the Site (as defined below). Should you have any questions concerning these Terms of Use or need technical support, you may contact us at info@smallslive.com.

PARTICIPATION IN THE ARCHIVE AND DOWNLOADING:

The Archive:

The SmallsLIVE Archive (the "Archive") consists of audio and audiovisual recordings (videos) produced by SmallsLIVE at the Smalls Jazz Club in the past (since 2007), now, or in the future.

Users of the SmallsLIVE's website ("Site") can access the Archive as subscribers ("Subscribers") and play (stream) the individual sets of multiple, combined musical performances ("Dates") by an individual artist and/or group ("Artist"). The Date may be audio only and/or audio-visual, and the embodiment of the Date in an audio or audiovisual medium shall hereafter be called the "Recording." Subscribers will pay SmallsLIVE a monthly subscription fee (the "Subscription Fee"), to be determined by SmallsLIVE. Subscribers will also have the option of downloading individual, artist approved, tracks embodied in the Recordings of each Date ("Tracks") for an additional fee to be determined by SmallsLIVE and sold as SmallsLIVE TRACKS.

Subscription fees will be placed in a revenue pool to be distributed to the Artists as specified in Paragraph 4 below ("Revenue Share"). Monies received by SmallsLIVE TRACKS from downloads of Tracks shall also be subject to the Revenue Share set forth in Paragraph 4 below.

Your approval of this Agreement applies to any Date past, present, or future in which you participated or will participate as a Leader or as a Side Musician as those terms are defined below.

ARTISTS' RIGHTS:

LEADERS & SIDE MUSICIANS: Each Date must have a designated leader ("Leader"), provided that in the event of a collective band, each member may be designated as a Leader. Any musician who plays on a Date who is not a Leader shall be deemed to be a "Side Musician."

PERFORMANCE FEE: The Leader is paid a performance fee for the Date at Smalls Jazz Club, under a separate booking agreement.

COPYRIGHT IN THE RECORDINGS: Except for SmallsLIVE's right, subject to paragraph 2(g) below, to include the Recording of each Date in the Archive as set forth herein the Leader of each Date shall retain all right, title and interest in and to each Recording including the copyright in the "sound recording" (as defined in the Copyright Act) in the Recording, and all renewals and extensions thereof, worldwide and for the full duration of the copyright. To effectuate this intent, SmallsLIVE and each Side Musician hereby transfer their interest in the copyright in each Recording to the Leader, including without limitation the authority to distribute or otherwise exploit each Recording as set forth in more detail in subparagraph 2(d) below. For avoidance of doubt, nothing in this Agreement will transfer the ownership or copyright in any underlying musical composition embedded in any Recording.

LEADER'S RIGHT TO EXPLOIT THE RECORDINGS: The Leader may use the Recording for any commercial or promotional purpose, including without limitation the right to sell, license or otherwise exploit the Recording or any portion thereof. The Leader shall have the exclusive obligation to make any payment required to the Side Musicians or any third parties, including any third party writers or owners of musical compositions. For the avoidance of doubt, SmallsLIVE shall not be responsible for any payments to or permission from any Side Musicians or any third parties.

ARTIST ACCOUNT: Every Leader and Side Musician will have an account (accessible by password) on the SmallsLIVE Site. From this account page, Leaders will be able to download their Recording(s) for personal use or commercial exploitation in accordance with Subparagraph d. above. Leaders may also use their account to "tag," i.e. add, the name of any Side Musician in regard to a Date for which SmallsLIVE inadvertently omits that Side Musician's name. Leaders and Side Musicians may also use the account to update personal info such as address, telephone, email, etc. Leaders and Side Musicians will also be able to set up their banking information to receive royalty payments from Subscription Fees and paid downloads and to see SmallsLIVE's metrics on usage and payout dates.

LEADER'S RIGHT TO KEEP DATES PRIVATE: Every Leader shall have the right to use his/her account to control which Recordings of Dates can be public, that is, accessed by Subscribers, and which Recordings of Dates shall remain private.

EDITING: Leaders shall have the right to "edit" their Recording(s) provided that any such edits shall be at their sole expense. SmallsLIVE is not responsible for editing, mixing and mastering of any Recording unless it is previously determined by SmallsLIVE and the Artist that the Date shall be a special project ("Special Project"). Special Projects are outside the terms of this Agreement and shall be subject to terms to be negotiated separately.

EDITED DATES: Leaders may "resubmit" their edited Recording for active use in the Archive, provided that the edited Recording must be a minimum of 20 minutes in length and must consist of at least two songs.

PAST DATES: You hereby agree to all the terms and conditions in this Agreement with regard to Recordings of Dates occurring prior to the date that you enter into this Agreement.

AUTHORIZED PAYEES: You shall have the right to assign your right to receive any income to you under this Agreement to any third party such as a business manager. Such authorization must be made in a writing signed by you and delivered to SmallsLIVE by certified mail. In case of your death or disability, monies earned under this Agreement shall be paid to your duly authorized representative after that representative has adduced any required legal documents confirming their authority.

SMALLSLIVE'S RIGHTS:

SmallsLIVE is hereby granted the non-exclusive perpetual right to include in the Archive any Recording of any Date in which the Leader or Side Musician participated or will participate in the future subject to the Leader's right to keep the Recording of any Date private in accordance with Subparagraph 2(g) above.

SmallsLIVE is hereby granted the right to live broadcast ("Webcast") each Date on the Site or any third party website or digital platform one time live and once as a rebroadcast. After that, a Recording of the Date, in Video/Audio will be added to the Archive for Leader's approval and use. SmallsLIVE shall have the right to make the Webcasts available for no charge to viewers or Subscribers, and to include advertising and accept sponsorship in conjunction with the Webcasts and the Videos.

No Leader or Side Musician may use "Smalls," "SmallsLIVE" or any logo or other mark associated with SmallsLIVE or Smalls Jazz Nightclub, in connection with the promotion, sale or license of any Recording, without the express prior written permission of SmallsLIVE.

You hereby give SmallsLIVE the right to use your name, image, likeness, and approved bio in the Site in connection with your Recordings, Webcasts and Videos, and in any advertising, promotion or marketing of such Recordings, Webcasts, Videos, the Site or the Archive.

Subscription revenue share & SmallsLIVE Tracks

Subscription Fees

All Subscription Fees collected from Subscribers for access to stream (but not download) the Archive shall be shared on a 50–50 basis between SmallsLIVE, on the one hand, and the Musicians (whether Leader or Side Musicians), on the other hand, after the deduction of operational Expenses (as defined below). All fees will be placed in a Revenue Pool.

The Musicians' share of the Revenue Pool will be determined by the number of minutes that the Recording of each Date is streamed within a pay period (either bi-annually or quarterly, to be determined by SmallLIVE). Each Musician who plays on any Date, whether as a Leader or as a Side Musician, will be credited the number of minutes that Subscribers listen to the Date(s). Musicians must be "Tagged" on the date to be credited with the Minutes. It is the responsibility of the Leader to tag all the Side Musicians on a date and the Side Musicians' responsibility to see that he or she does so.

The formula for determining a Musician's share of the Revenue Pool is:

Total Individual Musicians Minutes divided by the Total Archive usage minutes.

If, for Example in one three month period (pay period):

Peter gets 350 minutes listened to for all his dates in the Archive as Leader or Side Musician
Stacy gets 5000 minutes listened to for all of his date in the Archive as Leader or Side Musician
Grant gets 700 minutes listened to for all of his dates in the Archive as Leader or Side Musician
Tuomo gets 950 minutes listened to for all of his dates in the Archive as Leader or Side Musician
Miki gets 1200 minutes listened to for all of his dates in the Archive as Leader or Side Musician
Spike gets 30 minutes listened to for all of his dates in the Archive as Leader or Side Musician

Adding all these minutes together yields the Total Archive Usage, which in this example equals 8230 minutes.

To calculate the pay percentage attributable to each Musician ("Pay Percentage"), you must divide the individual minutes by the total usage.

Peter	=	.0425 (350/8230)
Stacy	=	.6075 (5000/8230)
Grant	=	.0851 (700/8230)
Tuomo	=	.1154 (950/8230)
Miki	=	.1458 (1200/8230)
Spike	=	.0036 (30/8230)

Payout = Revenue Pool Total x Individual Pay Percentage

Each Musician is paid an amount equal to the total amount collected from Subscription Fees (Revenue Pool) multiplied by his or her Pay Percentage.

If, by example, the Revenue Pool for the pay period is $500 then the payments would be:

Pete   = $21.25 (500 x .0425)
Stacy = $303.75 (500 x .6075)
Grant = $42.55 (500 x .0851)
Tuomo = $57.70 (500 x .1154)
Miki   = $72.90 (500 x .1458)
Spike = $1.80 (500 x .0036)

Use of the Archive will be measured in minutes rounded downward. For example, if a Subscriber listens to a Date for ten (10) minutes and thirty (30) seconds then Artist would be credited with 10 minutes.

Paid Downloads (SmallsLIVE TRACKS):

SmallsLIVE TRACKS is an Artist Curated Store for licensing and selling for download any Track(s) Leaders designate from their Archive recording. Any Leader of any Date may choose individual Tracks embodying one song to make available for paid download to Subscribers. Artist may edit the track themselves or ask SmallsLIVE to do so. Artist must provide Title, Composer and Publishing information. The MP3 will be offered to Subscribers at a price to be determined by SmallsLIVE in consultation with the Leader. The area of the site where such downloads will be available shall be called "SmallsLIVE TRACKS," although this name is subject to change in the discretion of SmallsLIVE.

SmallsLIVE shall share any monies it receives from such downloads with the Leader on a 50-50 basis after deducting any transaction costs.

The Leader shall be responsible for making any required payments to the Side Musicians, for mechanical royalties, or to any other necessary third parties.

The Revenue Share set forth in Subparagraphs 4.a and 4.b above, shall be the total compensation payable by SmallsLIVE for the rights granted under this Agreement.

SmallsLIVE retains the right to not publish a track for any reason and maintains the final decision on tracks placed in the SmallsLIVE TRACKS store.

EXPENSES:

SmallsLIVE will be allowed to deduct the following expenses from Subscription Fees:

Transaction costs (for examples, PayPal or credit card fees);
Licensing fees payable to performance rights organizations;

Hosting and bandwidth fees; and

Sales and local taxes, and other applicable taxes, levies or fees.

Other fees that may in the future become required for the continued operation of the streaming and download services set forth in this Agreement, including without limitation any fees to third party rights-holders.

TAXES: Each Artist who receives any monies under the Agreement shall be solely responsible for paying any applicable taxes.

ACCOUNTING: SmallsLIVE shall make payments to each Artist on a calendar quarterly basis 30 days after each quarter. Such payments shall be made by check or automatic deposit at the election of the Artist.

Notwithstanding anything to the contrary above, SmallsLIVE shall have no obligation to make a payment to an Artist if the amount due is less than ten dollars ($10) provided that when such monies exceed ten dollars ($10) any monies withheld will be paid after any pay period in which the total amount due to the Artist exceeds ten dollars ($10).

Every Musician will have access to on-line accounting pages by using a password to be assigned by SmallsLIVE. The accounting pages will set forth the amounts that have accrued for the Musician.

AUDIT: At any time within two (2) years after any payment is received by any Leader or Side Musician hereunder, that Leader or Side Musician shall have the right to give SmallsLIVE written notice of their intention to examine SmallsLIVE's books and records with respect to such statement. Such examination shall be commenced within one (1) month after the date of such notice, at the sole expense of such Leader or Side Musician, by any certified public accountant or attorney designated by such Leader or Side Musician, provided he or she is not then engaged in an outstanding examination of SmallsLIVE's books and records on behalf of a person other than such Leader or Side Musician. Such examination shall be made during SmallsLIVE's usual business hours at the place where SmallsLIVE maintains the books and records which relate to such Leader or Side Musician and which are necessary to verify the accuracy of the statement or statements specified in the notice to SmallsLIVE and the examination shall be limited to the foregoing. A Leader or Side Musician's right to inspect SmallsLIVE's books and records shall be only as set forth in this subparagraph and SmallsLIVE shall have no obligation to produce such books and records more than once with respect to each statement.

Unless notice shall have been given to SmallsLIVE in accordance with subparagraph above, each payment rendered to Artist shall be final, conclusive and binding the Artist and shall constitute an account stated. Artist shall be foreclosed from maintaining any action, claim or proceeding against SmallsLIVE in any forum or tribunal with respect to any payment or accounting rendered hereunder unless such action, claim or proceeding is commenced against SmallsLIVE in a court of competent jurisdiction within three (3) years after the date such payment is received by Artist.

Artist acknowledges that SmallsLIVE's books and records contain confidential trade information. Neither Artist nor Artist's representatives will communicate to others or use on behalf of any other person any facts or information obtained as a result of such examination of SmallsLIVE's books and records, except as may be required by law or judicial decree.

TERM, TERRITORY, AND TERMINATION: SmallsLIVE's non-exclusive rights as set forth herein shall be perpetual and shall extend throughout the world. You shall have a right to terminate this Agreement in regard to your grant of such non-exclusive rights upon notice of three months (3) months for future Dates only provided that SmallsLIVE reserves the right not to book you for future Dates. SmallsLIVE reserves the right to take down any Date from the Archive.

WARRANTIES AND INDEMNITIES: You warrant and represent that:

You are under no disability, restriction or prohibition, whether contractual or otherwise, with respect to (A) your right to enter into this Agreement, and (B) convey the rights granted to SmallsLIVE hereunder, to perform each and every material term and provision hereof, and to record each and every musical composition hereunder;

To the extent of your contributions hereunder, SmallsLIVE shall not be required to make any payments of any nature for, or in connection with, the acquisition, exercise or exploitation of rights granted to SmallsLIVE by you pursuant to this Agreement, except as specifically provided in this Agreement;

To the extent of your contributions hereunder, neither the Materials (as defined immediately below) nor any use of the Materials by SmallsLIVE will violate or infringe upon the rights of any person. "Materials" as used in this subparagraph means any musical, artistic and literary materials, ideas and other intellectual properties furnished by you, including any copyright, trademarks or rights of publicity contained in or used in connection with any Recordings made hereunder, which have not been supplied by the SmallsLIVE. Among other obligations, you shall not sample any third party work without the express written approval of SmallsLIVE;

All of your representations and warranties shall be true and correct upon execution hereof, and shall remain in effect in perpetuity. SmallsLIVE's use of Recordings or Materials hereunder shall not constitute a waiver of any of your representations, warranties or agreements in respect thereof.

You shall at all times indemnify and hold harmless SmallsLIVE and any licensee of SmallsLIVE from and against any and all third party claims, damages, liabilities, costs and expenses, including legal expenses and reasonable counsel fees, arising out of breach by you of any warranty, representation or agreement made by you herein.

SmallsLIVE warrants and represents that:

SmallsLIVE is under no disability, restriction or prohibition, whether contractual or otherwise, with respect to its right to enter into this Agreement, and to perform each and every term and provision hereof;

All of SmallsLIVE's representations and warranties shall be true and correct upon execution hereof, and shall remain in effect in perpetuity.

ASSIGNMENT AND RIGHT TO EXPLOIT ARCHIVE: SmallsLIVE shall only stream (in terms of the Archive) and sell downloads (in terms of SmallsLIVE TRACKS) exclusively from the SmallsLIVE website (www.smallslive.com). SmallsLIVE shall have no right to assign, transfer, sell or license this Agreement or any of its rights or obligations under this Agreement to any third party without consent of the Artist(s) and under a separate agreement.

AGREEMENT: This Agreement shall be fully valid and enforceable by the Leader or Side Musicians by clicking the "Accept" button in the Site and providing all the information required by SmallsLIVE in the Site.

ESCROW: If SmallsLIVE cannot locate any Leader or Side Musician at any time, it shall put any amount due to such Leader or Side Musician in escrow until the time that SmallsLIVE can find such person or he or she provides accurate information to SmallsLIVE.

NOTICE: SmallsLIVE may provide notifications, whether such notifications are required by law or are for marketing or other business related purposes, to you via email, mobile text message, written or hard copy notice, or through conspicuous posting of such notice on Site, as determined by SmallsLIVE in its sole discretion. SmallsLIVE reserves the right to determine the form and means of providing notifications to you.

JURISDICTION: This Agreement will be governed by the laws of the State of New York applying to contracts made and to be performed in New York. The exclusive jurisdiction for any claim, action or dispute with SmallsLIVE or relating in any way to your use of the Site will be in the state and federal courts of the State of New York.

<u>MISCELLANEOUS</u>: Should you have any questions concerning this Agreement or need technical support, you may contact SmallsLIVE at the following email address: info@smallslive. com

YOU ACKNOWLEDGE THAT YOU HAVE READ THIS AGREEMENT, UNDERSTAND IT AND WILL BE BOUND BY ITS TERMS AND CONDITIONS. YOU FURTHER ACKNOWLEDGE THAT THIS AGREEMENT, IN ADDITION TO THE SMALLSLIVE TERMS AND CONDITIONS, REPRESENTS THE COMPLETE AND EXCLUSIVE STATEMENT OF THE AGREEMENT BETWEEN US AND THAT IT SUPERSEDES ANY PROPOSAL OR PRIOR AGREEMENT ORAL OR WRITTEN, AND ANY OTHER COMMUNICATIONS BETWEEN US RELATING TO THE SUBJECT MATTER OF THIS AGREEMENT.

CHAPTER 9

MUSIC VIDEO PRODUCTION CONTRACTS

INTRODUCTION: BEFORE YOU SHOOT A MUSIC VIDEO, READ THIS LEGAL GUIDE

This chapter focuses on the business of producing music videos and contains a form agreement that can be used to hire a video producer, as well as releases for people and locations appearing in videos. Although MTV does not play many anymore, music videos on YouTube and other social media have become more important in breaking new artists than ever before. Before making your own video, though, it's important to know the legal ins and outs of producing them.

In the first part of this Introduction, I give a brief history of the music video followed by a survey of how successful artists have used and continue to use them to launch their careers. The second part of the Introduction offers a summary of business considerations in producing videos.

The History and Continuing Importance of Music Videos

Before Music Videos

Audiovisual presentations of music have existed since the first motion pictures containing sound. In fact, the first Hollywood "talkie," released in 1927, was a musical featuring Al Jolson called "The Jazz Singer." Before the invention of the video cameras, there were many musical short films featuring the performance of single songs, such as Frank Sinatra's patriotic "The House I Live In (That's America To Me.)" These films were sometimes shown before main features at movie theatres. In the 1960s, artists like the Rolling Stones and the Beatles started to make short form films of individual songs to promote their albums. The dawn of what we think of as music videos began in the 1970s. For example, in 1975, Queen commissioned the production of a video for their new single, "Bohemian Rhapsody," to show on *Top of the Pops*, a popular British TV show showcasing the week's top hit songs. In the U.S., *Video Concert Hall*, launched on November 1, 1979, was the first nationwide video music program on American television, predating MTV by almost three years.

MTV and the Birth of the Era of Music Videos on Television

In 1981, MTV launched by airing "Video Killed the Radio Star," and this began an era of 24-hour-a-day music videos on television.

The founders of MTV, including Robert Pitman (current chairman and CEO of iHeart-Media, Inc. (formerly Clear Channel)), convinced record labels to produce more videos and give them to MTV for free, just as they gave free records to radio stations. The pitch was that the videos would promote the labels' records and increase sales. The only money MTV paid the labels was a relatively small fee to secure exclusive rights to play select videos for a limited period of time. For instance, MTV paid Sony Music $4 million a year to select up to a dozen videos as exclusives for a six month period.

By the mid-1980s, MTV grew to play a central role in marketing pop and rock music. Many important acts of this period, most notably Madonna, Aerosmith, The Who, Phil Collins, John Mellencamp, and Billy Idol owe a great deal of their success to the seductive appeal of their videos. After years of controversy regarding the lack of diversity among artists on the network, MTV aired Michael Jackson's "Billie Jean," "Thriller," and other videos, which helped Jackson become the best-selling pop artist of all time.

But by the late '90s, MTV sharply decreased the number of videos it showed on its airways. Former MTV president Van Toffler explained: "Clearly, the novelty of just showing music videos has worn off. It's required us to reinvent ourselves to a contemporary audience." A decade later, MTV was playing an average of just three hours of music videos per day, preferring cartoons such as *Beavis and Butt-Head* and, later, unscripted reality shows such as *Jersey Shore*. MTV continued to play some music videos instead of relegating them exclusively to its sister channels (such as *MTV Hits*), but around this time, the channel began to air music videos only in the early morning hours and in *Total Request Live* or TRL, which aired the ten most requested music videos of the day, as voted by viewers via phone or online. As a result of these programming changes, Justin Timberlake implored MTV to "play more damn videos!" while giving an acceptance speech at the *2007 Video Music Awards*. Despite the challenge from Timberlake, MTV continued to decrease its total rotation time for music videos in 2007 and shut down *TRL* in 2008.

YouTube and the Rise of Cover Videos

YouTube was created by three former PayPal employees in February 2005. In November 2006, it was bought by Google for $1.65 billion. The online video sharing site is this generation's MTV. Artists like Beyoncé and Taylor Swift regularly have hundreds of millions of views for new videos, and their record companies and music publishers monetize them by allowing ads. YouTube keeps approximately 40% of the ad income, although the details of their formulas for arriving at the exact amount is not public record, and the balance is paid to the copyright owners.

YouTube allows you to share your videos with a worldwide audience. However, the thing that makes YouTube great for new artists—that it's so easy to upload and reach a huge audience—also makes it incredibly competitive. YouTube reports that hundreds of hours of video content are uploaded to its servers each minute. So, although you have a potential audience of millions that you can directly reach with your video, standing out in the sea of other content is a huge challenge.

One way new artists have used YouTube to attract attention is to "cover," that is, re-record hit songs. A good example of an artist who was discovered from making covers is Justin Bieber. Before he was the erratic "bad boy" that many love to hate, Justin Bieber was just a kid from Stratford, Ontario. At age 12, Bieber began to regularly post covers of hit R&B songs on his YouTube channel under the username "kidrauhl."

As his videos got more and more views, he was eventually discovered by talent manager Scooter Braun. After tracking Bieber down, Braun flew the then-13 year old to Atlanta to record some demo tapes. Braun then introduced Bieber to Usher, who reportedly beat out Justin Timberlake in a bidding war to sign the young YouTube star. After being signed by Usher, Bieber recorded his first album, released the single "One Time," and proceeded to have his face put up on tween bedroom walls everywhere. He's had 3 multi-platinum albums that have all reached #1 on the charts and continues to play to sold-out arenas all across the world.

Another example of how cover videos have launched careers is Vazquez Sound, a musical trio known for their covers of hits including Adele's "Rolling in the Deep," which has garnered over 172 million views. In September 2014, Vazquez Sounds released their first original album, which was an instant hit that earned them a nomination at the 2015 Latin GRAMMYs for "Best New Artist." Another example is the pop duo, Karmin. They broke a couple of years ago with a string of clever, sassy covers of hits by acts such as Lil Wayne, Nicki Minaj, and Katy Perry. Alessia Cara, a 19 year old Canadian singer and songwriter, is another example. She is currently signed to Def Jam and is best known for hit single "Here," which reached the Top 20 in the United States. Before her original album was released, though, Cara was known for her acoustic song covers on YouTube.

YouTube Musical Celebrities

Other Artists have made a career by producing original content for their YouTube channel. A prime example is Lindsey Stirling. She plays the violin, she dances and then she does them both at the same time. Stirling began posting videos of herself performing in 2007 after failing to be signed by a major record label. Now, she claims they are begging to sign her, but it's too late—she doesn't need them anymore. Explains Stirling: "It's a very loyal fan base that wants you to succeed because they found you. It wasn't some big radio station or record label that shoved art down someone's throat." Coming in fourth in Forbes round-up of the most financially successful YouTube personalities, Stirling raked in $6 million in earnings last year. She has also released two albums, *Shatter Me* and *Lindsey Stirling*, scored a book deal, and developed a lucrative touring career.

YouTube's New Subscription Service

YouTube recently unveiled its long-discussed paid subscription service, "YouTube Red." The new service offers ad-free versions of all current YouTube videos, and additional exclusive content from some of the site's top creators including PewDiePie and Lilly Singh, both of whom perform music as well as comedy. It launched on October 28 and costs $9.99 per month. YouTube Red will have a big emphasis on music, providing access to music streaming service Google Play Music and a new app called YouTube Music, which offers a Pandora-like personalized playlist based on a selected song or artist. Both music apps also have ad-supported versions that non-Red users can access.

Self-Made Indie Videos Launching Careers on Social Media Such as Vine & Instagram

Over the past several years, with the advent of smart phones with video capability as well as greater connectivity across social platforms, an entirely new phenomenon has occurred: singer songwriters as well as rappers catapulting themselves to recognition and commercial success by using self-contained performances on social media in addition to, or other than YouTube. One example is Shawn Mendes. In 2013, when he was 15, Shawn Mendes began posting cover videos on Vine and picked up millions of views. The next year, he was signed to Island Records and became the youngest artist to debut in the Top 25 with a song on the *Billboard* Hot 100.

Legal and Business Issues

Cover Videos

It is legally necessary to get a license from the owner of the song before making a cover video. However, YouTube has developed a system, Content ID, that deals with this issue. The system recognizes the identity of the cover song and then notifies the publisher. The publisher can then choose to order YouTube to take down the video, or let the video continue to play and "monetize" it. If they choose the latter, YouTube splits the advertising revenue with the publisher. It is important to note that, if the publisher chooses the second option, the artist performing the cover *will not* receive any of the fees generated by advertising.

Vine and Instagram do not employ Content ID. But, the music publishers have not, so far, cracked down on covers on these social networks. An argument could be made that the snippets played in these services are "de minimis," *i.e.*, too trivial to amount to copyright infringement. It can also be argued that these brief videos are "fair use." The argument would be that, under the doctrine of fair use, a person can use a brief excerpt of a copyrighted work if the new work is "transformative" of the original.

Work for Hire Production Contract

I was the Director of Business Affairs for TV & Video at Sony Music from 1991 to 2001. We produced about 250 videos each year I was there, and every video we commissioned was a "work for hire." Under the copyright law, a work for hire is defined as follows:

> (1) a work prepared by an employee within the scope of his or her employment; or (2) a work specially ordered or commissioned for use as a contribution to a collective work, **as a part of a motion picture or other audiovisual work**, as a translation, as a supplementary work, as a compilation, as an instructional text, as a test, as answer material for a test, or as an atlas, **if the parties expressly agree in a written instrument signed by them that the work shall be considered a work made for hire**. (emphasis added.)

In the case of works made for hire, "the employer or other person for whom the work was prepared is considered the author . . . [and] owns all of the rights comprised in the copyright." Recently, I worked with a small book publishing company that wished to produce a series of music videos to promote the new edition on one of its religious textbooks. The videos will feature songs by 12 different Christian rock acts. The agreement that we used to commission the videos was basically the same as Sony's work for hire agreement. I recommend to my artist clients the same business format for the production of their music videos. Re-published below is sample work for hire contract for producing a music video.

Releases

If you are either a new artist or a small label, and you wish to create a music video, in addition to using a work for hire agreement, you should also make sure that you will not have legal problems associated later on with any person or location depicted in your video. Although you should always have every side artist, model, dancer, or actor in your video sign a release, some judgment is required when determining whether to secure a location release.

Personal Releases

If a label is commissioning a video, the artist's appearance in the video will generally be covered by the recording agreement between the artist and the label, which usually includes a provision specifically addressing music videos and gives the label the right to use the video for any promotional or commercial purpose. If an indie artist is appearing in a video, obviously she will not need a release for her own performance. But whether the commissioning party is a label or an artist, they will want to have any *other* person appearing or performing in the video sign a personal release giving the label or the artist, as the case may be, the right to use the video, including that person's appearance and/or performance in all media. Usually, the production company will handle this responsibility.

An example of a personal release is included below. Personal releases do not vary very much, although some contain more legalese than others. The basic point of any personal release, however, is that the person signing the release grants the artist or label all rights to use their appearance and/or performance in the video.

Note that the person signing such a release may have recorded their audio performance as a background vocalist or musician. A separate contract usually covers that audio recording, but the release contained below would cover that audio performance as well. Also note that the release usually does not include financial remuneration, but if a musician, dancer or actor contributed a performance in the underlying audio track, there may be a separate agreement in which that person is compensated.

A cautionary tale about failing to secure proper releases: the producer of a video for an artist at a major record label used a picture of an old girlfriend from her Facebook profile in a spilt second of a still titled "Missing Persons" in a video featuring the artist singing about a romantic break-up. The ex-girlfriend noticed and was not pleased. She retained a lawyer who was able to negotiate a significant settlement.

Crowds and Audiences

If you are shooting in a public place, releases should be given to anyone wandering into the scene if they are recognizable. If they don't want to sign the release, you should avoid using that footage. If you are shooting in front of a live audience you can use a sign at the entrance to the performance area informing the audience that, by entering, they consent to appearing in the video. The sign should be large enough and displayed in a place prominent enough that anyone entering will notice. However, if a person from the audience is featured, or especially if they appear on stage, they should sign a personal release.

Location Release

The location release at the end of this article is for a venue that agrees to let you shoot your video at their location without a fee. It is particularly useful if there is a sign or logo that people would recognize. The release will make it clear that no consideration was expected for the use of the location. Of course, sometimes a location, such as a restaurant or bar, will require a fee. In that case, the amount to be paid can be inserted in the release.

Public Places

Generally, if public venues and landmarks such as the Empire State Building appear in the video, you do not need a release if the location is incidental to the action in the video. But if, for instance, you are shooting in front of a well-known place such as Nathan's hotdog restaurant in Coney Island, and their name appears prominently in the video, it would be wise to have the manager sign a location release.

Trademarks

The use of a trademark in a music video is generally protected by the First Amendment, but not always.

Likelihood of Confusion Test

The limited purpose of trademark protection set forth in the Lanham Trademark Act (15 U.S.C. § 1051 et. seq.) is to avoid confusion in the marketplace by allowing a trademark owner to prevent others from duping consumers into buying a product or using a service they mistakenly believe is sponsored by the trademark owner. Trademark law aims to protect trademark owners from a false perception that they are associated with or endorse a product or service. Generally, to assess whether a defendant has infringed upon a plaintiff's trademark, the courts apply a "likelihood of confusion" test that asks whether use of the plaintiff's trademark by the defendant is likely to cause confusion or mistake, or to deceive as to the affiliation, connection, or association of plaintiff's brand with defendant's product or service.

Applying these principals to music videos, the bottom line is that if a trademark is used in such a way that it is not likely to confuse a viewer into thinking that the brand sponsored the video, the producer has a First Amendment right to use the mark. The classic example is a rapper wearing a baseball cap or t-shirt. Just because the singer may be wearing a Yankees cap or Baltimore Orioles t-shirt doesn't mean that a reasonable person would think that the Yankees or Orioles sponsored or produced the video.

On the other hand, where a trademark is prominently featured, it may be reasonable to think that a brand is sponsoring the video. For instance, a number of brands are featured in the video for "Telephone" featuring Beyoncé and Lady Gaga. But in that case, the brands were actually sponsoring the video by paying for product placement. In fact, these days, many indie artists use brands to help pay for or at least defray the costs of their videos. But, if you have not received approval or received a sponsorship from a brand, it is important not to lead your viewers to believe that you have by drawing too much attention to the brand in your video.

Product Disparagement

Also called product defamation, trade libel, or slander of goods, product disparagement is any statement about a brand that is false and likely to adversely affect its profits. Product disparagement includes negative statements about a product or service, false comparisons of competing consumer products or services, and statements harming the reputation of an artist.

Applying these principals to a music video, it is important to note that showing a brand's name or logo in a negative context could prompt a demand that the video be changed or not shown at all. Consider this real world example: a record label made a video in the early '90s, when MTV was still playing videos, of a toy train running off the track and smashing into small models of people made of clay. During the video, close-ups of the artist as the conductor of the wayward train would appear. The video was lighthearted, and no one would think that the artist/conductor was actually running over real people. However, the name of the well-known U.S. railroad appeared on the toy train, and they were less than amused. In fact, they sent a letter to MTV demanding that they stop playing the video. The label agreed to take the name off the toy train by blurring it, but the railroad still insisted that the video be banned because the color of the toy train—a particular shade of yellow—was the same color as its actual trains. The label reacted by changing the entire color of the video to sepia which made the toy trains a different shade of yellow. Yet, the railroad still had a problem because the cars were still yellow. The label defiantly re-released the video. But, the railroad company initiated a lawsuit against the label and was able to persuade a federal judge to permanently enjoin the further exhibition of the video on MTV and any other outlet. Later, the label settled the suit by paying damages to the railroad in addition to agreeing to never using the video for any purpose again.

Artwork and Other Copyrighted Works

Best practice is to avoid using material protected by copyright. This will save you a lot of headaches, and possibly money. For instance, in the late 90s, Faith Ringgold, a successful contemporary artist, sued BET (*Ringgold v. Black Entertainment Television*) for airing an episode of a television series called *ROC* in which a poster containing her artwork (a quilt including a painting) appeared. In the scene, at least a portion of the poster was shown a total of nine times. In some of those instances, the poster was at the center of the screen, although nothing in the dialogue, action, or camera work particularly called the viewer's attention to the poster. The nine sequences in which a portion of the poster was visible ranged in duration from 1.86 to 4.16 seconds. The aggregate duration of all nine sequences was 26.75 seconds.

In addition to its appearance in the scene, there was also qualitative connection between the poster and the show. The poster included a painting depicting a Sunday school picnic held by the Freedom Baptist Church in Atlanta, Georgia in 1909, and was intended to convey "aspects of the African-American experience in the early 1900s." *ROC* was a television sitcom series about a middle-class African-American family living in Baltimore, and the scene in question was of a gathering in a church hall with a minister. The case was decided by a federal appeals court in New York. The court found that HBO's production staff "evidently thought that the poster was well suited as a set decoration for the African-American church scene of a *ROC* episode." The court concluded that from the standpoint of a quantitative assessment of the segments, the principal four-to-five second segment in which almost all of the poster is clearly visible, although in less than perfect focus, re-enforced by the briefer segments in which smaller portions were visible, constituted copyright infringement and held in favor of the artist and found BET liable.

On the other hand, the case of *Sandoval vs. New Line Cinema Corp* stands for the proposition that use of copyrighted artwork in the background of a scene may be "de minimis." As already noted in the section on Covers above, if the amount a work copied is so trivial as to fall below the quantitative threshold of substantial similarity, the copying is not actionable.

In *Sandoval*, the same court that decided the *Ringgold* case found that the use of the plaintiff's copyrighted photographs in the motion picture "Seven" was de minimis and therefore not actionable. The photographs appeared in the film for a total of 35.6 seconds, but they were primarily in the background and were never in focus. The court found that the "photographs as used in the movie [were] not displayed with sufficient detail for the average lay observer to identify even the subject matter of the photographs, much less the style used in creating them."

The court found that the use of the artwork was de minimis and held in favor of the defendant.

VIDEO PRODUCTION AGREEMENT

The agreement below contemplates that an Artist is hiring a production company to produce a promo video. The same agreement may be used by a label. An Artist may consider forming a corporate entity (i.e., C corporation, Subchapter S, or LLC) in order to avoid any personal liability in any agreement, including a video production agreement. In addition, an Artist would be wise to consult with an accountant or attorney about forming an LLC or S corporation for tax purposes including eligibility to deduct video expenses from their income.

This agreement ("Agreement"), effective as of _____, 2017, is between _____ ("Artist") with an address of _____, and _____ ("Producer"), with an address at _____.

WITNESSETH:

WHEREAS, Producer has recognized expertise in video production; and

WHEREAS, Artist wishes to engage Producer to record a music video featuring Artist performing a song titled "_____" (the "Video").

NOW, THEREFORE, in consideration of the mutual covenants and agreements contained herein, the parties hereto agree as follows:

1. PRODUCTION SERVICES

1.1. Producer shall provide Artist with the filming and production services (hereinafter "Production Services") described within this Agreement.

1.2. Principal photography shall begin _____. Producer shall make delivery of the Video to Artist no later than _____. "Delivery" shall consist of delivery of (i) a fully edited sound synchronized video master, and (ii) all other recorded elements created during production including but not limited to all audio tracks, video footage and outtakes. Delivery will not be deemed to have occurred until Artist accepts the Video as suitable for its commercial exploitation.

1.3. Producer shall provide the Production Services to Artist and/or its affiliates promptly with the degree of skill, attention and due care that is standard practice within the professional Production Services industry.

1.4. Producer and Artist agree that the budget attached in Schedule A shall represent 100% of the funds required to produce the Video (hereinafter "Budget"). This amount represents the Producer's total anticipated costs and profit.

The budget should include all costs for producing the video, including producer and director fees. For examples of music video budgets ranging from "shoestring" to "commercial/studio" budgets, see http://garrettgibbons.com/music-video-budgets.

1.5. If the Producer hires a director (hereinafter "Director"), the Director shall be an employee of the Producer for purposes of the production and delivery of the Video.

1.6. All employees and representatives of Producer providing the Production Services hereunder to Artist during the Term of this Agreement shall be deemed for all purposes (including all compensation, taxes and employee benefits) to be employees or representatives solely of Producer, and not to be employees or representatives of Artist or to be independent contractors of Artist.

1.7. The Video shall depict content to be included in a treatment or script to be approved by Artist prior to principal photography.

2.   GRANT OF RIGHT: WORK MADE FOR HIRE

This clause transfers all rights to the person (or company as the case may be) commissioning the video.

2.1. Production Services provided by the Producer and any other person providing such Services shall be deemed to be provided on a "work made for hire" basis as that term is defined under the U.S. copyright law. The Video and all other materials created or contributed by the Producer including all footage, outtakes and audio tracks (the "Materials"), shall be the sole property of Artist throughout the universe, free from any claims whatsoever by Producer; and Artist shall have the exclusive right to register the copyright in such Materials in her name as the owner and author thereof and to secure any and all renewals and extensions of such copyright.

2.2. Without limiting the generality of the foregoing, Artist and any person authorized by Artist shall have the unlimited exclusive right, throughout the universe, to manufacture or create copies of the Video or any other Materials by any method now or hereafter known, derived from the Video or the Materials and to sell, market, transfer or otherwise deal in the same under any trademarks, trade names and labels, or to refrain from such manufacture, sale and dealing.

2.3. Artist or any Person authorized by Artist shall have the right throughout the universe, and may grant to others the right, to reproduce, print, publish, or disseminate in any medium the name, portraits, pictures, likenesses and biographical material concerning Producer and Director any other person providing Production Services, as news or information, or for the purposes of trade, or for advertising purposes, in connection with promotion marketing and sale of the Video. As used in this Agreement, "name" shall include, without limitation, any of professional names.

3. COMPENSATION

3.1. The Parties agree that the Effective Date of this Agreement shall be as set forth at the beginning of this Agreement (hereinafter "Effective Date"). The parties acknowledge that the total amount of the attached Budget _____ Dollars ($_____). Within five (5) days of the Effective Date, Artist shall pay Producer 50% of the Budget, that is, _____ Dollars. The second payment of 25%, that is, _____ Dollars, shall be due upon completion of filming. The third and last 25% payment of _____ Dollars shall be due upon delivery of the Video and all other footage to Artist.

3.2. Overages. In regard to overages to the Budget, Producer shall not charge Artist any monies in addition to the approved Budget without Artist's prior written approval.

4. NOTICES

Notices, reports, accountings or other communication which Producer or Artist may require or desire to send to the other must be delivered EITHER by:

Certified mail, return receipt requested to the parties at the addresses first written above or other address to be designated by Producer or Artist; or

Electronic mail at the following addresses:

   (i)   for Artist: _____@____.com
   (ii) for Producer: _____@____.com

5. ASSIGNMENT

Producer may not assign this Agreement or any right or obligations under this Agreement. Artist may assign this Agreement or any of her rights or obligations hereunder to any person, firm, or corporation including a corporation in which Artist is a principal, provided that (i) Artist shall remain responsible for any payments required to be made under this Agreement, and (ii) the assignee has the necessary cash on hand to make any payments required under this Agreement.

6. WARRANTIES AND INDEMNIFICATION

6.1. Producer warrants and represents that it has the legal right to enter into this Agreement including the legal right to sign on behalf of the Director. Producer further warrants and represents that (a) all content contributed by the Producer shall be original and not interfere with or violate any rights of any third party; and (b) no content appearing in the Video, including artwork or photography, will interfere with or violate any rights of any third party.

6.2 Producer warrants and represents that he shall provide valid signed releases from any third party performing or appearing appearing in the video, and that he shall secure valid signed location releases from any location appearing in the video. Acceptable forms of release are attached hereto as Schedule "A" and "B" respectively.

The attached releases may be used as Schedules A and B. Note that the releases allow the Producer to assign the rights secured in the releases to the Artist.

6.3. Producer and each of its representatives, employees, contractors, agents and representatives hereby release, indemnify and agree to hold harmless Artist and her agents and representatives ("Producer Indemnitees") from and against any and all losses and/or damages which arise out of the Production Services.

7. TERMINATION

Artist may terminate this Agreement upon written notice in the event of a material breach by Producer, including late delivery of the Video, if such breach is not cured within ten (10) days of notice thereof. If such breach is not cured within that time, Producer shall not be entitled to any additional payments and, upon notice by Artist, Producer shall refund to Artist any monies previously paid.

8. MISCELLANEOUS

8.1. Governing Law. This Agreement shall be interpreted under the laws of the state of _____, and the parties submit to the exclusive jurisdiction of the courts of the state and federal courts located within _____ without regard to its choice-of-law rules.

The Artist should make governing law and jurisdiction his or her own state.

8.2. Relationship of Parties. Producer and Artist shall have the relationship of independent contractors. Nothing herein shall be construed to place Producer and Artist in the relationship of principal and agent, employer and employee, master and servant, partners, or joint venturers, and neither party shall, either expressly or by implication, have represented themselves as having any authority to make contracts in the name of, or binding on, each other, or to obligate the other in any manner.

8.3. Complete Agreement. Producer and Artist acknowledge that this Agreement represents the complete and exclusive statement of the agreement between the Producer and Artist with regard to the subject matter herein, and that it supersedes any proposal or prior agreement, whether oral or written, and any other communications between the Parties relating to the subject matter of this agreement.

8.4. Enforcement. If any provision of this Agreement shall be found invalid or unenforceable, then such provision shall not invalidate or in any way affect the enforceability of the remainder of this Agreement.

UNDERSTOOD AND AGREED:

[ARTIST's NAME]

_____

[NAME OF PRODUCTION COMPANY]

_____
Authorized Signatory

I hereby agree to all the terms and conditions set forth above and shall be personally liable for any breach of this Agreement by Producer:

_____
Name of President of Production Company

PERSONAL RELEASE

To _____
Address

Dear Sirs:

I understand that _____ ("Producer") is producing a music video containing the song "_____" featuring _____ (the "Video").

For good and valuable consideration, including my desire to appear in the Video, I irrevocably grant to Producer, its licensees and assigns the right to film, videotape, portray and photograph me, my likeness and my performance, and to record my voice and other sound effects, and the right to use them or any portion thereof, and my name and any biographical facts which may have been provided to you, in connection with the production of the Video and the advertising, promotion and publicity therefor, and all rights of every nature whatsoever in and to all films, video, portrayals, photographs, performances and recordings produced hereunder ("Material"), including without limitation all copyrights therein and renewals and extensions thereof, and the exclusive right to reproduce, exhibit, distribute and otherwise exploit the Material in whole or in part in perpetuity throughout the universe in all languages, in any and all versions (including digitized versions) and forms, and in any and all media now known or hereafter devised. Independently and apart from any consideration accruing to me hereunder, I hereby release Producer and Producer's authorized designees from, and covenant not to sue Producer and Producer's authorized designees for any claim or cause of action, whether known or unknown, for libel, slander, invasion of right of privacy, publicity or personality, or any other claim or cause of action, based upon or relating to the exercise of any of the rights referred to herein. I understand that nothing herein will require Producer or Producer's designees actually to produce or utilize any Material hereunder.

The point of this release is that the signor grants the right to use their appearance and/or performance in the Video and in any promotion of the Video.

This grant is irrevocable so that you may proceed in reliance thereon. This instrument contains the entire understanding of the parties, may not be changed or terminated except by an instrument by you and me and will be construed in accordance with the laws of the State of _____, provided that the courts of the state of _____ shall have exclusive jurisdiction to resolve any disputes arising from this Release.

Dated: _____

Authorized Signature

_____

[Print name]

LOCATION RELEASE

Property Owner: [Name]

Address: _____ _____

Phone: _____ Fax: _____

Email: _____ Contact: _____

Producer: [Name]

Address: _____ _____

Phone: _____ Fax: _____

Email: _____ Contact: _____

Your signature in the space provided below as owner or agent, will confirm the following agreement ("Agreement") between you as the Property Owner ("Owner") and Producer regarding filming of your property (the "Premises") described below in connection with a video containing the performance of a song titled "_____" (the "Video").

1. For good and valuable consideration, the receipt and sufficiency of which is hereby acknowledged, Owner hereby grants to Producer the right during the Term (as defined below) hereof to photograph and record at, the Premises (including, without limitation, the right to photograph and record both the real and personal property, all of the signs, displays, exteriors, and the like appearing therein, if any) for the period specified below.

> This location release contemplates that the Producer is not paying the owner of the location for use of the premises, but this release could easily be converted into an agreement under which the Producer does pay a fee.

2. As used herein, the term "Premises" refers to the premises located at: _____

_____

3. The term hereof (the "Term") shall commence from _____ am/pm to _____ am/pm on or about _____ and shall continue until _____, unless modified by the parties. The Term shall be subject to modification due to changes in production schedules. Owner agrees to consult closely with Producer's representatives to ensure scheduling is arranged which will allow for completion of the scenes planned to be included in the Video using the Premises. Owner acknowledges that Producer is incurring significant expenses in reliance on Owner's cooperation and participation in connection with this Agreement and that Owner may be held responsible for the actual and/or consequential damages incurred by any breach of this agreement.

4. Owner represents and warrants that: (a) Owner has the right and authority to make and enter into this Agreement and to grant Producer the rights set forth herein, without the obtaining of any consents or permissions from anyone; and (b) Owner shall take no action, nor allow or authorize any third party to take any action which might interfere with Producer's authorized use of the Premises. Owner hereby waives all rights of privacy or other rights of a similar nature with respect to Producer's use of the Premises. Owner shall indemnify Producer, its licensees and assigns, and their parent, affiliate, and related entities, shareholders, directors, officers and employees from and against any breach or claim of breach by Owner of any representation, warranty, agreement or obligation herein.

5. Producer shall leave the Property in as good condition as when received, reasonable wear and tear to be expected. Producer shall remove all of its material, equipment and personnel from the Property.

6. Producer agrees to indemnify and hold Owner harmless from damage to the Premises and property located thereon and for personal injury occurring on the Premises during the Term and from any liability and loss which Owner may incur by reason of any accidents, injuries, death or other damage to the Premises directly caused by Producer's negligence in

connection with its use of the Premises. In connection therewith Owner must submit to Producer, within three (3) days after Producer vacates the Premises, a detailed list of any property damage or personal injuries which Owner feels Producer is responsible, failing which Owner will be deemed to have acknowledged that there is no property damage or personal injuries for which Producer is responsible. Owner shall permit Producer's representatives to inspect any damaged property and to verify any claims for damages by Owner.

Paragraphs 5 and 6 clearly protect the location owner from potential harm that could happen during a shoot on his premises.

7. Nothing shall obligate Producer to photograph, to use such photography, or to otherwise use the Premises. Producer shall have the right to photograph, record and depict the Premises and/or any part or parts thereof, accurately or otherwise, as Producer may choose, using and/or reproducing the actual name, signs, logos, trademarks and other identifying features thereof and/or without regard to the actual appearance or name of the Premises or any part or parts thereof, in connection with the Movie and any other Movies produced by Producer.

8. (a) Owner acknowledges that, as between Owner and Producer, Producer is the copyright owner of the photography and/or recordings of the Premises, and that Producer, its successors and assigns have the irrevocable and perpetual right, throughout the universe, in any matter and in any media to use and exploit the films, photographs, and recordings made of or on the Premises in such manner and to such extent as Producer desires in its sole discretion without payment of additional compensation to Owner. Producer and its licensees, assigns and successors shall be the sole and exclusive owner of all rights of whatever nature, including all copyrights, in and to all films, programs, products (including interactive and multimedia products), photographs, and recordings made on or of the Premises, and in the advertising and publicity thereof, in perpetuity throughout the universe.

(b) The undersigned hereby gives to Producer, its assigns, agents, licensees, affiliates, clients, principals, and representatives the absolute right to use any names associated with the Property in the Video, or to promote the Video, all without inspection or further consent or approval by the undersigned of the Movie.

9. Producer may assign or transfer this Agreement or all or any part of its rights hereunder to any person, film or corporation; Owner agrees that it shall not have the right to assign or transfer this Agreement.

10. From the date of execution of this Agreement, through and including the date this Agreement may be terminated, Licensee shall keep or cause to be kept in force the following insurance:

Commercial General Liability Insurance, including public liability, contractual liability, bodily injury, and property damage insurance, each policy with a combined single limit of bodily injury and property damage liability of $1,000,000.00 per accident or occurrence. Owner shall be an additional insured. The policies shall provide that they cannot be canceled or reduced without thirty (30) days prior written notice to Owner. Automobile and mobile equipment liability insurance, including property damage, with a combined single limit of not less than $1,000,000.00 per accident. Owner shall be an additional insured. The policies shall provide that they cannot be canceled or reduced without thirty (30) days prior written notice to Owner.

All insurance policies required hereunder shall be with companies having at least a Best A+10 rating as of the date of issuance of the policy, and shall contain language to the extent obtainable, to the effect that (i) any loss shall be payable notwithstanding any act or negligence of Owner that might otherwise result in a forfeiture of the insurance, (ii) that the insurer waives the right to subrogation against Owner and against Owner's agents and representatives, including Owner's insurers, (iii) that the policies are primary and non-contributing with any insurance that may be carried by Owner. Producer shall furnish Owner with certificates evidencing the insurance on or before _____. All certificates of insurance required herein, and exclusions from coverage in all policies, and the actual liability policies are subject to the approval of Owner's Counsel.

Insurance is a good idea for both the Producer and the party commissioning the Video to have if shooting occurs at a location such as someone's house, in case there is damage to the property. The cost of the insurance should be included in the Budget for the Video.

---

11. This Agreement constitutes a binding agreement and is the entire agreement among Producer and Owner and supersedes all prior negotiations and communications, whether written or oral; representations and warranties, whether written or oral; and documents and writings, whether signed or unsigned, with respect to the subject matter hereof.

APPROVED AND ACCEPTED:

Owner or Owner Representative

Signature: _____

Print Name: _____

Producer or Producer Representative

Signature: _____

Print Name: _____

CHAPTER **10**

BAND AGREEMENTS AND
ESSENTIAL BUSINESS ACTIONS
A BAND (OR SOLO ARTIST)
CAN TAKE AT LITTLE TO NO COST
WITHOUT THE SERVICES
OF AN ATTORNEY

INTRODUCTION: ESSENTIAL BUSINESS ACTIONS ANY BAND OR ARTIST SHOULD AND CAN DO WITHOUT INCURRING LEGAL FEES

The first part of this Introduction discusses business actions a band can take at little to no cost without the services of an attorney. The second part examines the elements and benefits of an agreement between members of a band or musical group pertaining to important issues such as decision making, division of money (including performance and recording revenues), treatment of leaving members, and ownership of band property such as the band name, songs, and masters.

Band agreements usually require the services of an experienced music attorney to draft a legally enforceable contract. A sample band agreement provided by my friend and colleague, veteran music attorney Wallace Collins, is included in this article. If you take a glimpse at it, you will see it takes a lot of thought and work. A lot of experts, especially lawyers, advise clients to prepare and enter into a band agreement as soon as possible after the band's formation. They argue that this is the time when everyone in the band is getting along well, whereas it would be difficult to complete an agreement if there is already a dispute among the members. On the other hand, the vast majority of bands and music groups rehearse and perform at clubs and other venues on a part-time basis, and make little money, if any, at the beginning of their careers. It may not be worthwhile (i) to spend the time needed to discuss and reach consensus on all the complicated issues usually covered by a band

251

agreement, and (ii) to spend the money on an experienced lawyer to draft an enforceable agreement. As famed music manager and industry mogul, Irving Azoff, says in an interview presented later in this chapter, sometimes getting an agreement at the beginning of a band's career can be like a prenup; it can end a band's "marriage" before it even begins.

Here's the bottom line: if a band starts making good money, and it looks like they may have a real future, then they should consider taking the time and spending the money to create an enforceable band agreement. In the meantime, any band or musical group should take these basic business actions discussed in Section I below.

Essential Business Actions Any Band or Musical Group Should Take Without Incurring Legal Fees

These are the actions a band can and should take without using a lawyer:

- Sign a "split sheet" for every song written by more than one individual;
- Register all songs and masters with the U.S. Copyright Office;
- Register every song with the appropriate performing rights organization (PRO);
- Upload the set list of any live performance containing original songs for payment by their PRO; and
- Write up a simple agreement that no leaving member can use the name of the band without permission.

Make a Split Sheet for Every Song

What is a Split Sheet?

A split sheet states who owns what percentage of a song and sets forth the credit each person should receive. A split sheet should be created for each and every song that was created by more than one person and should be filled out and signed by all the writers before ever shopping it to a third party or trying to license it for placements. Every day around the world, songwriters collaborate on songs and never clarify who wrote what. But, if you are ever fortunate enough to license your song for a commercial, movie, or TV show, you may find yourself fighting over who receives what percentage of the revenues generated from your song.

Many songwriters and artists just want to create great music and may feel uncomfortable introducing a split sheet and dividing up shares of publishing when they're trying to be creative. However, it's a necessary part of the songwriting process. Have a meeting about split sheets prior to hitting the studio. This way everyone understands that it's not personal, it's just business. Doing this makes everyone feel as though their interests are protected, which can enhance creativity rather than inhibiting it.

How Do You Complete a Split Sheet?

Split sheets should contain the following information:

- The name of each writer;
- Percent of ownership. This is key. If the song makes money, this will determine how much each writer will receive;
- Credit for each writer, including who wrote the lyrics and who composed the underlying music;
- Everyone's signature;

Below is a sample split sheet:

WRITERS' SPLIT SHEET FOR SINGLE SONG

Date: _____

This is to confirm that we, the sole writers of the composition listed below, hereby agree among ourselves to the following writers' divisions:

Song Title: "_____"

Writers & % Ownership:

Writer Name: _____ Ownership % _____

Writer Name: _____ Ownership % _____

Writer Name: _____ Ownership % _____

Writer Name: _____ Ownership % _____

Credits:

Lyrics by: _____, _____

Music by: _____, _____

Produced by: _____, _____

If any samples are contained on this song for which the sampled writer(s)/ publisher(s) are to receive a copyright interest in and to the Composition and/ or payment of monies attributable to the Composition, then we agree that our own shares in the copyright and/or monies attributable to the Composition shall be reduced proportionately.

The following list of samples represent all of those samples embodied in the above composition:

Name of Song by Name of Writer

_____

_____

_____

This Agreement contains the entire understanding of the parties hereto relating to the subject matter hereof and cannot be changed or terminated except by an instrument signed by all of the parties hereunder. The validity, interpretation and legal effect of this Agreement shall be governed by the laws of the State of _____ applicable to contracts wholly entered into and performed entirely within the State of _____.

Signature below will indicate agreement of the above.

Read and Agreed: Read and Agreed:

_____   _____

Read and Agreed: Read and Agreed:

_____   _____

Registering Songs & Masters with the U.S. Copyright Office

Why Register?

Registration is not a prerequisite for copyright protection. Under the Copyright Act of 1976, a copyright comes into existence as soon as a work is fixed in a tangible medium of expression, and registration is not a condition of copyright protection. However, registration provides crucial benefits to copyright owners. Those benefits, which are set forth at the U.S. Copyright Office's website at www.copyright.gov/circs/circ01.pdf, include the following:

- Registration establishes a public record of the copyright claim;
- Before an infringement suit may be filed in court, registration is necessary for works of U.S. origin;
- If made before or within five years of publication, registration will establish prima facie evidence in court of the validity of the copyright and of the facts stated in the certificate;
- If registration is made within three months after publication of the work or prior to an infringement of the work, statutory damages and attorney's fees will be available to the copyright owner in court actions. Otherwise, only an award of actual damages and profits is available to the copyright owner;
- Registration allows the owner of the copyright to record the registration with the U.S. Customs Service for protection against the importation of infringing copies.

Of the reasons to register set forth above, the most important are that a copyright owner (i) cannot start a lawsuit for copyright infringement before registering, and (ii) cannot secure statutory damages or attorneys' fees without registering. With respect to (ii), the Copyright Act provides for statutory damages of up to $150,000 per infringement and attorneys fees. It is crucial that if the work has been published (that is released for sale), the registration occurs *prior* to any infringement. Otherwise, the plaintiff must prove actual damages, which can be difficult to quantify, or may equal a negligible amount unless the defendant earned a lot of money from the infringing work. Also, attorneys' fees are only available for published works that are registered prior to the infringement. Similar to other litigation, a lawsuit for copyright infringement can take a great deal of work and time on the part of the attorney. That is why attorneys' fees can add up. It would be difficult or impossible to retain the services of an experienced copyright litigator without the potential for recovering attorneys' fees.

Note that the only way to secure the benefits of copyright registration is to register with the U.S. Copyright Office. These benefits, contrary to a popular myth, cannot be obtained by sending a copy of your song or master to yourself (even by certified or registered mail).

How Do You Register?

To register a work, including a song or a master, you need to submit a completed application form, a nonrefundable filing fee, and a nonreturnable copy of the work. Here are answers to the most important questions regarding registration:

Where to apply?

You can find and complete the copyright registration application online at http://www. copyright.gov/eco (*eco* is an acronym for Electronic Copyright Office).

How much will it cost?

The basic fee for registering any work, including a song or master, was raised from $35 to $55 in May 2014. However, the fee is still $35 for registering a single work by a single author.

What else needs to be done?

It is also necessary to provide a "deposit" of the work. This can be done by uploading an MP3, or you can print out a "shipping slip" to be enclosed with a CD and mail it to the Copyright Office within 30 days of applying for the registration.

Is it possible to register a sound recording and a song in one application?

Yes. To register a master and a song in one application, click on "Sound Recording" in the drop down menu in the part of the application asking for the type of work to be registered.

Later in the application, there will be a page allowing you to claim music and lyrics as well as the sound recording.[2]

Any signatory to the split sheet can register the copyright in a song and/or master. They should include all the other signatories to the split sheet as joint "authors" in the application. Finally, the U.S. Copyright Office's website (www.copyright.gov) is an invaluable source of information not only on registration, but also on how copyright law protects songs and masters.

Registering with a PRO & Uploading Set Lists From Live Shows To Make Some Money

What is a PRO?

Any user of music that publicly performs a song must secure a license and pay a royalty to do so. Songwriters and their music publishers use Performing Rights Organizations (PROs) to collect these royalties. In the U.S., there are three: ASCAP, BMI, and SESAC. A fourth PRO, recently launched by music industry mogul, Irving Azoff, is Global Music Rights or GMR. The PROs collect public performance royalties from radio, television, the Internet as well as physical venues such as bars, nightclubs, concert halls, arenas, and other places where live or recorded music is played.

In order to collect public performance monies you must be a member of one of the three PROs. Anyone can join ASCAP or BMI. SESAC and GMR are selective. For advice on selecting a PRO see Chapter 6.

When a song is registered with one of the PROs, the PRO will require the person registering the song to indicate the percent ownership of each writer. If the band has a manager, she can perform this function. The registration should reflect the breakdown of ownership in the split sheet. Even if no split sheet was ever signed, the registration will itself be a record of the percent ownership of each member in the band. That's why each member with an interest in a song should check to see if the information supplied to the PRO is accurate.

---

[2] It is also possible to register more than one song and/or sound recording at a time by carefully following the rules established by the Copyright Office. See Circular 1, Copyright Basics, p8, http://www.copyright.gov/circs/circ01.pdf. However, it is important to note that, if a recording is not released as a single, but is merely contained in an album, the album may be deemed to be "one work," and statutory damages may be limited to one award per album. See the decision in *Bryant v. Media Rights Productions, Inc.*, 603 F.3d 135 (2d Cir 2010): "Based on a plain reading of the statute . . . infringement of an album should result in only one statutory damage award. The fact that each song may have received a separate copyright is irrelevant to this analysis." *Id.* at 141.

Live Performance Payments

Each of the PROs pays its writer and publisher affiliates for live performances at venues across the U.S. Basically, all the songwriter has to do is submit a set list of songs performed at any venue showing which songs were written by him or her. Generally, he or she must also provide the venue name, address, size of venue, and the dates of the performance. The songs must be registered first in order to complete this process. For more information on each of the PRO's live performance programs, go to:

- www.sesac.com/WritersPublishers/HowWePay/liveperformances.aspx
- www.bmi.com/creators/royalty/live_concert_royalties
- www.ascap.com/members/onstage.aspx

Anecdotally, I know a singer/songwriter in New York City who played shows at bars and restaurants and made about $200 a gig from passing the hat. She made $1,250 from SESAC by reporting her set lists for a single calendar quarter—one accounting period. Her name is Jennifer Sullivan, and for tips from Jennifer on making money from live performance, see Chapter 8.

Protecting the Band Name

Make Everyone Agree That Leaving Members Will Not Be Able to Use the Band Name

Even in the absence of a full-blown band agreement, a band or musical group can handle the issue of who owns the name by using a form such as this:

BAND NAME AGREEMENT

Date: _____

Re "_____" [Name of band]

This is to confirm that we, the sole members the above referenced band, hereby agree among ourselves that each member of the band is a joint owner of the name of the band, provided that no leaving member, whether that member leaves voluntarily or not, shall be able to use the name of the band in connection with the entertainment industry including the music business.

This Agreement contains the entire understanding of the parties hereto relating to the subject matter hereof and cannot be changed or terminated except by an instrument signed by all of the parties hereunder. The validity, interpretation and legal effect of this Agreement shall be governed by the laws of the State of _____ applicable to contracts wholly entered into and performed entirely within the State of _____. [Use the state where the band members reside]

Signature below will indicate agreement of the above.

Read and Agreed: Read and Agreed:

_____   _____

Read and Agreed: Read and Agreed:

_____   _____

Note that sometimes a band will want to handle ownership of the band's name in a different manner than in the sample agreement. For instance, where two of the members founded the band and then added a third or more members later, the founders may want to exclusively own the rights in the name, or they may wish to allow leaving members the right to use the band's name, provided that the leaving member uses the words "formerly of." For a band that wishes to treat the ownership or use of the band's name in a different manner than the sample agreement, it may be wise to hire a lawyer.

Consider Registration of the Band Name with the U.S. Trademark Office

A band should also consider registering their name as a trademark with the U.S. Trademark Office. (www.uspto.gov/trademark). In the U.S., it isn't necessary to register a mark to obtain protectable rights. You can establish "common law" rights in a mark based solely on use of the mark in commerce without a registration. However, owning a federal trademark registration provides a number of significant advantages over common law rights alone, including:

- A legal presumption of your ownership of the mark and your exclusive right to use the mark nationwide;
- The ability to bring an action concerning the mark in federal court;
- The use of the U.S. registration as a basis to obtain registration in foreign countries.

Registration fees depend on the kind of form you use and the number of "classes" you file for. Classes refer to goods and services for which you are using the mark. A band would always want to file under class 41, which includes entertainment services. You may possibly also consider filing for class 25, which includes clothing such as t-shirts and hats. The cheapest form is called "TEAS[3] Plus" and costs $225 per class. But, this form requires somewhat more

---

[3] Trademark Electronic Application System.

information and is slightly more difficult to complete than two other possible forms: TEAS Reduced Fee (which costs $275 per class), and TEAS Regular Filing (which has the least number of requirements, and costs $325 per class).

Unlike the other recommended business actions previously discussed in this article, it is advisable to use an attorney for a trademark application. Filing a trademark application, or even deciding on the right form to use, is a bit tricky, and experience in filling out the appropriate application and dealing with the Trademark Office is important. For instance, a failure to correctly list the goods/services with which you use the mark, or intend to use the mark, may prevent you from registering your mark, and you will not be given a refund of any fees paid.

Band Agreements

Why Bother?

When two or more people associate for the purpose of doing business, arguably they create a partnership in the eyes of the law. General partnership law applies to the association unless a written agreement states otherwise. General partnership law provides, among other things, that all partners equally own partnership property and share in profits and losses, that any partner can bind the partnership, and that each partner is fully liable for the debts of the partnership. In the case of most musical groups, a written agreement setting forth the arrangement between the group members as partners is preferable to general partnership law.

For instance, if one person decided to create a band and came up with the band's name, he or she may want exclusive rights to make the band's decisions and the right to fire any new band member. That person may also want a bigger percentage of band profits, especially if she pays more money than other band members for touring or studio time. As an example, I represent one person who started a band in China. He created the name and moved to the U.S., where he selected all new band members. He's the lead singer and writes all the songs. In this situation, it may be better to simply employ the other band members as freelancers and pay them a certain percentage of money from live gigs, but stipulate that he can replace them at will.

When Should a Band Have an Agreement?

When a time comes that a band is beginning to make decent money, and it's clear that they actually have a future together, that may be a good time to take the plunge. It will involve taking the time to consider the issues discussed below, coming to a consensus among all the members of the band, and then hiring an attorney to draft an enforceable agreement.

What Are the Basic Elements of a Band Agreement?

A band agreement is an agreement between the members of a band that covers basic business issues. The most important issues are:

- Decision making;
- Hiring and firing;
- Profits and Losses;
- Treatment of Leaving Members;
- Band name;
- Ownership of Songs and Masters.

Decision Making

The issue of control is very important. In most cases, each member will have an equal vote and a majority will rule. However, as set forth in the sample agreement provided by Wallace Collins, a particular member may have two votes, and the manager may have a tie-breaking vote. The agreement may also provide that certain matters such as requiring financial contributions from group members or incurring debts on behalf of the band require a unanimous vote. Again, there are endless variations, including situations where a particular member makes all of the decisions, or where new members do not have a vote on band business. For instance, a band could agree on what might be called a "reverse democracy:" each member has one vote but if any member voted against doing something then the band would not do it. In other words, this arrangement requires unanimous consent to proceed with an activity.

Hiring and Firing of Band Members

Another issue of control that must be decided concerns the hiring and firing of band members: how votes are calculated (e.g., will each member get one vote or will a particular member's vote count double or more) and how many votes are needed (e.g., a majority or a unanimous vote) to fire a group member and/or hire a new member. In most cases, a new member voted into the group will then be required to sign on to the band agreement. It must also be decided how to vote on any amendments to the band agreement since this may materially affect the relationship between the members after the group has started. In most cases, a majority vote will be deemed determinative, but some members may prefer a unanimous vote on such things as amending the agreement (as well as hiring or firing). This will have to be decided between and among the members of the group.

Profits and Losses

The band agreement should contain provisions regarding the sharing of profits and losses. One provision may pertain to revenues earned during the term while each member is in the group, and another may pertain to after the departure of a member or the break-up of the group. In most cases, a new group will have a provision that all profits from the group are shared equally between all members with an exclusion for songwriting monies (which each of the respective songwriter members would keep). Where an established group adds new members, the provision may provide that a new member gets a smaller percentage than the founding members.

Treatment of Leaving Members

The more complicated problem of revenue division arises after a member departs. The agreement may provide that the leaving member is entitled to his full partnership share of profits earned during his tenure but a reduced percentage (or no percentage) of profits derived from activities after his departure; or the agreement may provide for a reduced percentage for a short period of time after departure (*e.g.*, 90 days) and nothing thereafter. This is an easier issue to deal with regarding live performances than record royalties. In most cases, bands will agree that leaving members should receive their share of live performance profits during the time the member was in the band, even if it is received after the member's departure. But, the group also needs to determine what happens, for example, when a member performs on three albums but leaves before the fourth album is recorded. Although it might be acceptable to refuse to pay the leaving member any royalties on the fourth and future albums recorded by the group under a record contract the leaving member signed as part of the group, it might not be fair to refuse to pay that leaving member his share of royalties from the three albums that he did record with the band. Of course, this might vary depending on whether the leaving member quit or was fired. Another important financial issue is the question of the leaving member's share of partnership property such as band recording equipment or a sound system. Again, the agreement might specify a monetary payout to the leaving member if he is terminated but a forfeiture if the leaving member quits. If merchandise with the leaving member's name and likeness still in inventory is sold after the member leaves, a decision will have to be made about whether and how much the departed member might receive for the use of his name and likeness.

Buy-Out/Pay-Out Provisions

A band contract should contain a comprehensive Buy-out/Pay-out provision that deals with departing members. Whether the leaving member quits or is fired, the agreement may provide that the leaving member waives all rights in the intangible assets of the partnership (*e.g.*, the group name, the group contracts, etc.). If the member quits, he may waive any right to and benefit derived from the hard assets such as band sound equipment. If the leaving member is fired, the agreement might provide that he or she is entitled to the pro-rata percentage (*i.e.*, a proportionate share) of the current value of the hard assets. With respect to this payout, the band contract may provide that if the valuation exceeds a certain amount (e.g., $25,000) or would put the partnership in financial distress, the payout would be in a certain number of equal monthly installments (*e.g.*, over 12 months).

Again, this Buy-out/Pay-out provision can be as simple or as complicated as the band members deem necessary. There are as many variations in this as there are differences in personalities between the members of a group. Each member and each group, with the help of an attorney, has to find its own solutions.

Band Name

As previously discussed, an important issue is who owns the group name if one member leaves or if a group breaks up. Under partnership law, the partners would be the owners of the name and any member would arguably be permitted to use the name. Trademark rights are determined based on the use of a mark, not on who thought of it, so each of the members of the group would be an equal co-owner of the group name under trademark law. The end result could be chaos, with several bands all with the same name but different members.

One solution would be to use the brief agreement previously discussed. Or, the matter can be handled in the context of a full-scale band agreement. In most cases, the band agreement will state, as the short form agreement previously discussed does, that if a particular member leaves the band, either because he quits or is fired, he will not be entitled to use the band name. The band agreement could fine tune this provision by stating that the leaving member may describe himself as a "former member" of the band.

However, if one member thought up the group name, then the band agreement may state that only a group including that member can use the name. This will apply whether one other member leaves or if the group disbands.

Rights in the group name may also concern revenues in addition to the use rights, specifically as they concern merchandise such as t-shirts, caps, buttons, and posters. The band agreement may deal with how much each member of the band will receive from sales of such merchandise.

Ownership of Songs and Masters

We previously discussed how important it is to confirm who the writers of a band's songs are and that a split sheet can be used to confirm ownership. The band agreement could include a provision incorporating split sheets, or the agreement could provide that any song created by any member of the band would be jointly owned by all the band members. This would only make sense where the band operates as a collective, and every member is invited and does make contributions to the creation of each song.

The band agreement could also confirm that every member of the band is a joint owner of any recordings made during the life of a band. This makes sense if each member of the band is performing on recorded tracks.

Advantages of Forming an LLC and Entering into an Operating Agreement Instead of a Band Agreement

An alternative to a traditional band agreement would be forming a limited liability company (or LLC) and then drafting an "operating agreement" which would look pretty much the same as a band agreement, expect each member of the band would be a "member." The big advantage of this approach is that when the band enters into agreements with third parties, such as an investor, the personal assets of the band members would not be at risk. This is called "limited liability."

Role of the Lawyer

If each member of a band or music group could afford his or her own lawyer, then each lawyer could work out an arrangement on behalf of his or her client. In the real world, that will usually not be the case. Instead, after a band decides on the issues discussed above, they should engage an attorney to review their decisions and write up a legally enforceable agreement. An attorney cannot represent each member of the band. That would create a "conflict of interest" on the part of the lawyer. What an attorney can do is be a "scribe" who enforces the decisions of the band by preparing an agreement that is legally enforceable. Fees can range from a $1,000 to $5,000 or more depending on the lawyer and the complexity of the deal.

INTERVIEW WITH IRVING AZOFF

Irving Azoff has been one of the most successful managers in the history of pop and rock music, having managed acts such as The Eagles, Christina Aguilera, Journey, Van Halen, Steely Dan, Gwen Stefani, and many others. Since September 2013, he has been chairman and CEO of Azoff MSG Entertainment, a venture with The Madison Square Garden Company. He's also the head of a new public performance rights organization called Global Music Rights. Prior to this, he served as chairman and CEO of Ticketmaster Entertainment and was executive chairman of Live Nation Entertainment and CEO of Front Line Management. In 2012, he topped Billboard's Power 100 and was named the most powerful person in the music industry.

SG: Irving, thank you so much for allowing me to do this interview with you.

My pleasure, Steve.

SG: As you know I want to discuss the business side of being in a band, specifically, how to avoid or resolve disputes if they arise and the usefulness of a band agreement, and perhaps the limitations of a band agreement. First, you have been the manager of some of the most successful bands of all time, including The Eagles, of course. In addition to their fame for being brilliant musicians and songwriters, the members of The Eagles have been famous for legal battles with each other. Without revealing any confidences, can you tell us what you have learned about how to deal with conflicts between band members from your experience with the Eagles or any other bands that you've managed?

Yeah. First of all, the Eagles have had that reputation because they had that one big blowup when Don Felder left the band. But, the reality of the fact is that was the only real legal battle or real litigation that I remember the band really ever having. It was definitely a big, loud one. But different bands and different guys see it in different ways. Without really getting into names, some bands that look like they're bands, the key player or key leader may get 50%. In other ones, there have been agreements where certain guys have different percentages. And I've seen other ones where certain guys have percentages and certain guys are salaried, especially when guys leave bands and come back. Making music is an art form. Touring is an art form. These are creative people, and some of them have different creative thoughts. Some of them, it's all-for-one-one-for-all, 'we're all going to split the publishing equally, we're all going to split the writing regardless of who does it.' Others bands are 'I'm the lead singer. I get more than you.' There's no real right or wrong, it's how the interaction really works and what works in individual situations. I've seen situations where lead singers left the band and they did it by cycles. So, he got paid half of what he would've gotten for one cycle, and then the next cycle he gets a fourth, and then nothing after that. It can be different.

SG: Well, my next question is: is a band agreement useful?

I think you should write it down, I really do. By the way, the flip side of that is no matter what you write down, there are usually bad feelings when someone leaves the band. So it ends up with somebody hiring a lawyer and we live in an age where anybody can sue anybody for anything. Even if it's written down, it comes to interpretation. I think you're going to have less litigation if you do write it down, but you're not certain to have no litigation just because you write it down.

SG: Now, what is the role of the manager in resolving disputes before it gets to the point where people want to sue each other? As the manager, do you get involved in trying to resolve disputes between band members?

Different managers have different roles, and I as a manager have had different roles with different artists. Generally, my role is being the CEO of the band's business. They're the shareholders, and I am the CEO, and in times of turmoil, the shareholders kind of trump the CEO. But, as the CEO, you try and guide everybody through to a fair and reasonable resolution for everyone. Now, it doesn't help that a lot of times in our business, there are foreign substances and alcohol involved. The biggest time that things really get out of control is, more often than not, somebody's using.

SG: Right. Well, that is a problem in the music business or in any activity in life. Let me ask you this: one of the most important parts of the band agreement is that it tells you who has the right to use the name and what happens when somebody leaves and whether they can use the name or not. Usually the band agreement says you can't if you leave without permission. Can you give us an example of an issue that has arisen with the name of a band, without getting into confidential stuff, of course?

One in particular, and I don't represent any one here, but I have always watched with amusement what goes on with the name, The Beach Boys. It's changed over the years, and to my knowledge, Brian Wilson's never played a gig as The Beach Boys. Mike Love has, but I think there was also an Al Jardine group that did, so I'm not particularly sure. But there's an example of there must not have been something really agreed to up front, because it seems to have changed from time to time.

SG: If there's anything that is written down, it should be who owns the trademark or if a leaving member has the right or doesn't have the right to the name. That's a big litigation creation issue. Would you agree with that?

I would definitely agree with it. The first thing you should write down is: if we break up, what's going to happen to the trademark and the name?

SG: But on the other hand, for a band just starting up, a band agreement is probably not one of the top priorities. I know I think, and correct me if I'm wrong, something like 99% of bands are never successful enough to warrant a band agreement—well let's stop right there, do you agree with that?

I definitely agree with that, but I liken this to a young couple getting married. A lot of prenups ruin the marriage before it got started. So you never really know if it's a good or bad idea to talk about that upfront. Again, you're talking about a creative process. And mostly when I started in the '70s, most of them were equal splits. What the normal thing was in the '70s, and I think it works the best is, you have four band members who are splitting the money four ways, we own the name together, the guy who writes the song writes the song, and the publishing is the publishers.

SG: Right, and I think in the eyes of the law, if you don't have an agreement, that's the way it's going to play out, anyway. Except with respect to individual songs. So, to give a plug for the book that this interview will be included in, *The 11 Contracts Every Artist, Songwriter, and Producer Should Know*, in the band agreements part of the book, I've got what you can do and should do without a lawyer. And one thing you should do without a lawyer, and correct me if I'm wrong or if you disagree, is a split sheet for each song, so that everybody knows what the percentage of ownership is in that song. Agree or disagree?

I agree, but it's hard to do that upfront. You've almost got to wait 'til the end of the song to know who contributed what, and unfortunately there are a lot of disagreements at the end of the song: 'I wrote half, no you didn't, you know, I wrote most of the lyrics'. . . And then, of course, you have the current day argument with, 'how much is attributable to the track, how much is attributable to the melody, how much is attributable to the lyric?' In the old days, it used to be half melody half lyric.

SG: Yeah, that's no longer the case, with the complicated way songs are put together. You see a Beyoncé song, and you'll see ten writers and gosh knows who did what? But again, what's the role of the manager in that? Do you just try to avoid getting in between the creatives on the split sheet?

You know, look, you're asking for trouble later if you don't have an understanding, so I think the manager should get involved, often. Because you're kind of the CEO of the business, and if these guys are the creative guys, and if you see a potential business problem that could rear its head later, you better solve it now.

SG: Is there ever a case where the manager gets embroiled and over his head, and doesn't do a good enough job at keeping the peace or keeping neutral, and band members go and get their own managers?

Look, we're in a day and age it seems like all you've got to do to become a manager is slap the sign on the door that says 'manager,' so you end up, in my opinion, with a lot of people that don't really understand the business side of it, really, or are incompetent. So, it's a problem.

SG: I've seen that. One more question about managers, and we'll wrap up shortly, because I found this fascinating. I saw Freddy DeMann, the great manager of Donna and Michael

Jackson, and he said at the height of Michael Jackson's fame and success, he got a call from John Branca that he was fired, and he never found out why. Is that something that happens a lot?

Listen, the fact that they are creative people also gives them the creative license just to be crazy. So you never know what's going through an artist's head. I have a friend that got fired recently by a major superstar. He did an incredible, impeccable job, and I think that the artist just basically got jealous, is all I can read into it, as an outsider looking in. But you never know how, why, or what, you know? It could be a new girlfriend—who knows what it is? Who knows who, how, or why it happened? Look, arguably for me I've done a lot of things in my career. I've loved being a manager—it's my favorite thing I've done. I'm really intrigued and excited to watch the creative process and be the business side of that. And it comes with the territory. No matter how big your artist is, the advice I've given my son and I've given all the young managers is—I'm a guy who believes that you don't just manage one person, you need clout to really do well for anybody and, for your own peace of mind, you don't want one client that represents more than 30, 40 percent of your business because it's just what you said, you can wake up one morning and for no reason be gone.

SG: Well, you still love it?

Of course I love it! I wouldn't do it if I didn't love it.

SG: And the best part of it is . . .

Making a difference, and making people's dreams come true. When I sit down and decide if I'm going to work with somebody or not, the first thing I want to hear is, you know at this point it's really not about the money for me, and most major artists, I'm not really at the point where I can take new artists or understand guys just starting out, so. Artists don't come looking for a new manager because things are going great—they come because they think they can do better. So you've got to establish what it is you want to accomplish. For me, my goal is to help this person achieve these things—I actually physically make a list with him, and say these are the things if we sat down two years from now, that you'd say we've had a successful time together if we accomplish the following. And it's important to me that you put that down and you look at it, and if you think we can get there, you take the shot, because what you want, the greatest joy is when that artist goes out at the end of the two years—it's really how you judge a successful manager-client relationship. And one thing I would say especially to anybody going into the management business: make every decision on what's right for that artist's career move, and eventually that will be the right thing for your business. Put the client first.

SG: Well said. Who is your most active artist now? Who are you working with the most, or do you treat them all equally?

Currently, today, well we're having a busy summer. I can't imagine anybody being any busier than Gwen Stefani is right now. Journey and the Doobie Brothers are on the road, Joe Walsh is on the road, John Mayer's on the road with Dead and Company, Steely Dan's on the road, Don Henley's on the road—it's a busy time.

SG: So, in wrapping up, what's most fun for you? Because I know you're involved in a lot of different stuff, besides managing what's the most fun you're having?

We're really involved in a lot of stuff. You know, we started a new company with Tim Leiweke that's involved in the building side, which is very exciting. Our Global Music Rights business, which is a performing rights business, has been really fun. Everything we do has really been exciting and fun. You know, the management piece is still the meat and potatoes in what I do that has the most fun. I'm sitting here, and as soon as I finish with you, I've got a thing called the blue sheet trying to figure out where I'm going to travel the next two to three weeks so I can catch some of these wonderful shows and these artists that are on the road.

SG: That sounds great. Well, you are finished with me, so I'm going to let you go, but I've learned a lot and I hope my audience will, too.

Well, it was a pleasure to do this with you, Steve, and I've read with interest what you've written. I think you have a lot of worthwhile things to say, and I would recommend to the audience that they continue to listen to what you say and read what you write.

SG: Thank you Irving Azoff.

BAND AGREEMENT: EQUAL PARTNERS

This model band agreement has been graciously provided by Wallace Collins, Esq. (www.wallacecollins.com). Wallace is an entertainment and intellectual property lawyer. He was a recording artist for Epic Records before attending Fordham Law School.

This agreement (the "Agreement") is made and entered into this _____ day of _____, 2017, by and among the following persons:

[name/address]
[name/address]
[name/address]
[name/address]

The foregoing individuals are hereinafter each individually referred to as "Partner" and in the plural as "Partners." With respect to any gender reference in this Agreement, wherever required in this Agreement, the singular shall include the plural, and the masculine gender shall include the feminine and neuter.

1.   THE PARTNERSHIP.

The Partners hereby constitute themselves as a general partnership (the "Partnership") to be known as "_____" (the "Group") under the laws of the State of _____ for the purposes of live performances, creating sound recordings for use and commercial exploitation in all mediums and by any means whether now or hereafter devised of recording musical performances for reproduction ("Recordings"), exploiting and merchandising the names (both legal and professional) and likenesses of the Group and the members of the Group, using and commercially exploiting musical compositions composed by any Partner individually or jointly with any other person and recorded by the Group for the purpose of exploiting Recordings (the "Group Compositions"), and all other present and future activities of the Partners as members of the Group in the entertainment field during the term of this Agreement. Except as otherwise expressly provided herein, the Partnership shall have the exclusive right to the services of each Partner as a member of the Group in the entertainment field. The principal place of business of the Partnership shall be at such place as the Partners may determine pursuant to the provisions of this Agreement.

2.   THE NAME.

The Partnership shall do business as "_____" (the "Group Name") and any and all trademarks and related intellectual property rights therein and thereto shall be the sole and exclusive property of the Group.

3. DURATION OF PARTNERSHIP.

The term for which this Partnership is to exist shall commence as of the effective date hereof and shall continue until dissolved in any manner provided herein.

4. REPRESENTATIONS, WARRANTIES AND AGREEMENTS.

Each of the Partners warrants and represents to each of the other Partners that he is free to enter into this Agreement, and that he is under no disability, restriction or prohibition which will interfere in any way with his full compliance with all of his obligations under this Agreement. Each Partner warrants and represents that he has not done nor will he do any act or thing that will or might impair the full enjoyment by the Partnership of any of the rights granted to it under this Agreement or the commencement or continuation of the Partnership business in the manner herein contemplated. Each Partner further warrants and represents that he will not sell, assign, transfer or hypothecate any right, title or interest in or to any asset of the Partnership without the prior written consent of all other Partners. Each Partner covenants and agrees that he will perform the services provided to be performed by him hereunder diligently, fully and to the best of his ability during the Term of this Agreement, in a competent and professional manner, and will refrain from participating in activities which with reasonable foreseeability could limit or prohibit him from so performing. Each of the Partners acknowledges that preservation and enhancement of the value of the Partnership may be hindered by the failure of an individual Partner to apply himself diligently to the business of the Partnership or by actions in a manner injurious to the rights of the other Partners.

5. CONTRIBUTION.

As a contribution to the Partnership, each Partner is contributing his exclusive services as a recording artist with respect to Recordings embodying musical performances of the Group, his exclusive services as a musical performer in all media and on the live stage with respect to his activities as a member of the Group, his Merchandising Rights with respect to his activities as a member of the Group, his exclusive services as a songwriter and publisher with respect to the Group Compositions, and generally his exclusive services as a member of the Group within the entertainment field. No Partner shall be required to make any capital contributions except upon the unanimous agreement of the Partners.

6. PROFITS AND LOSSES.

(a) Subject to Paragraph 6(b) below, and unless agreed otherwise in writing by all of the Partners, the Partners shall share equally in all of the profits, losses, rights and obligations of the Partnership. Should any Partner at any time bear or satisfy a disproportionate share of the financial obligations of the Partnership, he shall be entitled to reimbursement therefore from the other Partners proportionately out of sums otherwise distributable to them as Partners.

"Net profits" (as hereinafter defined) shall be distributed in cash to the Partners from time to time, but only as expressly authorized by a vote of a majority of the then-existing Partners. "Net profits" as used herein shall mean all commissions, royalties (including Recording royalties but excluding the so-called "songwriter's share" and "publisher's share" of music publishing royalties), bonuses, payments (other than repayment of loans), fees (including synchronization fees), dividends, stock bonuses, interests or monies of any kind or nature which shall be paid to the Partnership or to any Partner as a result of the Partnership activities after deducting the sum total of all reasonable salaries, rent, promotional costs, travel costs, office expenditures, telephone costs, accounting and legal fees, entertainment costs, and any and all legitimate Partnership expenses incurred by the Partnership while conducting Partnership business. No Partner shall receive any salary, bonus or goods or other assets of the Partnership in excess of that received by any other Partner, except as set forth herein or otherwise upon the unanimous vote of all of the Partners.

(b) Notwithstanding anything to the contrary contained herein, and unless agreed otherwise in writing by all of the Partners, net profits arising from the copyrighting, publishing and exploiting of a particular Group Composition ("Publishing Profits," which includes, without limitation, the so-called "songwriter's share" and publisher's share" of music publishing royalties) shall be shared solely among the Partners who are the authors of such Group Compositions.

7. MANAGEMENT.

(a) Each Partner shall have the right to participate equally in the control, management and direction of the business of the Partnership. In exercising this control, management and direction, each Partner shall have the same vote as each other Partner. No Partner shall have the right to make any expenditure in excess of $100 or incur any major obligation (including, without limitation, borrow or lend money, make, deliver, accept or endorse any commercial paper, compromise or release debts owing to the Partnership, sell, lease, license, assign or hypothecate any Partnership property or enter into any contract for any purpose) on behalf of the Partnership, except as expressly authorized by a vote of three-fifths (3/5) of the then-existing Partners. No Partner shall hold or accept from any third party any gratuity or other consideration in consideration of his exercising or declining to exercise his rights hereunder in any manner. The Partners may, by 3/5 vote, delegate all or any of their management functions to one or more professional managers upon such terms and conditions as the Partners so voting shall designate.

(b) Notwithstanding anything to the contrary contained herein, but subject to any future agreement, if any, between the Partnership and a third-party co-publisher or administrator, the Partner(s) who is/are credited as the writer(s) of a particular Composition shall have the exclusive right to sell or grant rights (by means of license or otherwise) in respect to such Composition in his/their sole reasonable discretion; provided that any Partner disassociated from the Partnership pursuant to Paragraph 11 hereof shall thereafter retain the right to sell or grant rights in respect to any Composition for which he is credited as a writer, subject to Paragraphs 7(b)(i) and (ii) hereof and the continuing rights of the other Partners in any net profits derived therefrom as provided in Paragraph 6 hereof. A disassociated Partner shall keep the Partnership informed as to his address and telephone number for the purpose of transacting business in respect to the Compositions. If a Composition is co-written by a remaining Partner and a disassociated Partner and the remaining Partner seeks to pursue a commercial opportunity in respect to such Composition, he shall send the disassociated Partner written notice thereof by certified mail, return receipt requested. If the disassociated Partner does not respond within fourteen (14) days after the date of such notice, then the remaining partner shall have the authority to grant rights in such composition to a third party, subject to the disassociated Partner's right to share in any net profits in respect thereto as provided herein.

(c) Notwithstanding the foregoing, the Partner or Partners who are the authors of any Group Composition hereby grant the Group a mechanical license for use of the Compositions in any Group Recording at the full statutory mechanical rate.

8.   BOOKS OF ACCOUNTS AND RECORDS.

The Partnership books and records, together with all other documents and papers pertaining to the business of the Partnership, shall be maintained at its principal place of business or at such other place as shall be designated by the Partners, and shall be available for inspection at all reasonable times by any Partner or any designated representative of any Partner. The maintenance of such books and records shall be in accordance with generally accepted accounting practices and principles, consistently applied, and at the cost of the Partners, pro rata. The fiscal year of the Partnership shall end on December 31. The Partnership shall render yearly accountings to each Partner on the first day of February in every year during the term of the Partnership. At the sole cost and expense of the Partners, the Partners may retain any duly licensed firm of accountants and/or attorneys in connection with the business of the Partnership, including the rendition of said accountings.

9.   DISSOLUTION.

(a) This Agreement shall terminate, and the Partnership shall be dissolved, upon the first to occur of the following events:

(i)   The written agreement of all of the Partners to dissolve the Partnership; or

(ii)   By operation of law, except as otherwise provided herein. The addition of a new Partner (as provided in Paragraph 10 hereof) or the disassociation of a Partner (as provided in Paragraph 11 hereof) shall not terminate this Agreement, and it shall remain in full force and effect among the remaining Partners.

(b) Upon termination of the Partnership, the Partnership's receivables shall be collected and its assets liquidated forthwith (except as provided in subparagraphs (d) and (e) below). The proceeds from the liquidation of the Partnership assets and collection of the Partnership receivables shall be applied in the following order:

(i) First, to the expense of liquidation and debts of the Partnership other than debts owing to any of the Partners;

(ii) Next, to the debts owing to any of the Partners, including debts arising from loans made to or for such Partners, except that if the amount of such proceeds is insufficient to pay such debts in full, payment shall be made on a pro rata basis;

(iii) Next, in payment to each Partner of any financial capital investment made by him in the Partnership belonging to him, except that if the amount of such proceeds is insufficient to pay such financial capital investment in full, payment shall be made on a pro rata basis;

(iv) Next, in payment to each Partner on a pro rata basis of any of such proceeds remaining.

(c) The Partners shall execute all such instruments for facilitating the collection of the Partnership receivables and liquidation of the Partnership assets, and for the mutual indemnity or release of the Partners as may be appropriate under all then-present circumstances.

(d) Any property, including, but not limited to, the Group Name, all rights and interests in contracts, agreements, options, choses in actions and Merchandising Rights, owned or controlled by the Partnership at the time of dissolution from which income is being derived, shall not be sold, but shall be retained and distributed in the manner hereinafter set forth. After the payments provided for in Paragraph 9(b)(i), (ii) and (iii) have been made in full, any such property owned by the Partnership and the continuing earnings received as a result of the exploitation thereof shall be valuated by an accountant selected by the Partners who is experienced in the music industry. Said property shall then be distributed, as nearly as possible, among the Partners in a manner consistent with the terms set forth in Paragraph 6 hereof.

10. ADDITION OF A PARTNER.

A new partner may be admitted to the Partnership but only with the written consent of all of the Partners. Each new Partner shall be admitted only if he shall have executed an agreement with the Partnership under the terms of which such Partner agrees to be bound by all of the provisions hereof, as amended, as if a signatory hereto. Notwithstanding anything to the contrary contained herein, such new Partner shall have no right, title or interest in any of the assets or property of the Partnership existing at the time of his admission to the Partnership ("existing property") or in any of the proceeds derived from such existing property or from the sale, exchange, or liquidation thereof. Such new Partner shall have no interest whatsoever in the Group Name apart from the limited right to be known as a member of the Group, and upon the termination of the Partnership his interest in any assets, property, net profits and losses of the Partnership shall attach only to such assets, property, net profits and losses acquired by the Partnership after his admission to the Partnership. Such new Partner's capital contribution, if any, and share of the Partnership's net profits and losses shall be set forth in the written consent of all of the Partners approving the admission of the new Partner.

11.   DISASSOCIATION.

(a)   A Partner may become disassociated from the Partnership by reason of his death, his disability, his resignation or by the written vote of all of the other Partners. For purposes of this Agreement, a Partner shall be deemed disabled if he is unable to perform services as required hereunder for any reason for a period in excess of one hundred eighty (180) consecutive days, or two hundred seventy (270) days out of the year. If a Partner resigns, he shall give thirty (30) days prior written notice of such resignation to each of the other Partners. A Partner (or, in the event of disassociation by death, his executor or personal representative) who is disassociated shall be entitled to receive an amount equal to his proportionate share of the net worth of the Partnership as of the date of his disassociation, exclusive of any value attributable to the Group Name, but he shall not be entitled to any of the earnings of the Partnership received thereafter or any interest in the Group Name, nor shall he be subject to any of the liabilities of the Partnership incurred thereafter; provided, however, that such Partner shall be entitled to receive his applicable proportionate share (as set forth in Paragraph 6 hereof) of any royalties (other than any share of Publishing Profits provided for in Paragraph 6(b)(ii)(a) in respect to Group Compositions which are not written, in whole or in part, by the disassociated Partner(s)) earned from the exploitation of (a) any Recording recorded hereunder and embodying his performances, and (b) the Group Compositions which have been recorded by the Group prior to the date of his disassociation, as and when such profits are actually received by the Partnership, less his pro rata or other agreed share of any expenses and/or liabilities relating thereto.

(b)   The net worth of the Partnership shall be determined as of the date of the disassociation by an accountant selected by the remaining Partner(s) other than the Partnership's regular accountant, and other than the personal accountant of any Partner, which accountant shall be familiar with the music industry. The accountant shall make said determination in accordance with generally accepted accounting practices and principles, taking into consideration, among other factors, the fair market value of the assets of the Partnership other than the Group Name, its liabilities (including the disassociated Partner's entitlement to future royalties as provided in subparagraph (a) hereinabove), its past profits and losses. In the event of voluntary resignation, the determination of said accountant shall be final. However, if the disassociated Partner or his legal representative should disagree with the accountant's determination in the event of disassociation for any other reason, the disassociated Partner or such representative may within thirty (30) days after receipt of the accountant's determination submit the issue of the fair market value of the Partnership to arbitration in New York, under the applicable rules of the American Arbitration Association by one (1) arbitrator selected by such organization from its panel of arbitrators in accordance with its usual procedures. Unless the remaining Partner(s) elect to pay the disassociated Partner's share of the value of the Partnership sooner, said share shall be payable (without any interest accruing thereon) in twelve (12) approximately equal monthly installments commencing one month following the date of the final determination of said net worth; provided however, that if said share is in excess of $10,000 but less than $25,000, the remaining Partner(s) may elect to pay same in twenty-four (24) approximately equal monthly installments, and provided further, that if said share is in excess of $25,000, the remaining Partner(s) may elect to pay same in thirty-six (36) approximately equal monthly installments.

12. NOTICES.

All accountings and notices to be given hereunder, and notices of any action by the Partnership which has the effect of altering any Partner's share of profits or losses shall be given in writing, by personal delivery or by mail or by telegram at the respective addresses of the Partners set forth above, or at such other addresses as may be designated in writing by registered mail by any Partner. Notice given by mail or by telegram shall be deemed given on the date of mailing thereof or on the date of delivery of such telegram to a telegraph office, charged prepaid or to be billed.

13. PARTNERSHIP BANK ACCOUNTS.

One or more Partnership bank accounts may be opened and maintained by the Partners with such bank or banks as the Partners may determine and any checks or withdrawals from or against any bank account or accounts shall be upon the signature of any of any person as the Partners may unanimously select; provided, however, that such checks or withdrawals shall be subject to the approval process set forth in Paragraph 7 hereinabove.

14. ASSIGNMENT OF PARTNERS' INTEREST.

No Partner, or executor or administrator of a deceased Partner, shall sell, assign or transfer all or any portion of his financial or other interest in the Partnership or right to receive a share of Partnership assets, profits or other distribution without the prior written consent of all of the other Partners and any such purported sale, assignment or transfer in contravention of the foregoing shall be null and void. The Partners acknowledge that a part of the capital contribution of each Partner is the unique personal services required to be rendered for the exclusive account of the Partnership by each Partner, for which no presently adequate substitute exists; and that the other Partners are the sole and exclusive judges of the adequacy of any future substitution.

15. GENERAL PROVISIONS.

(a) Liability. The liability of the Partnership or the Partners arising out of any activities of the Partnership shall to the extent possible be covered by appropriate policies of insurance. In the event that any liability shall not adequately be covered by insurance, the amount of liability not so insured against shall first be satisfied out of the assets of the Partnership.

(b) Indemnity. Each Partner hereby indemnifies the other Partner(s) and holds such other Partner(s) harmless against and from all claims, demands, actions and rights of action which shall or may arise by virtue of anything done or admitted to be done by him (through or by agents, employees or other representatives) outside the scope of or in breach of the terms of this Agreement. Each Partner shall promptly notify the other Partner(s) if such Partner knows of the existence of a claim, demand, action or right of action.

(c) Successors and Assigns. Subject to the restrictions on assignments set forth in this Agreement, the provisions of this Agreement shall be binding upon and inure to the benefit of the heirs, executors, administrators, successors and assigns of the Partners.

(d) Severability. If any term, provision, covenant or condition of this Agreement is held to be illegal or invalid for any reason whatsoever, such illegality or invalidity shall not affect the validity of the remainder of this Agreement.

16. CONSTRUCTION.

This Agreement shall be governed by and construed in accordance with the laws of the State of New York. In the event of any action, arbitration, suit or proceeding arising from or under this Agreement, the prevailing party shall be entitled to recover reasonable attorneys' fees and costs of said action, suit, arbitration or proceeding. This is the entire understanding of the parties relating to the subject matter hereof and supersedes all prior and collateral agreements, understandings, and negotiations of the parties. Each party acknowledges that no representations, inducements, promises, understandings or agreements, oral or written, with reference to the subject matter hereof have been made other than as expressly set forth herein. Each Partner acknowledges that he has consulted with legal counsel of his choice with respect to the contents of this Agreement prior to execution hereof, and has been advised by such counsel with respect to the meaning and consequences hereof. This Agreement cannot be changed, rescinded or terminated except by a writing signed by each of the

Partners. The titles of the paragraphs of this Agreement are for convenience only, and shall not in any way affect the interpretation of any paragraphs of this Agreement or of the Agreement itself.

NOTWITHSTANDING THE REPRESENTATION OF THE PARTNERSHIP BY WALLACE COLLINS AS LEGAL COUNSEL, EACH OF THE PARTNERS HAS BEEN ADVISED OF THEIR RIGHT TO RETAIN INDEPENDENT LEGAL COUNSEL IN CONNECTION WITH THE NEGOTIATION AND EXECUTION OF THIS LEGAL DOCUMENT AND EACH PARTNER HAS EITHER RETAINED AND BEEN REPRESENTED BY SUCH LEGAL COUNSEL OR HAS KNOWINGLY AND VOLUNTARILY WAIVED RIGHT TO SUCH LEGAL COUNSEL.

IN WITNESS WHEREOF, the parties hereto have executed and sealed this agreement on the date first above written.

"PARTNERS"

_____
Name

_____
Name

_____
Name

_____
Name

CHAPTER 11

INVESTMENT AGREEMENTS

INTRODUCTION: HOW TO STRUCTURE A FAIR DEAL

Early in their careers, many artists face the decision of whether to take the big leap and quit their day jobs in order to pursue their dreams full time. But, without the steady income from a day job to provide funding to cover the cost of recording, videos, tours, and other expenses, quitting can be a tough choice to make if the artist has no other source of income. So, an artist may decide to approach their family members or other people they know to invest money in their career. This article explains the best way to structure an agreement for that investment.

In essence, an investment agreement involves someone who believes an artist will be successful and is willing to make a "bet" by giving the artist money to further their career in return for a percentage of profits (if and when the artist makes money). This article addresses the deal points of an investment contract from the point of view of both the artist and the investor. Below is a discussion of the main deal points in a typical artist investment contract. At the end of this chapter are a pro-artist agreement and a pro-investor agreement. Once you finish reading this section, you'll be ready to call that rich, eccentric uncle and form a fair investment agreement so that you can quit your job and follow your dream!

Amount of Investment

The amount of money invested varies with the identity of both the investor and the artist. I have drafted agreements ranging from $25,000 to $2.5 million. Sometimes an investor is so eager to help an artist's career, or just so wealthy, that she isn't very concerned about losing the investment and doesn't even ask for the protections in the "pro-investor" form that is included in this article.

Some agreements provide for installment payments rather than a lump sum up-front. Paying in installments gives the investor greater control because then she can stop making the installments if the artist does not comply with the contract. For instance, if the contract requires expenditure of funds for a specific purpose and the investor learns or merely suspects the artist is spending the investor's money for expenses not authorized in the agreement, then she may stop paying the installments.

Rate of Return

Most investors hope to be repaid and make a profit. Generally, this is handled in the following manner: the investor receives a percentage of monies that the artist earns minus expenses such as recording costs. That percentage, or "rate of return," varies from case to case, but an important factor in calculating a fair rate of return is the amount of the investment. If the amount provided is a large sum, the investor is justified in asking for a higher rate of return such as 40 or even 50%. But, if the investment is relatively small, the rate of return should be scaled down so that the artist retains the opportunity to take on other investors. For instance, if the investment is only $25,000, a fair rate of return would be 10 to15%. Repayment may be made on a monthly, quarterly, or semi-annual basis, and an investor will normally have the right to audit the artist's books.

Cap on Return

The investor's total possible return is usually limited in one of two ways: first, the return may be limited to an amount that equals a multiple of the investment, typically 100% to 250%. For instance, if an investor puts in $25,000, the cap may be a multiple of 100% (such as $50,000). In this model, the artist is free of the obligation to continue to pay the investor after the investor has made 100% profit.

Another way of capping the investor's return is to limit the period of time during which an investor is entitled to receive the return. That period of time is subject to negotiation. If the amount invested is very high, such as a million dollars, it may be fairer to apply a long duration such as ten years. This rewards the investor for the significant amount invested because there is no cap on his potential return. The investor's attorney may also insist that even a long term should be extended until the investor at least makes his money back plus a reasonable profit.

Control

Whether a contract is pro-artist or a pro-investor, the agreement should address decision making and approval. A pro-investor agreement would either state the particular purpose for which the investment can be used, such as production costs for a set number of masters, or at least give the investor the right to approve expenditures of his investment. A pro-artist agreement would state that the artist can use the money in her discretion, giving her the widest latitude to decide how best to use the money as the circumstances of her career change.

Source of Income

An artist may earn income from a variety of sources including record sales, live performances, touring, merchandise, publishing, and endorsements. Whether the investor recoups his or her investment from all these sources or just selected income streams is subject to negotiation. For example, if your rich aunt pays money toward recording masters and manufacturing CDs, in a highly pro-artist agreement, she would be repaid only from downloads, streaming and CD sales because these are the streams directly attributable to her contribution, and not from live performances, merch sales, or any other income streams. On the other hand, from an investor's perspective, the repayment should be from all income sources because investment in one sector assists income generation in another. However, it is to an artist's benefit to limit the recoupment on the investment to the income streams directly related to the investment.

Affirmation of Risk and Limited Liability

A pro-artist agreement may include a clause stating that the music industry is a highly speculative business and that repayment of the investment cannot be guaranteed.

Also, it is in an artist's interest to enter into the agreement not as an individual but via a "furnishing company." To accomplish this, the artist must create an entity such as a corporation or an LLC that will conduct business on behalf of the artist. This will protect the artist's personal assets by creating "limited liability." This means that a disgruntled investor who sues the artist for breach of the agreement can only try to secure repayment from assets in the artist's furnishing company. Property owned by the artist as an individual including bank accounts, stocks, a house, and car are all insulated from any claims. However, an investor may be able to "pierce the corporate veil" if he can prove fraud on the part of the artist. For instance, if the artist moves the furnishing company's assets into his personal account the investor may be able to go after those funds to recover his money.

Creating a furnishing company can also have tax benefits such as proof that the artist is in a legitimate business rather than a hobby so that expenses can be legitimately deducted as business expenses. An artist should consult with a knowledgeable accountant regarding tax issues and should strongly consider consulting an attorney regarding formation of the corporate entity.

Conclusion

Third party funding can be a welcome push to an artist's career provided the agreement between an investor and artist is well drafted. Both the artist and the investor are well advised to seek knowledgeable counsel to protect their interests and help structure a deal that is fair to both parties.

PRO-ARTIST AGREEMENT

This investment agreement ("Agreement") is entered into as of _____ ____, 2017 by and between: _____ (the "Artist") a corporation with an address at _____ furnishing the services of _____ ("Artist") and _____ ("Investor") with an address at _____.

> Note that the Artist is entering into this agreement, not as an individual, but via a "furnishing company." See the discussion regarding "Limited Liability" in the Introduction.

WHEREAS the parties to this Agreement seek to advance the career of Artist, they agree as follows:

1. INVESTMENT: Investor agrees to invest a minimum of Two Million Dollars ($2,000,000) (the "Investment") and a maximum of Two Million Five Hundred Thousand Dollars ($2,500,000) pursuant to the terms of this Agreement. The Investment shall be paid directly to Company. The parties agree that the Company shall use the Investment to advance the career of the Artist in the Entertainment Industry (as defined below) and to satisfy the goals set forth in the marketing plan attached as Schedule A (the "Marketing Plan"), provided that Company reserves the right to change the Marketing Plan if Company reasonably believes that such changes would enhance the career of the Artist.

> A marketing plan is a comprehensive blueprint that sets forth a company's (or in this case an Artist's) advertising and marketing efforts for a period of time. It includes a budget and specifications of what the Artist intends to do with the money. For instance, it may include amounts for hiring a publicist, and/or an indie radio promoter. It will also include detailed estimates of the Artist's earnings. These projections may be key in an investor's decision to support an artist.
>
>   Note that in this pro-Artist agreement, the Artist reserves the right to use the Investment for other expenses than in the Market Plan presented to the Investor if the Artist feels that the money could be better spent on other activities as the circumstances of the Artist's career change.

2. PAYMENT DATES:

(a) Five Hundred Thousand Dollars ($500,000) shall be payable to Company upon execution of this Agreement. Said amount shall be paid to a bank account ("Account") owned by Company as a check payable to Artist.

(b) Company shall have the right to withdraw funds from the Account in accordance with the purposes of this Agreement.

(c) Investor shall replenish the Account at any time that there is less than $20,000 in the Account. For the avoidance of doubt, if at any time there is less than Twenty Thousand

Dollars in the Account Investor will place at least enough money in the Account so that it will equal Five Hundred Thousand Dollars ($500,000).

(d)   It is understood and agreed that Investor shall not pay any Expenses directly but rather that Investor will make sufficient funds available for Company to pay Expenses.

(e)   The parties hereto agree that the purpose of Investor replenishing the Account is to allow Artist to pay Expenses to advance the Artist's career, and the parties anticipate that at least Two Million Dollars ($2,000,000) will be required to invest in the Artist in order to generate Net Profits as defined below provided that if additional funds are required up to the amount of Two Million Five Hundred Thousand Dollars ($2,500,000), Investor shall make such additional funds available.

Although this is a pro-Artist agreement, the investment is so large that a limited number of installments is reasonable.

(f)   The Company shall have full discretion and the right to exercise independent judgment without approval form Investor with respect to paying any individual expense up to Seventy-Five Thousand Dollars ($75,000). For any individual expense in excess of Seventy-Five Thousand Dollars, Investor shall have the right to approve such expense, provided that approval shall not be unreasonably denied if the Expense is in the best interests of advancing Artist's career.

This is a reasonable control on spending.

---

3.   INVESTMENT RETURN: As consideration for the Investment, Investor shall receive a total of forty percent (40%) of "Net Profits" (as defined below) earned by Artist from the Entertainment Industry. Such consideration shall be referred to herein as the "Investment Return."

This rate of return is on the high side but is in proportion to the large sum invested.

---

4.   COMPANY: Company shall use best efforts to launch, sustain, and advance the Artist's career in the Entertainment Industry. It is agreed at all times during the Term of this Agreement that the Artist shall be a shareholder and an officer in the Company.

5.   DEFINITIONS:

(a)   "Net Profits," for the purposes of this Agreement, shall mean Gross Earnings as defined below minus Expenses. "Gross Earnings," for the purposes of this Agreement, shall mean all income actually received by Company or Artist from the Artist's activities in the Entertainment Marketing including performance fees, sponsorship fees, endorsement fees, advances, guaranties, recording royalties, salaries, bonuses, deferred compensation, union payments, equity or shares in corporations or partnerships, shares of profits, or any other form of compensation or income. Notwithstanding anything to the contrary in the foregoing: (i) the Investment shall not be deemed to be Gross Earnings, and (ii) salaries, benefits including insurance and pensions, and/or any other fees paid to employees or agents of Company or Artist shall not be deemed to be Gross Earnings.

(b) "Expenses," for the purposes of this Agreement, shall mean (i) any actual recording or video production costs paid to unaffiliated and unrelated third parties in connection with Artist's recording or video recording of the Artist, (ii) any actual tour support costs, including sound, lighting, equipment rental, transportation, accommodations and lodging paid in connection with Artist's live performances, (iii) any actual bona fide documented payments to any third party in connection with advancing the Artist's career in the Entertainment Industry such as monies paid in connection with marketing, public relations, publicity, branding and image consulting, website development, artist management, marketing management, booking agents, accounting and legal fees, photography, wardrobe and styling, radio promotion, manufacturing and packaging, digital distribution or any other out-of-pocket expenses incurred in connection with the Artist activities in the Entertainment Industry; (iv) any monies needed to maintain corporate offices and a recording studio including rent, furnishings, recording equipment, electricity, phone, any computers, etc., (v) up to Five Hundred Thousand Dollars ($500,000) for any salaries and/or benefits paid to employees or agents of the Artist, and (vi) all taxes payable by the Artist including federal, state and city income taxes, and sales taxes.

(c) "Entertainment Industry," for the purposes of this Agreement, shall mean Artist's activities in the entertainment industry as follows: (i) live performance as a music performer or dancer; (ii) music recordings and records including sale, lease or rental of music recordings in any media throughout the world now know or hereafter developed; (iii) music videos and concert films; (iv) all aspects of motion pictures and the motion picture Marketing including performance, directing, writing and producing; (v) all aspects of television and the television Marketing including performance, directing, writing, and producing, (vi) licensing music recordings for television, movies, commercials, and electronic or video games; (vii) merchandise of any sort including clothes, posters, stationary, etc., or endorsements of any product or service; (viii) any project associated with digital entertainment content involving the Internet, mobile or any other technology now known or hereafter developed; (ix) all aspects of book publishing including writing; (x) all aspects of live theatre and the theatre Marketing including acting, performing, directing and producing. For the avoidance of doubt this Agreement does not pertain or apply to any income received on behalf of any other artists or individuals except the Company or Artist.

6. <u>CAP ON INVESTMENT RETURN</u>: Notwithstanding anything to the contrary herein there shall be a cap of ten (10) years (the "Term") from the date of this Agreement. For avoidance of doubt, the Investor's right to collect monies from Artist shall terminate ten (10) years from the date of this Agreement so that there shall be no obligation to pay Investor any share of any monies received by Company or Artist after said date.

The long term is in proportion to the large investment.

7. <u>ACCOUNTING AND PAYMENT</u>: Company shall account to Investor on a semi-annual basis starting _____ ____, 2017 and continue so long as Net Profits are earned, by furnishing statements and any payments due to Investor after deduction of permissible Expenses. Each such accounting statement shall include a description of any transaction subject to this Agreement including identification of any third party, the amount paid and the nature of the products and/or services for which payment was made. Each such accounting statement shall cover all relevant transactions for the immediately preceding semi-annual period.

8. <u>AUDIT</u>:

(a) Investor shall have the right, at any time, to give Company written notice of Investor's intention to examine Company's books and records with respect to each royalty statement. Such examination shall occur no more than once each year and be commenced no sooner than one (1) month and no later than three (3) months after the date of such notice, at Investor's sole cost and expense, by any certified public accountant or attorney designated by Investor, provided that he or she is not then engaged in an outstanding examination of Company's books and records on behalf of a person other than Investor. Such examination shall be made during Company's usual business hours at the place where Company maintains the books and records which relate to Investor, and which are necessary to verify the accuracy of the statement or statements specified in Investor's notice to Company. Company shall have no obligation to produce such books and records more than once.

(b) Unless Investor provides a notice to examine Company's books and records within six (6) months of receipt by Investor of any royalty statement, each such statement rendered to Investor shall be final, conclusive and binding on Investor and shall constitute an account stated. Investor shall be foreclosed from maintaining any action, claim or proceeding against Company in any forum or tribunal with respect to any statement or accounting rendered hereunder unless such action, claim or proceeding is commenced against Company in a court of competent jurisdiction within one (1) year after the date that such statement or accounting is received by Investor.

(c) Investor acknowledges that Company books and records contain confidential trade information. Neither Investor nor Investor's representatives will communicate to others, or use on behalf of any other person, any facts or information obtained as a result of such examination of Company's books and records, except as may be required by law or judicial decree.

9.   LEGAL COUNSEL: Investor hereby acknowledges that he has sought and received legal advice from independent counsel or that he has voluntarily waived his right to independent counsel with respect to the terms and provision contained in this Agreement. Investor acknowledges that the Entertainment Industry is a highly risky business and that he may not be re-paid or earn any Net Profits.

Note that the contract makes clear that the Investor may never recoup his investment.

---

10.   INDEPENDENT CONTRACTOR: Investor and Company shall have the relationship of independent contractors. Nothing herein shall be construed to place Investor and Company in the relationship of principal and agent, employer and employee, master and servant, partners, or joint venturers, and neither party shall have expressly or by implications, represented themselves as having any authority to make contracts in the name of, or binding on, each other, or to obligate the other in any manner.

11.   NOTICES: Notices, reports, accountings or other communication which the Investor or Company may be required or desires to send to the other, must be delivered EITHER by

(a) certified mail, return receipt requested to the parties at the addresses first written above or other address to be designated by Investor or Company.

(b) electronic mail at the following addresses:
      (i) for Company: _____@_____
      (ii) for Investor: _____@_____

12.   ASSIGNMENT: Investor may assign this Agreement or any of his rights hereunder to any person, firm, or corporation including a corporation in which the Investor is a principal, provided that (i) Investor shall remain responsible for any payments required to be made under this Agreement, and (ii) the assignee has the necessary cash on hand to make any payments required under this Agreement. Notwithstanding the foregoing, Company may not assign this agreement or any of its obligations herein.

13.   ENTIRE UNDERSTANDING: This Agreement constitutes the entire understanding between the parties with reference to this matter, and supersedes all prior agreements, written or oral. This Agreement cannot be modified except by written instrument signed by the parties.

14.   GOVERNING LAW: This Agreement is made, and is to be construed under the laws of the State of New York with respect to contracts to be executed and performed in this State.

15. <u>ENFORCEMENT</u>: If any provision of this Agreement shall be found invalid or unenforceable, then such provision shall not invalidate or in any way affect the enforceability of the remainder of this Agreement.

AGREED TO AND ACCEPTED:

INVESTOR   COMPANY f/s/o ARTIST

By: _____   By: _____

Name: _____   Authorized Signatory

PRO-INVESTOR AGREEMENT

This investment agreement ("Agreement") is entered into as of _____ ____, 2017 ("Effective Date") by and between: _____ (the "Artist") residing at _____ and _____ Inc. (the "Investor") a corporation with an address at _____.

WHEREAS the parties to this Agreement seek to advance the career of Artist, they agree as follows:

Note that the Artist is entering into this agreement as an individual, not as a company. This will expose the Artist's personal assets to liability.

---

1.   INVESTMENT: Investor agrees to invest Seventy Thousand Dollars ($70,000) (the "Investment") pursuant to the terms of this Agreement. The Investment shall be used for the specific purposes set forth in Paragraph 2 below. The investment shall be made in two installments as follows: (i) Thirty-five Thousand ($35,000) upon execution; and (ii) provided that Artist strictly complies with all his contractual obligations herein, Thirty-five Thousand ($35,000) within ninety (90) days of the Effective Date.

Note that the Artist must strictly comply with the contract if he is to receive the second installment.

---

2.   EXPENDITURE OF THE INVESTMENT: Artist agrees to use the Investment for the following specific purposes only: (i) produce two (2) albums of recorded music featuring the Artist; and (ii) implement the marketing plan attached as Schedule A (the "Marketing Plan"). Company shall have approval over any other use of the Investment that Artist may desire.

Unlike the pro-Artist agreement, the Artist in this case cannot change the marketing plan if she feels that changing circumstances dictate that the monies should be spent in a manner that the Investor has not approved.

---

3.   INVESTMENT RETURN: As consideration for the Investment, Investor shall receive a total of forty per cent (40%) of "Net Profits" (as defined below) earned by Artist, and that sum shall be referred to herein as the "Investment Return." The Investment Return shall be paid by Artist to Investor on a semi-annual basis as set forth in more detail below.

The rate of return is relatively high compared to the amount of the investment.

---

4.   ARTIST: The Artist shall use best efforts to launch, sustain, and advance the profitability of his career.

5. <u>DEFINITIONS</u>:

(a) "Net Profits," for the purposes of this Agreement, shall mean Gross Earnings as defined below minus Expenses. "Gross Earnings," for the purposes of this Agreement, shall mean all income actually received by Company or Artist from the Artist's activities in the Entertainment Marketing including performance fees, sponsorship fees, endorsement fees, advances, guaranties, recording royalties, salaries, bonuses, deferred compensation, union payments, equity or shares in corporations or partnerships, shares of profits, or any other form of compensation or income. Notwithstanding anything to the contrary in the foregoing: (i) the Investment shall not be deemed to be Gross Earnings, and (ii) salaries, benefits including insurance and pensions, and/or any other fees paid to employees or agents of Company or Artist shall not be deemed to be Gross Earnings.

(b) "Expenses," for the purposes of this Agreement, shall mean (i) any actual recording or video production costs paid to unaffiliated and unrelated third parties in connection with Artist's recording or video recording of the Artist, (ii) any actual tour support costs, including sound, lighting, equipment rental, transportation, accommodations, and lodging paid in connection with Artist's live performances, (iii) any actual bona fide documented payments to any third party in connection with advancing the Artist's career in the Entertainment Industry such as monies paid in connection with marketing, public relations, publicity, branding and image consulting, website development, artist management, marketing management, booking agents, accounting and legal fees, photography, wardrobe and styling, radio promotion, manufacturing and packaging, digital distribution or any other out-of-pocket expenses incurred in connection with the Artist activities in the Entertainment Industry; (iv) any monies needed to maintain corporate offices and a recording studio including rent, furnishings, recording equipment, electricity, phone, any computers, etc., (v) up to Five Hundred Thousand Dollars ($500,000) for any salaries and/or benefits paid to employees or agents of the Artist, and (vi) all taxes payable by the Artist including federal, state and city income taxes, and sales taxes.

(c) "Entertainment Industry," for the purposes of this Agreement, shall mean Artist's activities in the entertainment industry as follows: (i) live performance as a music performer or dancer; (ii) music recordings and records including sale, lease or rental of music recordings in any media throughout the world now know or hereafter developed; (iii) music videos and concert films; (iv) all aspects of motion pictures and the motion picture Marketing including performance, directing, writing and producing; (v) all aspects of television and the television Marketing including performance, directing, writing, and producing; (vi) licensing music recordings for television, movies, commercials, and electronic or video games; (vii) merchandise of any sort including clothes, posters, stationary, etc., or endorsements of any product or service; (viii) any project associated with digital entertainment content involving the Internet, mobile or any other technology now known or hereafter developed; (ix) all aspects of book publishing including writing; (x) all aspects of live theatre and the theatre Marketing including acting, performing, directing and producing. For the avoidance of doubt this Agreement does not pertain or apply to any income received on behalf of any other artists or individuals except the Company or Artist.

6.   DURATION OF THE INVESTMENT RETURN: Notwithstanding anything to the contrary herein, the Investor shall be entitled to the Investment Return for a period of ten (10) years (the "Term") from the date of this Agreement, provided that the Term will continue after that period (the "Extended Term") if the Investor has not received at least one hundred percent (100%) of the original Investment of Seventy Thousand Dollars ($70,000). For avoidance of doubt, the Extended Term will continue until the Investor has received at least One Hundred and Forty Thousand dollars ($140,000).

Note that the cap of ten years is long compared to the amount of the investment. Also, note that the investor is guaranteed at least 100% return no matter how long it takes.

---

7.   RIGHT TO MAKE ADDITIONAL INVESTMENT: The Investor shall have the right to invest up to an additional One Hundred Fifty Thousand Dollars ($150,000) at any time(s) before the expiration of the Term ("Additional Investment"). The Investment Return for such Additional Investment shall be the same as for the original Investment, that is, forty percent (40%) of Net Profits. The Investor shall have the right to receive the Investment Return on such Additional Investment from the time the Additional Investment is made for a duration of seven (7) years (the "Additional Investment Term"), provided that the Additional Investment Term will continue after that period if Investor has not received at least one hundred percent (100%) of the Additional Investment. By way of example, if the Investor chooses to an additional Seventy-Five Thousand dollars ($75,000), he would be entitled to 40% of Net Profits for seven (7) years from the date of that Additional Investment, provided that the Additional Investment Term would continue until the Investor has received at least One Hundred Fifty Thousand dollars ($150,000) in connection with that Additional Investment. The purposes for which such Additional Investment shall be used shall be mutually approved by the parties at the time the Additional Investment is made. The Investor shall have the right to make an Additional Investment in any amount or at any time in his discretion provided that the total Additional Investment shall not exceed One Hundred Fifty Thousand dollars ($150,000) without the approval of Artist. If the Investor makes more than one Additional Investment, the Additional Investment Term for each Additional Investment shall start from the date of the Artist's receipt of each Additional Investment. At no time would the Investor's Rate of Return exceed forty percent (40%) of Net Profits.

This provision gives the Investor the right to make additional investments. In this manner, the Investor can put more money in if the Artist starts making a lot of money. In that case, the Investor greatly increases his chances of a good return on his investment.

---

8. ACCOUNTING AND PAYMENT: Artist shall account to Investor on a semi-annual basis starting _____ ____, 2017 and continue until the expiration of the Term by furnishing statements and any payments due to Investor after deduction of permissible Expenses. Each such accounting statement shall include a description of any transaction subject to this Agreement including identification of any third party, the amount paid and the nature of the products and/or services for which payment was made. Each such accounting statement shall cover all relevant transactions for the immediately preceding semi-annual period.

9. AUDIT:

(a) Investor shall have the right, at any time, to give Artist written notice of Investor's intention to examine Artist's books and records with respect to each accounting statement. Such examination shall occur no more than once each year and be commenced no sooner than one (1) month and no later than three (3) months after the date of such notice, at Investor's sole cost and expense, by any certified public accountant or attorney designated by Investor, provided that he or she is not then engaged in an outstanding examination of Artist's books and records on behalf of a person other than Investor. Such examination shall be made during Artist's usual Marketing hours at the place where Artist maintains the books and records which relate to Investor, and which are necessary to verify the accuracy of the statement or statements specified in Investor's notice to Artist. Artist shall have no obligation to produce such books and records more than once every year.

(b) Unless Investor provides a notice to examine Artist's books and records within six (6) months of receipt by Investor of any financial statement, each such statement rendered to Investor shall be final, conclusive and binding on Investor and shall constitute an account stated. Investor shall be foreclosed from maintaining any action, claim or proceeding against Artist in any forum or tribunal with respect to any statement or accounting rendered here-under unless such action, claim or proceeding is commenced against Artist in a court of competent jurisdiction within one (1) year after the date that such statement or accounting is received by Investor.

(c) Investor acknowledges that Artist's books and records contain confidential trade infor-mation. Neither Investor nor Investor's representatives will communicate to others, or use on behalf of any other person, any facts or information obtained as a result of such exami-nation of Artist's books and records, except as may be required by law or judicial decree.

10. LEGAL COUNSEL: Artist hereby acknowledges that he has sought and received legal advice from independent counsel or that he has voluntarily waived his right to independent counsel with respect to the terms and provision contained in this Agreement.

11. INDEPENDENT CONTRACTOR: Investor and Artist shall have the relationship of independent contractors. Nothing herein shall be construed to place Investor and Artist in the relationship of principal and agent, employer and employee, master and servant, partners, or joint venturers, and neither party shall have expressly or by implications, represented themselves as having any authority to make contracts in the name of, or binding on, each other, or to obligate the other in any manner.

12. NOTICES: Notices, reports, accountings or other communication which the Investor or the Artist may be required or desires to send to the other, must be delivered EITHER by:

(a) Certified mail, return receipt requested to the parties at the addresses first written above or other address to be designated by Investor or Artist.

(b) Electronic mail at the following addresses:
    (i)   for Artist: _____
    (ii) for Investor: _____

13. ASSIGNMENT: Investor may assign this Agreement or any of his rights hereunder to any person, firm, or corporation including a corporation in which the Investor is a principal, provided that (i) Investor shall remain responsible for any payments required to be made under this Agreement, and (ii) the assignee has the necessary cash on hand to make any payments required under this Agreement. Artist may not assign, sell, transfer or convey this Agreement or any of its obligations herein without the written approval of the Investor.

14. ENTIRE UNDERSTANDING: This Agreement constitutes the entire understanding between the parties with reference to this matter, and supersedes all prior agreements, written or oral. This Agreement cannot be modified except by written instrument signed by the parties.

15. GOVERNING LAW: This Agreement is made, and is to be construed under the laws of the State of New York with respect to contracts to be executed and performed in this State.

16. ENFORCEMENT: If any provision of this Agreement shall be found invalid or unenforceable, then such provision shall not invalidate or in any way affect the enforceability of the remainder of this Agreement.

17. LIABILITY: It is the intention of this Agreement that Artist shall be individually for complying with every provision of this Agreement.

AGREED TO AND ACCEPTED:

INVESTOR   ARTIST

_____   _____

Authorized Signatory   [Artist's name]

Print Name _____

ACKNOWLEDGMENTS

I would like to express my appreciation to the following individuals for their assistance, support, and encouragement in writing this book: Kathryn Matt, Valentina Osoria, Brooke Weinberg Esq., Wallace Collins Esq., Linda Lorence, Amy Dadow, Dr. Vanessa Caskey, Irving Azoff, Spike Wilner, Ricky Gordon, Eric Kulberg, John Paige, Aicha Cisse, Jennifer Sullivan, Karly Shonova, Robyn Mundell, Kendall Minter Esq., Darlene Brooks, Paul Resnikov, Ayesha Acquah, Rastiningdyah Sryantoro and Xocoa Sharma.

ABOUT THE AUTHOR

STEVE GORDON (www.stevegordonlaw.com) is an entertainment attorney with over 25 years of experience, including ten years as Director of Business Affairs/Video for Sony Music. His current and recent clients include emerging and major record label artists; managers; music and television producers; entertainment companies such Time Life Films, Shout Factory, and Soul Train Holdings; and cultural institutions such as the Smithsonian Institution and the new National Museum of African American History and Culture. He also represents television, film, and web based producers and production companies.

Other areas of his practice include providing expert services in litigation; counseling producers of and participants in reality TV shows; registering trademarks and copyrights; and supervising copyright infringement and contract litigation.

Steve also operates a music clearance service for producers and distributors of feature films, documentaries, ad campaigns, musical theater, concert programs, audio compilations, and music based apps and websites.

Steve is the author of *The Future of the Music Business* (Hal Leonard 4th ed. 2015). The book provides a legal and business roadmap to artists, entrepreneurs, and music industry professionals for success in today's music business. Steve updates the book at www.futureofthemusicbusiness.com.

Also an educator, Steve frequently lectures on entertainment law and music business issues and is the recipient of two Fulbright scholarships. As a Fulbright scholar, he taught courses on music business and law at Bocconi University in Milan, Italy, and Tel Aviv University in Israel.

His CLE video for Lawline, "Thicke v. Gaye: Will the Jury's Decision Have a Chilling Impact on Creativity?" won the "Best Program" award at the most recent the Association for Continuing Legal Education conference.

Steve is a graduate of New York University School of Law.

ABOUT THE EXECUTIVE EDITOR

Ryanne Perio is a graduate of Columbia Law School and a former legal intern at Atlantic Records and SAG-AFTRA. She is currently an associate at Wilmer, Cutler, Pickering, Hale and Dorr, where she specializes in intellectual property and complex commercial litigation.

ABOUT THE ASSOCIATE EDITORS

Blair Maclin is a junior at the University of Massachusetts Amherst.
Eric Dickstein attends The Dalton School in New York City.